A

IN OLD ALASKA

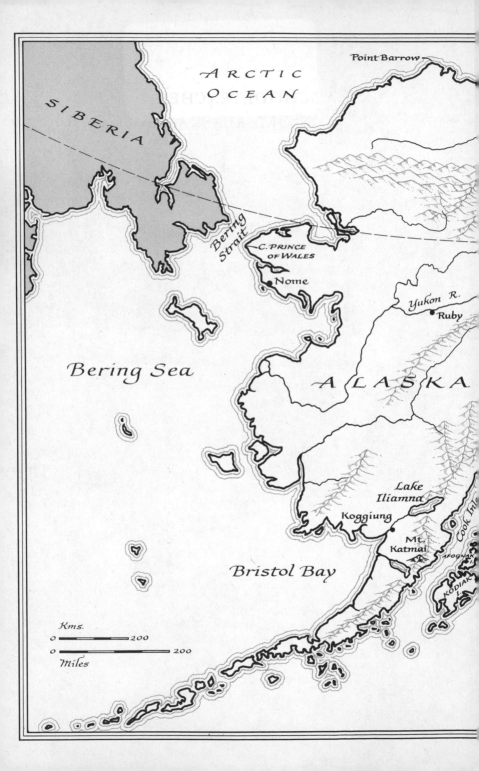

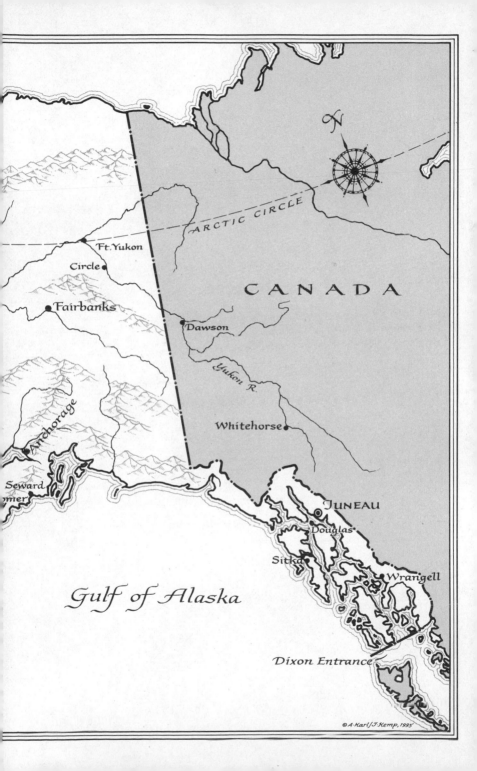

N

ARCTIC CIRCLE

CANADA

Ft. Yukon

Circle

Fairbanks

Dawson

Yukon R.

Anchorage

Whitehorse

Seward
omer

JUNEAU

Douglas

Sitka

Wrangell

Gulf of Alaska

Dixon Entrance

© A. Karl / J. Kemp, 1995

A SCHOOLTEACHER
IN OLD ALASKA

◄◦►

The Story of Hannah Breece

*Edited and with an Introduction
and Commentary by
Jane Jacobs*

VINTAGE BOOKS

A Division of Random House, Inc.   New York

FIRST VINTAGE BOOKS EDITION, JANUARY 1997

Map research by James K. Jacobs and Robert H. Jacobs
Photo on page v: Hannah Breece about to embark, at age fifty-two,
for a remote Alaskan Indian fishing village. Beside her is Joe Kackley, an
Alaska guide born in Ohio who was part-owner of the chartered boat,
and his two Dena'ina native assistants.
Hannah Breece collection

The Library of Congress has cataloged the Random House edition as follows:

Breece, Hannah: the Story of Hannah Breece
A schoolteacher in old Alaska: the story of Hannah Breece /
by Hannah Breece; edited and with an introduction and
commentary by Jane Jacobs.
p. cm.
Includes bibliographical references and index.
ISBN 0-679-44134-4
1. Breece, Hannah, 1859–1940. 2. Teachers—Alaska—Biography.
3. Eskimos—Education—Alaska—History.
I. Jacobs, Jane. II Title.
LB2317.B586A3 1995 371.1'092—dc20 [B] 95-2486

Vintage ISBN: 0-679-77633-8

Random House Web address: http://www.randomhouse.com/

Book design by Oksana Kushnir

Printed in the United States of America
10 9 8 7 6 5 4 3 2 1

FOREWORD

To be openly proper and conventional yet also openly daring is a way of being that was seldom available to women in the past. Some who did pull off this trick without being either aristocratic or rich were Americans on the frontier. Hannah Breece was one of these women.

To her great-nephews and great-nieces, of whom I was one, she had the glamour of a storybook heroine. She camped out with Indians! She held a hundred wild dogs at bay by herself and escaped them! She traveled in a kayak wearing bear intestines! A bear almost ate her right from her bed, and this time the dogs saved her!

Hannah Breece was no rash or spry young thing in a band of spry young things when she experienced exotic perils. She was a middle-aged woman essentially on her own. Her job was serious and responsible: teaching Aleuts, Kenais, Athabaskans, Eskimos and people of mixed native and European blood in Alaska from 1904 to 1918. She was forty-five years old when she went to Alaska and fifty-nine when she completed her assignments there, a fact to remember when we observe her, in her memoir of those years, scaling cliffs, falling through ice or outracing a forest fire. That was part of the daring. She did those things encumbered by long and voluminous skirts and petticoats. That was part of the propriety.

While her memoir is not a diary, it is diary-like in its mingling of domestic matters, work, public events and chance encounters. At the time of which she writes, all Alaska had fewer than 65,000 persons, and for some of those years closer to 55,000, both native and white, but that small population assayed high in outré or otherwise extraordinary characters who come matter-of-factly into her story: gold prospectors and fur traders; tribal chiefs and wise men; ladies in black silk and dressy hats meandering among the stumps and briars of primitive Seward; bounders who took off in boats after fathering children; Russian Orthodox priests; tellers of strange tales.

The self-portrait that emerges from her memoir jibes exactly with my memory of her when she was elderly. In personality and character she much resembled the fictional Jessica Fletcher portrayed by Angela Lansbury in the television series *Murder, She Wrote*. That is, she was forthright and spontaneous but with wondrous funds of self-control; she did not shrink from making judgments but was so intuitively sympathetic in most instances that her judgments could be taken in good part. She was inexhaustibly interested in the ordinary—or better yet, extraordinary—minutiae of daily life. While she was not one who used charm in a conscious way to get what she wanted—she was anything but manipulative— people liked being around her, in part because of her resourcefulness and dependability and in part because she was good, lively company. She even looked somewhat like Angela Lansbury with her soft, rounded cheeks, regular features and intelligent, engaged eyes. However she was not elegant, although she could have been had she so chosen.

Some of her stories have resonances for us she could not have imagined. The story of Gregory echoes against Lenin's tomb with its lines of visitors gazing at a preserved corpse.

The tribulations of the Russian bishop, who was too liberal, and Miss Vonderfour, who fell out of favor with the Czarina, merge into those of other dissidents under other regimes. Now and again she relates bits of short stories for which only the reader can try to supply missing parts. How in the world did penniless Mrs. Miller get from Wales to the Klondike, and whatever possessed her to acquire that awful husband? Hannah is not telling, either because she did not know or, more likely, because the facts would have reflected badly on Mrs. Miller. What is one to make of the deplorable Reindeer Man? What I made of him was an uprooted fellow, not too bright, who dreamed of a coquettish woman at his beck and call and conned distant bureaucracies into collaborating with his fantasy. Imagine his horror when solid, middle-aged Miss Breece materialized in the wilderness and (I am looking at this through his eyes) brazenly commandeered all the men in sight to do her bidding.

In some ways—this was part of the propriety again—she was formal, hewing to the etiquette of her time. For example, she did not address even old and good friends by their first names, nor did they address her as Hannah. She was Miss Breece. Her Alaskan pupils and their parents and fellow villagers addressed her as "Teacher," much as we would say "Professor" or "Doctor." Her letters found in government archives are often in pencil on lined schoolchildren's notebook paper, but even so not informal; they begin, "Sir: I have the honor to address you . . ." and those she received start with "Madam: . . ."

But in other ways she was radical—this was part of the daring. She was inventive with teaching methods and projects. She had to be; often enough, at the time pupils entered school, she and they had no language in common. Sometimes her pupils' opportunities for schooling were so short that at the same time she was teaching them, she was devising ways for them to continue by teaching each other. We catch her, in 1911, pre-inventing on a small scale a 1930s New Deal–type work-relief program when she had to contend, on her own responsibility, with how to dispense famine relief without doing the recipients harm.

Her memoir shows her as always consistent in some of her enthusiasms: championship of women and pride in women's accomplishments; the desirability of good, homemade bread; appreciation of the natural environment and concern for its preservation; scorn for superstition. She herself was devoutly religious and respected others' piety. But she drew a fine and severe line between what she deemed religious beliefs and what she deemed superstition, and this did not necessarily accord with other folks' fine lines between the two.

Although she worked closely with missionaries in several assignments and civic efforts, her attitudes were in some respects subtly different from missionaries' preoccupations. For instance, she enjoyed and appreciated love of finery, whether it was manifested in ancient costumes of feathers and fish skins, the embroidered robes of a bishop, beaded belts and moccasins, the draping of wedding veils, or her own handsome fur boots trimmed in beaver. The silk and satin party dresses that Athabaskan women made for themselves would doubtless have fallen, from a missionary viewpoint, into the category of what the Episcopal archdeacon of the Yukon called "glittering trash." But to admiring Miss Breece they were evidence that the women had an excellent sense of style and were "natural-born dressmakers."

In one of her causes it is fair to say she was fanatic. She was an implacable, relentless prohibitionist. She became so, she once told me, by having seen the effects of alcohol on families and communities while on earlier teaching assignments on Indian reservations in the Rocky Mountains. She pronounced alcohol "the curse of the north" and at one point in her memoir we see her, like a Carry Nation, personally dumping a barrel of home brew down a riverbank.

Her own family and upbringing hardly could have been more conventional. She was born in 1859 in Catawissa, Pennsylvania, a very small town on the Susquehanna River, and was brought up there and in the pretty and placid county seat, Bloomsburg. She was the eleventh of twelve children of Mary Ann Case and Daniel Breece, a small businessman and farmer. Her middle name, which she used only as an initial, was Elizabeth. She took pride, in her later years, in a distant family kinship to Samuel Finley Breese Morse, inventor of the telegraph, a connection of which he was surely oblivious. Otherwise there is no record of anything the least unusual about her family, and certainly not her upbringing.

Like two of her sisters, one of whom was my grandmother, she graduated from the Bloomsburg academy and normal school for teacher training and at the age of twenty began teaching, as was expected of her, in Catawissa and then in Bloomsburg elementary schools. But unlike her sisters she did not end her teaching career after some ten years by marrying. In due course she became an elementary school principal and began taking summer courses in anthropology at the Summer-School for Teachers of the University of Chicago. This led to a commission by the U.S. Department of the Interior to teach on various Rocky Mountain reservations and then to travel by covered wagon in the southwest, explaining to Indian communities the educational opportunities open to them. After four years of teaching Navajos, Utes, Hopi and Sioux, she was selected to join the handful of Alaskan teachers employed by the Department of the Interior and was sent in 1904 to an existing but problem-plagued school in the Kodiak archipelago.

From that point on, she pretty well chose her own assignments, the more remote or otherwise difficult, the better.

When she got her first post in Alaska, with twenty-four years of teaching experience already behind her, her salary was six hundred dollars a year. After five years she passed up a salary of a hundred dollars a month to take a post she preferred at ninety dollars a month, which—since a year included three months of unpaid vacation—came to $810 a year. The average salary of Alaskan schoolteachers from 1993 to 1994 was $47,390, and for a top teacher, which she was both in seniority and responsibilities, an average of $57,677. But we cannot understand her income simply by translating it into modern terms. The Alaskan educational funds were chronically inadequate. She was paid enough to get by with prudent and careful attention to her expenses. The very few luxuries she allowed herself tended to be gifts for others.

Her sacrifice of ten dollars a month to get the post she wanted can be best understood as a 10 percent pay cut in a salary adequate but not munificent. When she writes that fox skins ranged in price from a dollar fifty to seven dollars, this represented roughly half her day's pay at the time to half a week's. When she tells that a trained dog team cost six hundred dollars and adds "an enormous sum," she was not exaggerating; that would have been considerably more than the cost today of a new pickup truck. The rich woman from Seattle who had fifty thousand dollars would be worth several million in today's terms, which is why she could well have afforded the gift of an infirmary or even—considering the technological simplicity of hospitals at the time—a small hospital.

Although Hannah was at peace with herself in most of her enthusiasms and attitudes, one major perplexity surfaces and becomes more troubling with time. She seldom mentions it outright, but there it is, sneaking in.

When she arrived in Alaska she had utter faith that American civilization held the keys to overcoming ignorance, poverty, disease and superstition, four foes from which she hoped to help deliver "Uncle Sam's less fortunate children." Given the time in which she lived, her boundless faith was justifiable, or seemed so. The great crisis of her early childhood, the Civil War, had been won by her side, including soldiers from among her extended family and friends; the Union was saved; slavery was abolished; education was spreading; immemorial plagues were gradually being overcome or mitigated; marvels like the telegraph were tumbling from inventive minds; ordinary life in towns like Bloomsburg and cities like Chicago was improving amazingly; the poor and downtrodden from many other parts of the world were finding hope and better lives for their children in America. To be sure, there were problems; she knew that. But given the reality of so much unprecedented progress, what further splendors could not be accomplished? One of the patriotic hymns Hannah loved was "America the Beautiful," especially its last verse:

> "Oh beautiful for patriot dream
> That sees beyond the years,
> Thine alabaster cities gleam
> Undimmed by human tears.
> America, America,
> God mend thine every flaw,
> Confirm thy soul
> With self control
> Thy liberty with law."

She believed in the essential promise of what she sang.

On the other hand, she could not avoid seeing that civilization was bringing along with it intractable disruptions, temptations and exploitations. Her fourth post, to the lawless settlement of Fort Yukon, forced her to confront the real, stark possibility of the bad aspects of imported civilization outrunning and overwhelming the good aspects. And compounding such contradictions between what she was working for and what was happening was her increased appreciation of the capacities and traits of people she had been taught to regard as inferior because their circumstances of life were poor and primitive. This accounts, I think, for the curious way in which her memoir ends. After Fort Yukon it loses exuberance— somehow her heart goes out of it. Yet, at the close, in defiance of disappointments and fears, she rouses herself to affirm that yes, the beautiful patriot dream is destined to triumph.

After she left Alaska, Hannah taught for several years more in a public elementary school in McMinnville, Oregon, a town she first visited in 1915 and chose as her ideal place for later retirement. During her retirement there, and then after 1932, in the home of her brother-in-law and younger sister in Bloomsburg, she occasionally gave talks about her Alaskan experiences, and in response to urgings from her audiences that she write them down, she retrieved her Alaskan letters to family and friends and from these put together a manuscript.

It would be more accurate, though uncharitable, to say she threw together a manuscript. Reading it was a bit like contemplating a box of jigsaw-puzzle pieces. The fragments were fascinating but maddeningly unassembled. After the manuscript was rejected, each time with kind words about the interesting material, she asked me to help her get it published; I was twenty-one at the time and my only qualification was the production of a few short magazine and newspaper articles.

I told her I thought the manuscript required reorganizing

and rewriting. She agreed, but at the age of seventy-seven did not feel equal to undertaking this and asked me to do it. I did a revised draft, which we sent off to some admirers who liked it, and to publishers who did not.

I did not like it either. For one thing I lacked sufficient craftsmanship and knew it. For another, I had a conflict I did not discuss with her; it was too formidable. Some of her assumptions and assertions, to my mind, were imperialist, chauvinist and racist—white man's burden stuff (although she did not care for Kipling). They set my teeth on edge. It would not have been honest to omit them from what, after all, was her memoir, not mine, but I hated including them.

After she died in 1940 at the age of eighty—still bright, good company until her last few days—I set aside the manuscript and the abortive draft drawn from it. But in addition to my mother's periodic reminders that I ought to get back to it, the manuscript on its own account persisted in the back of my mind. It had hooked me; so had the notion that some time I should try to do it justice. To complete a project hanging about in one's head is good. But to dally more than fifty years? Well, it is more leeway than one has a right to expect.

The assumptions and assertions that bothered me so long ago still set my teeth on edge. But now I see them as necessary to her story. They were inherent to her times. Without these condescending white-man's-burden assumptions one cannot understand why she was sent to Alaska or why she went.

But if my old cavils no longer were obstructions when I returned so belatedly to her manuscript, I discovered new frustrations. These were primarily unaccountable holes or gaps in her story. For example, she described a hazardous lake-and-river business trip to a Bering Sea settlement with only the vaguest explanation for undertaking it. Later she told of a thousand-mile round-trip on a Yukon steamer, followed by an arduous dogsled journey in the dead of winter, with no more explanation than that she had to go to court "in the interests of the native people." What was that all about? (The raunchy particulars can be found in the commentary section about troubles in Fort Yukon, p. 228.)

In the summer of 1994 I accompanied three other kinfolk of Hannah's to Alaska. Our quest was to see what the communities she described were like now, and along the way to try to fill the gaps in her story that we were not able to explain with accessible library materials. We were given most generous help by many Alaskans, especially by John Branson, historian of the Lake Clark National Park and Preserve; by Marian Johnson, director, and Alice Ryser, archivist, of the Kodiak Historical Society's Baranov Museum; and the staff of the Consortium Library of the University of Alaska in Anchorage.

As might be expected after a lapse of some eighty to ninety years we found immense changes in Hannah's communities today, but also some similarities. Our joint observations of both are sketched out in the epilogue.

The chief surprises—jolts!—involved material I had not even suspected was missing. The Reindeer Man was not merely a lonely fellow intent on conjuring up an amiable lady. He was a cog (and a crook) in a grand fiasco—a government- and missionary-sponsored social-engineering and economic megaproject. Sheldon Jackson, the man who selected Hannah as an Alaskan teacher, was more powerful, peculiar and controversial than one could guess from Hannah's bland mentions of him. The bureaucracy under which she worked, far from being as reliably efficient and flexible as it appears in her telling, was capable of driving her to the brink of fear and despair. In a couple of instances her retelling of what she heard may be the only documentation bearing on minor but mystifying bits of history.

Why did Hannah omit what she omitted? Some fragmentary notes I found from my last conversation with her threw some light on this question, as well as upon the moral standards she set for herself.

Hannah was not a tattletale. From childhood I had been aware of that; it was one reason she could be trusted with confidences and also the reason she discouraged a child, or anyone else, from running people down behind their backs. In our last talk, in response to my prodding, she told me that when a birth occurred in Iliamna village, the mother lay down on straw and moss in a trough and "everybody gathered around to worry along with the mother about the pain." I asked why she didn't include this in her writing. Well, she replied, it was so out of accord with decorum (there's the propriety again), and also those people would not want to be humiliated or held up to ridicule. One can interpret this as a case of cultural Eurocentrism, but to Hannah it was a case of protecting people's dignity.

In the same conversation she confessed she had lied about her age in this village. She was fifty but when asked she said forty. Women there were so old and wrinkled by the time they were forty they scarcely could have believed her true age; if they had, it would have made them sad, or ashamed of their own appearance. Only Epheme, the blind sage—whom we meet in the memoir—was not fooled. He told her she had been to too many places to be only forty. At the age of eighty, she still felt a little uncomfortable remembering this long-ago lie, and was still amused and relieved to recall that at least one person had seen through it.

Hannah was a truth-teller. Reading her, we can rely on everything being true as far as she knew. But she was not a teller of the whole truth. She had no intention of using her memoir to denigrate persons to no purpose. When she does come down hard on anyone, the reason is outrage and it is never casual.

I have no scruples against being a tattler for the purpose of supplementing her story and its background, but have kept all supplements, these or others, distinctly apart from her account. In my editing, I have done what she expected of me: improved organization, removed repetition and digressions that interrupt the flow, fact-checked distances, names, spelling, vegetation—the customary assistance an editor can give an inexperienced writer. The story she chose to tell, and the vividness with which she set it on paper, are all Hannah's.

Jane Jacobs
Toronto, January 1995

CONTENTS

COMMENTARY

Puzzles, Tangles, Clarifications

MAPS AND PHOTOGRAPHS

MAPS

PHOTOGRAPHS

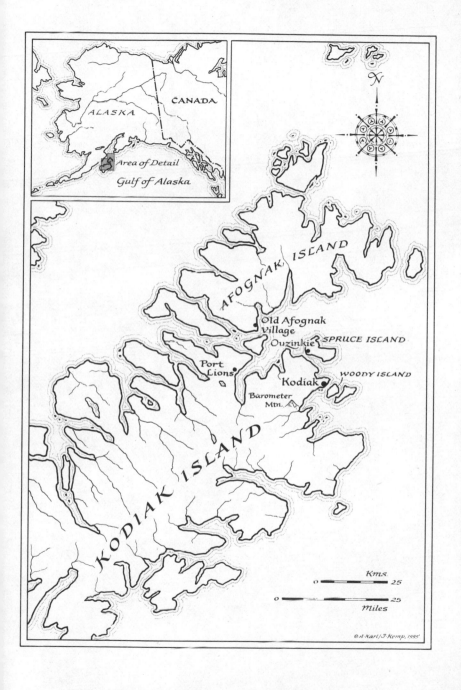

ALASKA

CANADA

Gulf of Alaska

Area of Detail

N

AFOGNAK ISLAND

Old Afognak
Village

Ouzinkie

SPRUCE ISLAND

Port
Lions

Kodiak

WOODY ISLAND

Barometer
Mtn.

KODIAK ISLAND

Kms.
0   25

0   25
Miles

© A·Karl / J·Kemp, 1995

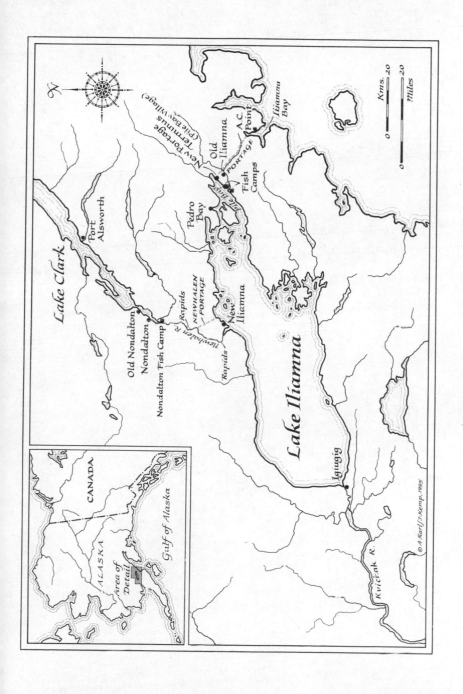

Lake Clark

Lake Iliamna

Port Alsworth

Old Nondalton
Nondalton
Nondalton Fish Camp

Rapids
NEWHALEN PORTAGE
New Iliamna
Rapids

Newhalen R.

Pedro Bay

New Portage Terminus
(Pile Bay Village)
Old Iliamna
PORTAGE
A.C. Point
Iliamna Bay
Fish Camps

Old Iliamna

Igiugig

Kvichak R.

Kms. 20
Miles 20
0
0

© A. Karl / J. Kemp, 1995

CANADA

ALASKA

Area of Detail

Gulf of Alaska

HANNAH'S ALASKAN CHRONOLOGY

SCHOOL YEAR		SUMMER	
1904–05	Afognak	1905	Afognak
1905–06	Afognak	1906	Kodiak, Wood Island, Seward and Iliamna
1906–07	Wood Island	1907	Wood Island
1907–08	Wood Island	1908	Wood Island
1908–09	Wood Island	1909	Kodiak, Seward and Iliamna
1909–10	Iliamna	1910	Nondalton
1910–11	Iliamna	1911	Nondalton
1911–12*	Iliamna	1912	A.C. Point, Seattle and Fort Yukon
1912–13	Fort Yukon	1913	Fort Yukon
1913–14	Fort Yukon	1914	To Wrangell at some point
1914–15	Wrangell	1915	Visit in McMinnville, Oregon
1915–16**	Wrangell	1916	Possibly McMinnville
1916–17	Douglas	1917	Possibly McMinnville
1917–18	Douglas		

*To April 1912
**Some time after October 1915

Hannah, probably en route to Alaska from Seattle, at the age of forty-five. The outfit she is wearing is most likely the inappropriate "traveling suit" in which she disembarked for Afognak. *Photocopy of an unlocated photograph in the possession of Rev. David E. Robison, courtesy of Mary D. Robison.*

MEMOIR

by *Hannah Breece*

1

Prelude to My Assignment

When Uncle Sam sent me to Alaska in 1904, the land where I was to spend the next fourteen years was still in many ways almost as Russian as American, although we had owned it since 1867. Yet it was also a land that, if any place on earth, approached the American ideal that all men are created equal. In its polyglot population, mothered by dozens of nations, there was said to be a higher percentage of college men than in any other country: There were men, and women too, for whom book learning was still vital, but also men who had long since forgotten their once-prized diplomas, and many who could not decipher their own mother tongues. Recommendations, credentials and diplomas belonged to the past and unimportant reputation of an individual. What stamina, what ingenuity, what knowledge or mechanical ability do you possess for the here and now? That was the important thing. It was truly the land where "A man's a man for a' that."

It was also a society of genuine chivalry. I could depend on respect and protection as a woman, and as a teacher I was even venerated. This code, running through the veins of Alaska, made it possible for me to travel far by dogsled, riverboats and foot trails to remote locations, into some of which no woman of European descent had previously found her way. I could dwell anywhere, no matter how distant from civilization.

Uncle Sam understood the situation or he would never have sent a woman to do the work.

The official in Washington who chose to send me and who was my supervisor during the early years was Sheldon Jackson. His title was U.S. General Agent of Education in Alaska: that is, he was head of the Alaska division of the Bureau of Education in the Department of the Interior. Dr. Jackson had spent years exploring Alaska, beginning before the time that the United States had so much as appointed a governor. He concentrated on learning what sorts of populations had come along with our acquisition of Russian America. Its new American name, Alaska, selected after much debate in Congress, was taken from an Indian word meaning "great country."

When I took up my work there I had already taught for twenty years in my native state of Pennsylvania, and for four years on Indian reservations in the Rocky Mountains. I prepared myself as best I could with summer-school university studies of primitive races. But perhaps I learned more to make me ponder during a single day's stopover in Sitka during the steamer voyage northward from Seattle.

Sitka was the quaint old Russian capital and at this time was still the American capital too. Most of its large store of Russian archives had still not been translated. One old Russian building had become the Sheldon Jackson Museum, filled with treasures Dr. Jackson had collected during his explorations. At a time when American knowledge of Alaska was extremely vague, he had the foresight to realize the value of displays reaching back into prehistoric times.

As I looked at this great feast, I thought of how our own inventors have all civilization to back them up when they make something tangible which has first existed only in their minds. They have seen parts of what they will use to make something new. They have mathematical knowledge and all types of subtle measurements to draw upon. But inventions by people of primitive races lacked these multiple points of contact. I was impressed by the ways these inventions had been contrived to overcome hard circumstances, and also by the values they expressed. There were boats large and small of many different ingenious designs and diverse materials, some of them like boats I was eventually to travel in myself. Some garments were made of feathers arranged in beautiful patterns or else sheening off into the richest of hues. Other garments were fashioned from golden skins of fishes, splendid furs and well-tanned leather. Skins patterned with bright beads were made into blankets and dresses. Glossy mattings were made from bark peeled off the roots of spruce and cedar. There were many, many implements, coming down from unknown time, for cooking and building, for fishing and hunting, for warfare, for amusement, and of course carved totem poles telling their mute, stately stories of legendary family trees.

It flashed through my mind that these wonders were clues to the hidden powers of the minds of the people to whom I was being sent, to help them overcome ignorance, poverty, disease and superstition. My job was to bring them benefits now available to them from civilization and from Uncle Sam's care for his less fortunate children.

Welcome to Afognak

Valdez, which in 1904 was the most important Alaskan center for gold and copper mining, at the head of Prince William Sound, was the terminus of the excursion steamer I had boarded in Seattle. From here my trip continued to the westward on a much smaller steamer, the *Dora*. This staunch little vessel was to be a faithful link to the outside world through almost all my Alaskan years. The *Dora* sailed a lonely course over thousands of miles of ocean. In many seasons no sister craft sailed along or across her course. She glided in and out among the islands and peninsulas like a phantom from another world.

Along our way she stopped at tiny villages to unload freight, mail and occasionally passengers. Unloading lumber was tedious but it gave us time to go ashore. I had never imagined a settlement so nearly built on nothing as Ellamar, a little mining town at the Copper River. About a square yard in front of each cabin was made usable by pounding glass bottles upside down in the soft earth. Planks were laid between these little solid places, for the moss-covered earth was deceptive. Stepping on it meant a struggle to gain solid footing, and to step into one of the many sinkholes could mean death. There was a plan to drain and plank the town if the copper held out long enough to warrant it. I brought back to the ship with me

some reindeer moss, shells, flowers and seaweed. The governor of Alaska, John G. Brady, who was aboard, asked if I had
left any of Ellamar ashore.

In Seattle I had heard much talk about the important city of
Seward at the head of one of the inlets we traveled. But we
passed it by without even stopping, and to my surprise it
seemed to consist of only two houses. It was still a dream city,
based on the hopes of promoters trying to raise capital for a
railroad to link the site with the Arctic Circle.

The *Dora*, which Hannah called "a faithful link to the outside world
through almost all my Alaskan years." *John Newlund, Kodiak Historical Society*

Finally, after I had been on the boats for sixteen days out of Seattle, we approached my destination, Afognak, on an island of the same name just north of the large island of Kodiak. The *Dora* had no freight or other passengers for Afognak and had not planned to stop there until it received instructions from Dr. Jackson in Washington. A storm was coming up, and the bay was rocky and treacherous, so the *Dora* anchored many miles offshore.

I was told I must climb down a rope ladder thrown over the steamer's rolling, tossing side and from there jump into a rowboat. I told the crew I simply would not do it. Governor Brady asked me what I proposed to do since there was no other way for me to reach Afognak. Before boarding the *Dora* I had done a little studying of routes and transportation so I answered that I would stay on the *Dora* until the next town with a wharf, then make my way on a small schooner capable of reaching the Afognak shore. Governor Brady and the captain consulted together and decided they would lower a rowboat with me and my baggage in it. In later years I was to go down and up that slippery, tossing rope ladder many a time, but at this point I was too fearful. In fact, I was in terror even within the small boat as it swung out and over the water. It was the first time I had ever been on a rough sea in a small boat. Nor was I well enough acquainted with what to expect to have dressed properly. I wore a hat and a traveling suit. Mr. Inglis, the purser, handed me an oil coat and a sou'wester. A good thing because the storm was rising, the waves crashing and mounting, and the rain was soon falling in torrents. When the little boat slapped the water, Mr. Inglis, who looked like a wisp of a boy, and a cheerful Irish sailor named Pat joined me via the ladder. The captain called to them to lose no time and hurry back. All the passengers, about thirty, stood on deck calling out good wishes and singing; the last strains coming over the water were "Pull for the shore."

We were headed toward a bluff which stood high above the beach. Atop it I could make out a large white building which Mr. Inglis told me was the U.S. government schoolhouse and teacher's residence. Nearby was a charming white cottage. Mr. Inglis inquired where I was going to stay the night and I told him Dr. Jackson had written me to go to Mrs. Pajoman.

My attention was then caught by a row of white men standing in front of the schoolhouse. I plumed myself that they had come to welcome me, and in all that rain too! We had a dreadful time landing the rowboat in the breakers and struggling up the bluff, leaving my luggage behind under a tarpaulin. I wondered why the welcoming committee did not come to our aid. It had vanished. Nobody was in sight.

Then a young boy appeared on the scene. Heaven bless boys. When or where was anything unusual that a boy did not appear? Later I learned that the men had received no word a teacher was coming, and when they saw a strange woman arriving for no reason they fled and sent the boy, Albert Petellin, to learn what was up and do the honors. "Sure, Teacher," he said with a smile, "I will get someone to help, we will put your things in the dry."

Mr. Inglis said he did not intend leaving me just yet. He knew Mrs. Pajoman, he told me, and thought he had better introduce me. So up a steep trail we went, to the pretty white cottage. I caught a glimpse of a woman's face peeping from behind a curtain and Mr. Inglis apparently saw it too for he remarked that Mrs. Pajoman was at home. But when he knocked on the door there was no response. Again and again he knocked and after fifteen minutes or so I urged him to return to the boat, but he assured me he had no intention of leaving until he knew I had a good place to spend the night.

After half an hour the lady gave in and opened the door a crack, then reluctantly allowed us to enter. She was a very short, chubby woman with black hair and bright black eyes and the dark complexion of an Aleut. If she had not looked so troubled she would have seemed a pleasing person. Her living room was certainly pleasing. It contained a prettily dressed bed, a piano, some books and a few comfortable chairs. That she had a cultivated taste for books and music was evident from her conversation as well as her surroundings. She spoke excellent English with only a slight accent.

Plainly I was not a welcome guest. I was puzzled and then the light dawned on my tired brain. I asked, "Mrs. Pajoman, did you teach this school last year?"

She replied that she had been the teacher for the past eight years. The mystery was solved. She had probably thought I would return to the steamer if I could find no place to stay the night. I expressed my regret at her disappointment and told her I only knew that I had been sent here. She said she herself did not much mind being replaced. She did not care about the school, but her husband would be very angry at the loss of her salary.

Mr. Inglis asked her to take us to the schoolhouse, some fifty feet away. The building made a good appearance from the outside, but inside it was in terrible condition. The eight large windows, four on each side, were hung with faded, ragged, dirty, stringy old curtains. One could see, by searching out small protected ledges, that at one time the walls had been painted gray, but smoke and long years of accumulated dust covered them and the ceiling. The floor was even worse, the boards all splintered and worn out. As furniture there were two plank benches without backs. A single board slab, much warped and hacked, seemed to be the writing table but it was too high to use from the benches and had no shelf for putting away a book or pencil. The stove looked good but its pipe was rickety and disreputable with rust. I thought it was no credit to a great country like ours to be supporting such a miserable-looking institution. The teacher's quarters were not much better, but I could imagine fine possibilities in both sections of the building. The view from what would be my living room was magnificent and I determined not to think of the place as it was, but as how it could be.

Mr. Inglis looked concerned as he inspected the teacher's quarters. He commented that I couldn't stay there, it had no furniture and was too dirty. Then he turned to Mrs. Pajoman and told her I would have to stay with her that night. She said she supposed I could, and only then did Mr. Inglis leave.

Back at the cottage, Mrs. Pajoman told me her husband owned a store and a schooner, the *Mattie,* named for her. All her earnings went into his businesses. She had hardly any pupils at school, she said. The first two years' attendance had been pretty good but during the last six years children had become too lazy to bother.

Finally I inquired whether she wanted me to take off my hat and stay the night. She repeated that her husband would be very angry but there was no place else for me to go. Then she boiled potatoes and fried salmon and we had a good supper together. I supposed Dr. Jackson expected me to make my own judgments and I consoled myself with the thought that if everything had been fine, any teacher could have gotten along. Instead of pitying Mrs. Pajoman—poor little woman—I steeled my heart and pitied the children who had been running wild. Mrs. Pajoman's father was an Aleut who had become a Russian priest; her mother was a Russian from Siberia. She had attended school in the United States, where she was educated with the object of returning to help her people. She played the piano well and, as I was to learn, her singing voice was exceptionally beautiful.

That night, exhausted, I slept in the pretty white bed near the piano. In the small hours I was awakened by loud knocking. Through the glass in the door I saw the silhouette of a great shaggy head with a big pipe in its mouth. It was the ogre! I called out to Mrs. Pajoman. The ogre heard me and went to the other door.

He was not at all the monster I had imagined, for at breakfast he was pleasant in his manner. He looked Slavic, with white hair, blue eyes and a light complexion. He calmly told me that in only about three weeks the steamer would come from the west and I could return on it. Other teachers had come, he said, and when they heard what a community this was they had gone home and his wife continued with the school.

I smiled benignly and made no answer. But I thought, If you expect to call after me, "Here comes the teacher, going back!" you will be disappointed.

Organizing the School

At eight the next morning I set out to hunt up the children, taking along as my Aleutian interpreter Albert Petellin, the boy on the bluff.

Afognak village was actually two villages, two and a half miles apart, each on a shallow bay with a wooded cape jutting between them that concealed each settlement from the other. A marsh lay between the two, and there one had to keep to a plank walk because quicksand, sinkholes and the deep moss were treacherous. As we passed over the marsh, eight immense eagles soared above us, so close that I could see white feathers on one. Albert said that it was a young one. A chattery little river spanned by a rustic bridge also separated the settlements. One was Aleut, the other was thought of as Russian.

Along a bit of paved road straggled the church, the school, a store, the Russian Orthodox church and the priest's house. Halfway between the church and the school, maintaining its lawful distance from each, was a pretentious saloon. As I passed it I thought, Here you are, ready to tear down what each institution can do for the good of the people.

My instructions from Washington had been to make special efforts with the Aleutian children because the school was supported principally for them. My plan for the morning was to visit every home in both villages. Albert and I had to omit a few homes in the Aleutian village because those families were still in the summer fishing camp. The island, which was about fifty by thirty miles but with many deep inlets, rose in hills and steep mountains, so its many rivers were short but they were rich salmon grounds.

Wherever people were home I was greeted and entertained courteously. Parents and each child shook hands with me and offered the best chair or box in the room. The Aleut houses were all furnished scantily and crudely but they had plentiful bedding, all piled on one bed during the day. In some houses the pile almost reached the ceiling. The Aleuts had lived on these islands centuries before the Russians arrived.

Part of the Aleut village at Afognak. *Special Collections Division, University of Washington Libraries*

Houses and garden plots in the Russian village at Afognak. The schoolhouse and teacher's residence are not visible. *Special Collections Division,
University of Washington Libraries*

They were neither Eskimos nor Indians. Physically they resembled Japanese although they were darker, shorter and
stockier, with the protective layer of fat common to people in
the far north.

Albert could not speak Russian, so three young mothers
who had completed second grade and spoke English were my
interpreters in the Russian village. Homes there were a
marked contrast to the Aleuts'. Some boasted plush-covered
chairs and tête-à-têtes in peacock blue or scarlet. Although
the squared-off-log walls were not plastered, they were neatly
papered on a cheesecloth backing. I was impressed by a sense
of whiteness whenever we entered a best room: floors were

sanded and scoured white; rugs were strips of pure white canvas; curtains were white lace brightened with pinned-on paper flowers. I never saw so much crochet work in my life; it adorned every available piece of furniture, and the white bedspreads were crocheted or knitted. A typical best room contained a bed, a table, some chairs (including a rocker), a sewing machine, some sort of music box and at least one accordion. In the center of the building, so it kept all the rooms warm, was a wood-burning Russian heater with thick clay walls. Once it was fired up, the heat it stored kept the place warm all night, which is why the indoor plants the Russian villagers loved did not freeze.

Every house had a holy corner, as they called it, with a religious print, painting or hammered brass depicting either the Virgin or an apostle, and a little shelf with an incense lamp and a bottle of holy water. This corner, they told me, was never disturbed. When a house was abandoned, or the last member of a household had died, the holy corner remained until the house fell or was torn down; then the nearest relative took custody of the holy objects.

The best room of each house had a life-sized portrait of the Czar, and almost always one of the Czarina too. The only other pictures were cut out from the labels of fruit or vegetable cans. Mr. Sheratine, the reader of the church, who ranked next to the priest, had a room entirely ceiled with labels from salmon cans: hundreds, they looked like thousands, of fish swimming overhead on the hot ceiling.

The Russians were part Russian, or part European of another nationality, and part Aleut. They were regarded by themselves and seemingly by the Aleuts as the higher social class. They were also thought of as richer, but it seemed to me that the value of the boats, seines and hunting equipment I had noticed in the Aleut village represented at least as much investment as the Russians' houses and furnishings.

After I had made the rounds, the three young Russian women helped me make a list of children in both villages. With this in hand, I returned to the Aleut village to talk with the chief. On my way I passed the store again and asked the Danish storekeeper to furnish my quarters, giving him an idea of the requirements. He promised to have it done that afternoon so I could move in by night.

Next, I asked the chief to call a meeting of his people and explain why the children should go to school. I suggested several reasons to place before them. The principal one was that the Russian children were surpassing the Aleut children. Why should other children put theirs to shame? Then I presented the practical side. It was foolish not to take advantage of opportunities that could be useful in life. I next stopped at the priest's house to see Albert's uncle, Father Petellin, who was an Aleut himself, and asked him to attend the chief's meeting.

By this time it was two o'clock in the afternoon. I knew people expected school to open the next day, but pupils could not come into that dirty room. So after a bite to eat I rounded up six large girls and as many boys who were not only willing but glad to clean the schoolroom. When the ragged curtains were pulled off and the big panes of glass clean and bright, the improvement was enormous. We could do little with the walls and ceiling but we scrubbed the floor and benches. I was pleased. The school only needed the benches to be filled with boys and girls to make it cheerful, for pupils are the principal thing in a school anyway.

The pupils came, from both villages. But the Aleut children were a ragged, unkempt lot and the Russian village children treated them shamefully. During the first week, when I was teaching little children a game during the recess period, the Russian pupils rounded up every single one of the twenty Aleut children, big and small, and before I knew it the Aleuts were fleeing to their village with the Russians in pursuit. Then the Russian children came back triumphantly. Now they had the school to themselves.

I asked the Russian children to tell me about the situation and listened to their scorn and complaints. I laughed along with them and told them I did not wonder they had chased the Aleuts away, they were so ragged and dirty. I reminded them that I had not seated them alongside the Aleut children but kept them apart as far as that was possible.

But then I asked how many had a grandmother or grandfather who lived in the Aleut village. While I could see they were thinking about that, I proposed a compact with them. If I tried to be patient and was willing to teach such ragged pupils, would they help me tame them and teach them? If we all worked together, I said, soon there would be no dirty Aleut section in our nice school. I pictured how it could be when the Aleuts were clean and neat and could talk English and we could be like one big school family. How many would like to train the Aleuts?

Everyone volunteered to help. So at once I sent three or four of the ringleaders to bring back the children they had just driven away. Rather to my surprise, every Aleut child was willing to return.

That night I wrote to friends in Seattle giving the name, age and description of each Aleut child and the clothing needed. I knew very well that children should not be "spoiled." But there is another side to the question of not helping for fear of spoiling. These children felt like nobodies because the others treated them so basely. I was willing to risk spoiling. When the Aleut parents realized how their children could look when they were clean and nicely dressed, I was sure they would keep up the improvement. I had already been impressed with how proud the parents of both villages were of their children and how anxious they were for them to learn.

In about six weeks the boxes from Seattle arrived on the *Dora*. I had worried that the clothes might be too fancy and inappropriate, but my friends were sensible people and I need not have been anxious. The boxes were wonderful: a complete set of clothes for each child, underwear and shoes and stockings, dresses of serge and other good serviceable cloth; even hair ribbons were not forgotten. For the boys there were stout corduroy suits for best wear and overalls for school. I think it was the first time some of the children had clean, warm underwear. I did not give out the clothing until I knew the children had all been taken to the *banya*, the Russian-type steam bath used by both villages.

After this time, one could hardly tell to which village a child belonged. Best of all, the Russian children were not jealous, because they took credit for the change and prided themselves on it. Of course, by now, all the children had been sitting and playing together, not apart.

I had also written strenuously worded letters to Washington, listing what we needed: school desks and blackboards, books and writing materials, bookcases and cupboards, white cambric curtain materials to modify the glare from sun shining on water, and I especially asked for songbooks and an organ. The same shipment that brought the Seattle boxes brought everything except the organ. That was refused. I would have to get it some other way. In the mail was an authorization for a new floor and repainting.

In my own luggage I had brought a box of playthings: cloth

animals, toy wagons, a little stove, a set of play dishes, a little tub and washboard and broom. We set apart a good-sized square of space at one side of the big room for the playthings, and although I did not call it a "project," it served this purpose. When little ones were through with their study, they went to this place and kept house. It was one way I could deal with them and still have time to teach the older ones.

One evening a week the older boys had a sort of club in which they'd look over books and magazines and play games for an hour or two. They had never seen popcorn. One evening, when two Russian boys, Emil and Fedotia, and Johnnie Tawnashak, the Aleut chief's son, were popping corn, Johnnie refused to eat it; he said the devil must be in it because nothing but the devil could make it turn itself inside out.

Johnnie was fourteen, and ever since his mother had died four years previously he had had to do the cooking for the family and take care of two younger children. He had never been to school and it required a great deal of persuading to induce him to give it a trial. All at once, during an evening session, the connection between the object and the written word dawned upon him. He jumped up, thumped his hand on the desk and exclaimed, "I can learn! I understand. I always go to school now!"

Johnnie had entered school too late to have the benefit of the Seattle clothing boxes. One day I noticed him looking intently at the Russian boys. He did not come to school the next day nor for several days after that and I feared he had left. He was a fine-looking boy, tall and straight, and had many good traits. I knew an education would enliven his countenance and he would be a handsome man. When he returned, his hair was cut and brushed until it shone and he was wearing a new overall, new shoes, new cap and a happy expression. When I asked where he had been, he said he was working because he didn't have enough money to buy everything he needed. He had gone to the forest and trapped a fox.

On Saturday mornings I had classes in making bread for the older girls, and as a result many families began to make loaves instead of hard pilot bread. Each Saturday afternoon the girls had a sewing party. After the walls and ceilings had been white-enameled, they made new curtains for the windows with ruffles down their center edges and ribbons to tie them back. Each girl in turn prepared simple but pretty refresh ments for these parties. The school was always open and seldom empty because it was the only public room in the community except for the saloon.

Thanksgiving Day was the occasion for everyone to come and hear the children recite and to admire the refurbished school. Mrs. MacDonald from the Russian village, who had been educated in San Francisco and had become a good friend of mine, rented her organ to the school for special occasions like this, and Mrs. Pajoman played and sang beautifully for everyone's enjoyment, which I thought generous of her.

The whole life and spirits of the town seemed to be changing for the better. The men put up a tall flagpole and raised flags for stormy as well as fine weather, so for the first time ever, the Stars and Stripes were floating over Afognak. As the days grew dark, the great round moon rolling up from the ocean made our long nights as charming as a marble palace, all sprayed and spangled in silver.

By November pupils were flocking in; or I should say flooding in, because many were coming in boats from scattered places. When attendance reached more than a hundred, I had to divide the school into two sessions: mornings for small children, afternoons for older ones. Sometimes the younger ones would stand outside in the afternoons and howl, but if I had tried to teach so many at once, none would have learned anything. Four teachers were needed here, I informed Washington, which responded promptly with sufficient additional desks, books and other educational supplies, but sent not even one additional teacher, then or the next year either.

On the whole, things were going well but problems did crop up. As winter wore on, it seemed to me the Aleut children were looking wan and they tended to get restless or listless. One day several found some laundry starch I had used and set out to throw away. They ate it ravenously. I bought a sack of flour and made a thick porridge, adding native cranberries that were small, dark red and had a very rich flavor, along with some sugar. The children loved this experimental dish, so each morning Aleut pupils came early and had all the porridge they wanted. Their main food was fish, and plenty of it, but evidently a supplement was needed. Children seldom learn well when they are undernourished. With the daily porridge their restlessness disappeared and it seemed to me they were learning twice as fast as they had been. They were bright, and wanted to learn.

Even when children learn eagerly, it is hard for them to unlearn things that have been ground in since infancy. I prided myself that they had learned the government of the United States was their government, and that it was headed by the president, who was elected by the people. We voted in school from time to time about what should be done, so they had a concept of voting.

One day, wording my query a little differently from the form I had previously used, I asked, "Who says which man shall be president of the United States?" With one accord they chorused, "The Czar!"

The Sunday School Crisis

Afognak was once a Russian convict island, mostly for debtors. Those exiled had to find their own living, as well as wives for themselves. Then in recent times, only some dozen or so years before I arrived, a party of about thirty men of European and American birth or ancestry came to the island and married women who were Aleut or part Aleut and part Russian. These men joined the Russian village and raised families there. It was they who had become sufficiently dissatisfied with Mrs. Pajoman's school to send complaints to Washington. Now some of them pressed me to start a Sunday school, which in any case I had hoped to do. There had never been one in Afognak.

I attended the Russian church because it was the only one. It still practiced many of the very old customs discarded by other Orthodox churches. The services were in language so archaic that even Father Petellin himself did not understand it. All Sunday morning the children had to stand perfectly still. If they so much as stirred, some old man walked up and gave an ear a sly, hard twist, so the children stood there and listened without understanding. This may have been good discipline, but it was certainly not a joyous occasion. Every Sunday night there was a dance in the saloon, which to my mind was not a good influence.

The Scandinavian and other non-Russian fathers in the Russian village were not in sympathy with the church, although they did not oppose it or interfere with their wives' religion because when they married they had had to sign an agreement to that effect.

On Sunday afternoons there was nothing for the children to do, and although I did not intend to proselytize I did long to teach them to love the Bible and understand its essential truths. So when some of the fathers asked for a Sunday school I wrote a letter to a Presbyterian journal in the States, explaining the situation and asking for what we needed, from lesson cards to an organ. I emphasized the children's love of pictures. My letter was printed and received a splendid response; everything to make the school a success was sent us, many pictures and even an organ! It kept me busy writing letters of appreciation, but it was a pleasure to discover how kind strangers can be. They even sent things for us to put away for the Christmas tree.

I had already discovered, hidden away, a hundred New Testaments. Mrs. Pajoman told me they had been sent long ago from Washington but she was afraid the priest would be angry so she had hidden them. Far from being angry, Father Petellin was pleased when his children brought one home.

The mothers came to Sunday school with their children, and quite often the fathers came too. The men were good singers, and Mrs. Pajoman attended regularly to help with the singing. Everybody dressed up, and the parents seemed as pleased to get their lesson cards and Sunday school story-papers as the children were. The Sunday school pictures adorned many a home; indeed some rooms were newly papered to set them off grandly.

I was careful not to antagonize the church. It would not have been right in any case, but I also knew I could do nothing for the people without the church's goodwill. Old Peter Chichenoff took both his daughters out of Sunday school and I went to his store and asked why. He replied that the Russian God was all right, but the American God was no good. I explained that there is one God only. He said, "Is that true?" I assured him it was, and he decided they might return.

After it started, the Sunday school flourished throughout the rest of the winter and the spring, but then one summer day Father Petellin called, much excited. He begged me to close the Sunday school, promising that if I would only agree he would give me any other aid I asked. I was surprised, since his own children attended. He assured me nothing was wrong with it, but it must be stopped.

When pressed to tell me the real trouble, he said I was getting too much hold on his people, which might be all right as long as I was there but it might be bad if another teacher came who was not friendly. Then he added that the children liked my Sunday school better than his church service.

Father Petellin was easily swayed in his opinions, and I noticed that just before coming to me he had visited Mrs. Pajoman. But I knew he was in earnest about doing his best for the people, or at least his best to please the Czar, from whom he got a neat fifteen hundred a year. He was simply attending to his own line of business, or so I surmised.

But finally the real trouble emerged. Bishop Innocent, the bishop of all Alaska and the Pacific Coast states, was coming to Afognak in a month. Father Petellin exclaimed that the Czar paid Bishop Innocent thirteen thousand dollars a year!

While he talked on, I did some thinking. I had thirty fathers in the Russian village to reckon with. Would he agree, I asked, to postpone any decision until the bishop came to Afognak, and would he agree to abide by the bishop's decision if I agreed to do the same? Meanwhile, I would not hold any Sunday sessions until after the bishop's arrival.

Plump little Father Petellin nearly bubbled over with joy. That was good! Very good!

The fathers who had requested the school wanted me to ignore the priest's demand and continue to ring the bell as usual on Sundays. But a Sunday school in a fight, in my opinion, is worse than no Sunday school at all. I reasoned with them and they agreed to keep quiet and wait.

On its next visit the *Dora* brought in its cargo fifty beautifully dressed kid-bodied dolls as Christmas presents for the girls. I had asked friends in the States for them in the spring, explaining that it would be best to ship them in summer. Along with presents came decorations. Now the ocean may howl, thought I; everything for Christmas would be packed in the window chest of my living room.

The *Dora* also brought the bishop on that trip. People from all the nearby islands gathered on our beach, hundreds and hundreds of them, all dressed in their Sunday best. As the rowboat bearing the bishop came into sight, cannons boomed, guns banged and the church bells pealed. Otherwise there was not a sound. When the bishop landed, people passed before him in line, bowing low and kissing his gloved hand.

He was accompanied by an entourage of monks, priests and readers who formed a procession led by the bishop and followed by the crowds, who dispersed and went home when the visitors entered the priest's house.

Early in the evening the church bells pealed. I went with the rest to see what they did when a bishop was there. They had built a platform about eight feet high in the center of the church. Upon the pinnacle of this structure was a seat, and there sat the bishop. On each side, standing on a ledge just high enough so their uplifted hands reached the top of the bishop's head, stood two men. Between them they held an immense metal crown, not touching his head but directly over it. There those two stood by the hour and never moved a muscle. I remained until ten, and they were still in that position. The bishop was dressed in the most gorgeously embroidered satin robe.

Before the service began, a monk went about with a whisk broom and basin of water, sprinkling the pictures, walls and people with holy water. He kindly asked me if I wished water on me too. I told him I did not, but that I would move out of his way. He told me to remain where I was, then spoke in Russian to people near me, and they moved away until they had been sprinkled, then returned to their places.

After a long ceremony read by a priest, the bishop blessed each person without speaking a word. A church official held a bowl of water before him, and all the officials, beginning with the monks down to the readers, passed before him in line and mounted the steps to the throne. The bishop dipped his finger in the water and made a cross on each forehead. He used a brush instead of his finger to mark the cross on all the other people, each in turn. I left during this long procedure.

I had intently studied the bishop from afar. Even though he was like a little god stuck up near the ceiling, and in spite of all that seemed new and strange, I came to the conclusion that he had a good face. I would not bank on the monks, judging from their countenances, but I would on the bishop.

In the morning Father Petellin came to tell me the bishop would meet me in his home at ten. I was there on time but no bishop appeared. I had a good chance to examine his exquisitely embroidered gowns, for they were spread in the living room. At noon Father Petellin came in and said the bishop would not see me, he was too busy. He consoled me by saying he thought the bishop would send for me again and then tell me whether I could have a Sunday school.

I had to give myself a pinch to find whether I was really not in Russia instead of the good old United States. I found I was not in Russia and with that I found my spunk. I informed Father Petellin that it would be inconvenient for me to come again. He should tell the bishop that if he wanted to talk with me he could come to the government school. If he did not come, I said, I intended to resume the Sunday school.

Father Petellin, greatly agitated, said everybody had to come to the bishop, he would not come to see me. I said he was at liberty to adhere to his custom and I would adhere to mine. If the bishop thought it best not to come, I would act independently. Then I went home.

Late in the afternoon, the reader was sent as a herald to announce the bishop. Down the road came the whole procession of gowned officers. My house had two entrances, one of which I did not use. Of course they came to the wrong one and marched in where I had five chickens safely cuddled away in a box for the night to protect them from a weasel. The frightened chickens set up an awful clatter.

I could not help laughing at this comedy in the midst of the pomp and display. The bishop enjoyed it too and laughed when I said the poor chickens felt they were doomed with so many preachers coming in on them. He answered in the same vein, but the monks and priests in his entourage were solemn.

I stated the case of the Sunday school and the bishop asked me to tell him just what we did. I showed him the lessons and hymns and gave him a synopsis of the work. He turned to Father Petellin, who was fidgeting in his chair, and asked why he

did not want the Sunday school. All Father Petellin could answer was that the people liked to come to it better than they
liked to come to church, and he did not want it in the village
anyway.

The bishop said he thought they should be glad someone
was willing to teach the children and that he considered it a
wonderful opportunity. He could not understand why there
had been objections. He turned to the reader and inquired if
he had come to the Sunday school and tried to help me. Mr.
Sheratine was in a box, for the poor fellow had been afraid to
come. He answered, "I was there once."

"Once!" the bishop repeated. There was a whole sermon in
the word as he pronounced it.

He told Father Petellin that he should come to the Sunday
school and observe the methods, then try to use them. If the
children liked them so much, they would then like his church
too. It was settled that I was to continue the Sunday school. I
was glad for the sake of the children, but resolved not to hurt
the pride of Father Petellin. I was sorry for him, and determined to encourage the children to go to church regularly.

The bishop was curious about our Christmas exercises. I
told him what we did and then opened the chest and showed
him the decorations and gifts. He thought it almost too good
to believe that people far away had sent such beautiful gifts to
children they had never seen. He commented that it was a
very unselfish way of giving. He was especially delighted with
the dolls. Like a child, he piled his arms full of them and tried
to select the prettiest, but they were all so pretty he thought
he could not choose. He joked, "I almost wish I were a child,
to get one."

But the monks and priests were not pleased with him in this
lighter vein. I was afraid for the bishop. If I could read between the lines, he would have trouble with his home coun-

try. For one thing, he objected to Father Petellin continuing to teach Russian. He said that this was America and the children should be taught the language of their country. I heard that he said the same thing at the Russian school for girls in Kodiak, which was supported by the Czarina and where no language but Russian was allowed.

Almost a year after the visit I asked Father Petellin what he heard of the bishop. He had been recalled to Russia, that was all Father Petellin knew.

5

The Seasons

Gardening was responsible for the difference between the Russian and Aleut diets. Gardening had been brought to the island by the Russian convict settlers, and the Russians told me some of the gardens were a hundred years old. They grew a variety of vegetables but potatoes were their chief crop, cultivated by an ancient and laborious method. About a foot of surface soil was removed from the plot and set aside, then a thick layer of kelp, which the families gathered in dorys, was laid down. On top of that went the seed potatoes, then the topsoil was replaced. The potatoes multiplied prolifically, and when the women dug them in the fall they were clean and smooth. Many Russian families also kept a cow from the old Russian stock: short legged and heavyset, covered with yellowish-brown hair that extended over the eyes and face. Households with a cow grew hay in little jagged places between rocks, trees and stumps.

The Aleut villagers did not garden because they left for summer fishing camp and stayed there until fall. This did not mean they entirely lacked green and growing things. In spring they gathered wild celery and tender, mild wild onions that grew in marshy groves; they ate wild rhubarb all summer, wild parsley and wild rice. But they shunned wild potatoes, and in winter lacked vegetables.

When summer came I plotted out a large school garden with wide flowerbeds along the sides and rows of vegetables in the middle. The Agricultural Research Station in Sitka sent us seeds and plants. I taught the children to plant the garden our way, for I speculated that there might be more gardening if the work was easier: no taking off the earth and putting it back again.

We grew beets, turnips, carrots, parsnips, cabbage, radishes, onions, lettuce and, of course, potatoes. It rained almost every day and the summer sun shone for such long hours that growth was rapid, which made the vegetables exceptionally tender and delicious. They made good school treats. Turnips in this climate were as fine grained and tender as apples, and the children ate them like apples.

When school started again in the fall, I had hoped Washington would send another teacher or two. However, the newly passed Nelson Law interfered. On the whole, this was a good law; it provided for citizens in unincorporated towns to manage their own schools and choose their own teachers, like citizens in incorporated settlements. The governor of Alaska would issue teacher permits to qualified applicants. Teachers chosen by Nelson schools would be paid from U.S. Treasury funds sent to the governor. The law applied to places with at least fifteen white children, and in law a child was defined as white if the father was white.

Afognak came under the new law. However, a prerequisite was that the citizens had to bond for the school and its equipment; this had not yet been done in Afognak, so it was too late to establish a Nelson school that winter.

When I requested additional teachers, I wrote Washington about the circumstances. Word came back that I was to admit only Aleuts. Think of it! All those other children to lose a winter's schooling.

I would not stand for that. I wrote again asking that all children be admitted, and I would do the best I could, as I had the previous year. The reply came that I would be permitted to take them in but they were to be considered visitors and no mention made of them in my reports.

More than fifty visiting children every day! But they never knew they were visitors. I simply announced all children were to come to school, and then my practice was to classify and grade them all, make out two separate reports and send both to Washington.

How could I have told Ephram Derenoff that he was only a visitor? His mother, bringing along a friend as interpreter, came to inquire about the progress of her other son, Elijah. I assured her he was well behaved and was learning, and inquired why his older brother was not in school. I told her that since Ephram was fourteen, there was no time to lose. When he grew to manhood he would be ashamed that he could not speak or read English.

She was surprised that I knew about Ephram. She said they did not know how they could spare him, but she would talk to his father and they would send him to school if they could. Ephram came the next day and every day after. Luckily he had a start in the primer and a good idea of the sound of the letters, which saved much time. He worked early and late and was quickly reading well in the Third Reader and supplementary papers.

What touched my heart was the way his parents managed to send him. Mrs. MacDonald told me that Ephram had lived on a small offshore island by himself, to make hay and tend the family's cattle. He fed them when it was too stormy or the snow too deep, hunted game for himself, and lived in a shack.

What could they do? Ephram's father had to get wood from the forest for fuel, and fish from the sea. He had to shoot a bear from time to time for leather to sole their boots. Mrs. Derenoff could do none of these things but she could feed the cows, so she left their home in the Russian village to live all winter by herself in the desolate shack. Could any mother and father make greater sacrifices to educate a child?

I had another new pupil from a lonely island home, a ten-year-old Aleut. She was the quaintest little thing. Her mother had been to the store and bought bright, silky material with a pattern of large flowers and made her a new gown in which to enter school. It was gathered at the neck and reached to the floor, with wide kimono sleeves. She looked exactly like a Japanese, indeed like a big Japanese doll.

We had a special wax doll with golden curls that had been given me by a little girl in Seattle; she had other dolls but this was her best and favorite and she was determined to send it to little girls in Alaska. Not wanting to do less than such generosity deserved, I used the doll as a mascot. The girl who had been the most faithful student each day was allowed to take it home and keep it all night. All year the doll was in one or another home and was never broken, nor were its clothes soiled, for the older girls loved laundering them.

The little doll-like Aleut girl was so entranced with our wax doll that I let her hold it, although she had not earned the right. There she sat and hugged it all day long. At night she was determined to take it home. The other girls were willing, and through an interpreter she promised to take good care of it. But the next day she did not bring it back and from then on utterly refused to part with it, she was so desperately in love with that doll. I knew how she felt, for my dolls were the same to me. She was too undeveloped to reason out the matter with us; all she realized was that she wanted the doll and would not give it up.

So I threw philosophy to the winds and put the matter to a

vote. The girls voted to give the doll to her. I think the child
in Seattle would have had it so too. When this little girl has
been in school a few years, she will look back on the incident
and put it in proper perspective. It was good for her not to
have one cross word or look to remember, for not an item of
that first day in school would be effaced from her memory as
long as she lived.

Summer and fall were lovely seasons on Afognak. The summer dawn came as early as two in the morning, announced by
amethyst mingling with the dark blue of night, and then a
great burst of gold. The sky was so blue, the grass so green,
the air warm and mild. Every stump was covered with fern-
like moss, and air-moss floating from the trees gave the forests
a tropical air. Dandelions, the chief wildflowers, were as
large, brilliant and wide-petalled as asters.

The chain of islands and mountains to which Afognak belongs is unstable, and the animals were aware of instability before people felt it. One Saturday when I was at home alone my
attention was aroused by an unusual stillness on sea and land.
A weird, yellowish light was cast from a muddy-yellow, low-
hanging cloudbank. Suddenly, from upstairs, or so I thought,
came a grinding noise. It flashed through my mind that the
house must be on fire and the rafters falling, but running to
the head of the stairs I saw nothing was wrong. Outside the
dogs were yelping, and on the bluff was a little Russian cow
frantically pawing the earth. By this behavior I knew it must
be an earthquake. An instant later came a trembling, followed
by another. These slight earthquakes were common, and terrifying even when they did no more harm than shake the
dishes.

Quakes, of course, carry the possible threat of tidal waves.
The Aleuts had chosen their village site more prudently than
the Russians. Behind the Aleut settlement was a clear run to

mountain slopes rising steeply inland, but between the Russian village and the mountain behind it lay a fearsome, bottomless lake.

In winter, when people wanted fresh fish they needed only to row three miles out to sea, and with immense hooks and lines catch huge dogfish. They used whale oil for shortening.

All winter trappers harvested beautiful furs, chiefly thickly furred fox but also marten, mink and ermine. I saw so much fur worn and hanging about that I came not to care for it, but my friends in the States did and I sent them fox, which ranged in price from one-fifty to seven dollars a skin, and ermine, which were twenty-five cents each. As for myself, I bought an immense Kodiak bear skin with brown, silky fur and had it tanned for a rug fourteen feet long.

My first winter in Afognak was mild, registering no lower than ten below zero. Every child who could brought a potted plant to school and none of them froze. Every house in the Russian village had a flower window that year with roses blooming all winter, some of them climbing to the ceiling. In the school building we used coal, which was mined on the coast and which burned furiously, keeping both the schoolroom and my quarters comfortable.

But my second winter on the island was bitter. The blizzards began in early fall and returned at short intervals all winter. One was so severe I could not step out of doors for three days, nor could anyone else. The house was not built for weather so cold and winds so fierce. When the storm began I pushed my cot close to the heater and took the Kodiak bear rug off the floor and curled up under it. I ate very little because everything was frozen. I could not read because my hands would surely have frozen if I had tried to hold a book.

On the third day the storm abated and an old man from the Aleut village came panting to my door with a pail of water. He knew my spring would be frozen. He had taken water from a hole in the river ice and carried it two miles. In the meantime I'd had some melted snow. It requires very cold weather for ocean water to freeze, but that winter the entire bluff and seashore were one mass of ice.

6

Russian Ceremonies

On Afognak, church rituals took precedence over every-thing else. For a week during my second winter I could not get a child into school because the church was celebrating a strange and special festival at the frozen lake.

Father Petellin and the reader, Mr. Sheratine, had gotten people to make a large tent of spruce boughs on the lake ice. Inside the front of the open tent was a stand with the open Bible on it, and a large gilded cross. In front of this altar or pulpit was a round hole in the ice, cut down to the waterline. The church had borrowed all the American flags from the school, and these were floating gaily from the tent.

Father Petellin and Mr. Sheratine stood in the rear of the tent and conducted the service. All the people of both vil-lages, large and small, old and young, including even little babes in arms, congregated before the tent every day, all day, for a week, sometimes kneeling for long periods on the ice in the dreadful cold.

One day I heard the firing of guns and wondered what it meant, until Johnnie Tawnashak showed up at my home, quite troubled, and asked me to explain to him why in the Sunday school lessons God was up and the Devil down, but in the church it must be that the Devil is up and God down. I asked him why he thought so and he replied that that morning

Father Petellin had told them to shoot up into the air to shoot the Devil, and when he baptized, he baptized down. I spoke to Father Petellin and asked him why he was teaching these poor, ignorant people that they could shoot the Devil. He was a little ashamed, I think, but said it was an old custom. I suggested that some of these old customs might be abolished because as people became enlightened, they were doing some thinking for themselves and those things would have to be explained. I surmised there would be no more Devil-shooting.

For the last act of the week's ceremonies, Father Petellin immersed the gilded cross in the water, letting it down through the hole in the ice. This was supposed to make all the lake holy, but for that afternoon only. The people filled pitchers, bottles and containers of all sorts from the lake and carried them home for a supply of holy water to last all year.

I did not understand such ceremonies and neither did the people. However, anything that creates a good or pure thought is not lost, and surely the week's ceremonies did create a longing to do what is right. Only, I do wish the priest and the reader had to doctor all the colds of the younger ones and the aches and pains of the older ones caused by prolonged kneeling and standing on the ice. I am sure I made enough onion syrup for youngsters after the rites were over to scent all the water in the lake, even if it could not make it holy.

Near the end of the winter another priest and his wife moved to Afognak temporarily. Their children were all grown and married, living elsewhere. He had been suspended from his church charge because he was frequently intoxicated. He explained that he had to travel hundreds of miles by dog team and began drinking on those trips, then could not stop. If he reformed during six months in Afognak, he was to be given another church. I invited him and Father Petellin, with their wives, to dinner one Saturday afternoon. The ladies spoke only Russian and I entertained them mostly with pictures. After dinner they wanted to wash the dishes and I went into the living room but found it was empty. Then I noticed smoke rising behind the open door. The two priests in their long black robes were crowded behind it, smoking cigarettes. I called their wives in to enjoy the ludicrous sight, and all five of us had a good laugh. I told the men they need not go behind the door to burn their incense. But did this not show how childlike they were, ashamed to take their after-dinner smoke before me, so they hid?

Food in the Russian village was delicious, especially at holidays. For a dish they called *peruk,* the women mixed salmon, cooked rice, hard-boiled eggs, diced bacon, parsley, onions and butter, put it in a baking dish, poured cream gravy over it and covered the top with pastry. They told me this was served as a first course in Russia, but in Afognak it was seldom made because it was expensive and then was the first and every other course.

Weddings were the most elaborate social events of the village. The custom was for the groom to pay for whatever clothes the bride chose to buy at the store and charge to his account. The gown was usually bright-colored silk with rows of white lace sewn around the skirt. The stores kept on hand bolts of filmy bobbinet, and the women certainly did know how to drape a wedding veil: It was attached to a wreath of paper roses on the bride's head and cascaded so the bride was entirely enveloped from the crown of her head to her feet.

Mary Petellin, one of my pupils, a niece of the priest and older sister of Albert who had helped me so well as interpreter of Aleut, married Jack Nielson, the son of the storekeeper. She was eighteen, very pretty, tall and graceful, and made a most beautiful bride. Like other women in Afognak, she had small and dainty hands and feet, and she wore fine wedding shoes.

The length of a ceremony varied, according to the price the groom paid Father Petellin. Judging from the length of Mary and Jack's ceremony, the groom must have paid a good round sum.

No wedding invitations were sent out, as it was understood by custom that every person in the village where the bride or groom lived was invited and everyone attended, the old and young, the lame, the halt and the blind. Of course I went too. In this case, since neither the bride nor the groom lived in the Aleut settlement, nobody from the Aleut village was included.

This was a very fashionable wedding. The festivities began with everyone assembling in the bride's home for the procession to the church. Father Petellin and Mr. Sheratine led, Mary and Jack followed, then came the godfather of the groom. (If a groom had none, Father Petellin would appoint a godfather, usually one of the groom's friends of his own age, which was considered a great joke, but the appointed godfather was always a good sport and played his part with gusto. At one point this entailed hitting the groom over the head with a loaf of bread.) The bride's godmother followed, and then the guests flocked along any which way, a medley of shouting and laughing people soon crowding about the bride and groom. The crowd went into the church first, then the bridal party, and last, Father Petellin and the reader.

Everyone stood and all fell silent. Then the service began with chanting followed by an hour of reading by Father Petellin in an unknown tongue. Even Father Petellin did not know what he was reading. Nevertheless it was impressive.

Mary and Jack then started on their figurative journey of life. One man stood just behind Mary, another behind Jack, holding heavy metal crowns over the couple's heads. Everyone marched with them around the church, time and again, with the crown-bearers racing along, struggling to do their part with dignity. (This was difficult in weddings in which they were shorter than the bridal couple.) This lasted about half an hour.

Next followed another long ceremony, which ended with Mary going to the front of the church and kneeling for about fifteen minutes before the picture of the Madonna.

After the church services the whole crowd followed the couple to Jack's godfather's home. This is when the groom was hit over the head, three times, with a loaf of bread, which had a cross scored on it.

The great feast, the wedding dinner, was served in the bride's home with her family officiating, but the feast was organized, managed and paid for by Jack. Such a feast generally cost the large sum of two or three hundred dollars. No wedding presents were given by anyone. I suspected there would be plenty of wine, so instead of going to the dinner I slipped away to my home as we passed the school, but in about an hour I was sent for, so of course I went. It would have been too impolite to refuse.

Mary's home, of course, was not large enough to accommodate everybody at once. When I arrived, crowds had already eaten and crowds were waiting to eat. Each of three tables seated about a dozen persons. They placed me at the same table as Father Petellin and his wife, a charming woman, beautiful, sweet and womanly. The tables were loaded with everything good that the country afforded and were set about with great dishes of oranges and apples. A man at our table rose and asked me if I preferred that no liquor be served at the table where I sat. I replied that I didn't want to interfere and was willing to excuse myself, but that I did not wish to eat at a table where there was drinking. They said I must stay, so I ate as quickly as I decently could, then excused myself. Father Petellin, I heard later, was angry because as soon as I left the liquor was brought on again and nobody asked whether or not he objected. I was also told that my pupils' fathers would have been disappointed with me if I had not objected.

That night, following the feast, there was a great dance in the saloon. The revellers did not straggle home until morning.

The entire next week was a holiday for everyone. All day long the bride and groom paid visits. In each home of the village a tea table was spread and the young couple went about drinking tea and eating raisins, nuts, cake and candy. Then they danced all night, every night. By the time the week was ended, the bride's finery was pretty well draggled out.

The law specified sixteen years as the legal age for marriage but some people evaded the law. One who did was my pupil Daria Taludin, from the Aleut village. Daria had been the poorest child in school and I had a hard time teaching her to mend her clothes and come to school halfway neat. One thing I could not tolerate was that there were nearly always feathers sticking to her hair from the pillows. Many a time I sent her home to tidy up. She was fourteen but seemed such a little girl with her short dresses and braided hair. Poor child, she lived all alone with an old grandmother who was stone blind. One morning I went to the Aleut village and told Daria that she could not come to school again until her old, discouraging one-room house was cleaned and she was wearing a clean, mended dress. After school that day, when I neared her house, Daria came running to meet me, proud to show her clean dress. What a transformation! The room was spic-and-span and so was Daria. She had accomplished so much, I suspected the neighbors had helped her and I hope they did.

At most Daria was fifteen, and perhaps still fourteen, when

Jack Keegan, a well-to-do and very likable Irishman about forty years old, asked her to marry him and she accepted. Mr. Keegan told his friends he thought he would have a better wife than any of them if he trained Daria to be a good housekeeper. Probably because of the age problem, I heard nothing of the engagement until the wedding was at hand.

Such a change in Daria; the transformation was even greater than that of her home the first time she cleaned it. Here she came, swishing along in a dress that touched the floor, with her hair all done up on the top of her head. The wedding was the usual one, with paper roses and long veil, and Jack Nielson, whose own wedding had so recently been celebrated, was appointed the groom's godfather. I thought he would knock Jack Keegan's head off with that loaf of bread. All week the festivities went on, there was eating and drinking in the day and dancing all night, and at the week's end Daria was a full-fledged society lady of the Russian village.

Another proposed wedding was giving me great anxiety. About the time I came to Afognak, a beautiful young girl named Lavia fell in love with a transient prospector. I had never spoken to him but had often seen him. He was of medium height, had black hair and a black mustache. Lavia was blue eyed and fair haired. These two eloped, running away to a government justice of the peace (or as such an official was called in Alaska, a commissioner) to be married. Since they had not been married in the church, Father Petellin did not recognize the marriage.

In the summer, a daughter was born to this child wife. The young man stepped into a boat, telling Lavia he must go out to the *Dora,* lying in the harbor, to transact some business. He boarded, sailed away and was not seen again. Lavia never faltered in her belief that he would soon return, but no one else believed that and nobody knew whence he came or where he went.

Lavia's family decided she should marry an old paralytic by the name of Squartsoff, who could barely shuffle along and who lived alone except for his nine-year-old son, Nicholai, in Ouzinkie on a nearby island. Of course she would have Nicholai and her own daughter for company, but I protested to her parents and Father Petellin. The match was so absurd and inhumane I did not think they would dare force it. Nevertheless, two years later, after I had left Afognak, Lavia's parents did force her into the marriage. I heard that she was a good mother to Nicholai, teaching him to read and write. So they lived for a time and then a young Aleut, who had long been in love with Lavia, came to camp on the island.

Not surprisingly, his company was welcome to the lonely and resentful girl. One night these two murdered the old man while he slept and tossed his body into the ocean. When the tide brought it back the next day they again threw it to the waves and once more the tide returned it. Then, with Nicholai watching them, they dug a grave, and after the body was buried they threatened the boy with the same sort of death if he ever told what he had seen.

Some days later Nicholai's uncle came to the island to visit and asked where his brother was. "I daren't tell," whispered the terrified Nicholai. His uncle soon had the story and notified the police.

A Secret Service agent came to Wood Island, where I was teaching at the time, and asked me what I knew of Lavia and her family. I told him the circumstances and it modified matters a little. The court in Valdez where they were tried judged the two more as children than as hardened criminals, and so instead of being executed they were sentenced to life imprisonment.

Lavia's mother had a friend write a letter to me, asking if I could ever be her friend again after her daughter had done such a terrible thing. Poor thing, she had really thought she was doing the best for her disgraced daughter when she had forced that awful marriage. This was the same mother, Mrs. Derenoff, who had spent the winter on a lonely island, tending the cows, so her son Ephram could get an education.

If ever justice could be rendered in such a case, that dapper young man who abandoned Lavia and left her with a daughter would be called to account.

Funerals were solemn and sad in Afognak, as everywhere. Mrs. Malutin died during my second winter there. She was a young mother who had befriended me on my first visit to the Russian village, when I walked into her kitchen, a stranger, while she was cutting up whale meat for a stew. Her kind countenance had impressed me and she was true to her looks, for she did many kind little acts in the village.

There she lay after death, on a sheet-draped board held upon the seats of two chairs, with a tiny dead infant on her arm. Her husband sat with his face bent low over a three-year-old on his knee, beside him the two other children, Darie and Johnny, looking much older than their years. The "old woman" who ministered to all families in trouble sat in front of a small stand on which lay an open Bible, while the reader, Mr. Sheratine, monotonously droned out Slavonic words, on and on, and I thought again what reaching out there is for the Light, by whatever means people have.

All the while, the village women were coming in, one by one, each enveloped in a large black shawl draped so that it almost covered her face. They seated themselves in rows on the floor, moaning and swaying in unison. Outside in the vestibule, the men were making the coffin. The sound of the hammering accompanied the low wail of the women and the chanting monotone of the reader.

When the box was finished, the men covered it with blue calico and lined it with white muslin, and on the center of the lid was placed a cross sewn of muslin. The next morning I brought lace and ribbon to trim the pillow, and the other women brought the prettiest blossoms they had from indoor plants to lay around her body.

The people, including the immediate relatives, stood back while the funeral procession started toward the church. Two altar boys led, the first carrying a large lighted candle in a brass candlestick, the second bearing the Greek cross. Then followed two men carrying on their heads the lid of the coffin surmounted with a wreath of flowers at each end. Four men behind them bore the coffin on two wide strips of muslin. Over the body had been thrown a gaily striped shawl. The reader followed, carrying a large open Bible, and last came Father Petellin, holding a gold-covered cross. Alongside the coffin walked a man carrying hammer and nails. All the while, the church bells pealed mournfully.

The family and all the rest of the community straggled along behind in any order, all singing a hymn in a minor key. When the body was placed in the church, incense was burned. Then came a rite that horrified me. Every man, woman and child walked up and kissed the corpse upon the mouth. Even infants in arms were held up and their little mouths placed on the mouth of the dead woman. I made a mental note to protest to Father Petellin that this should never happen again.

As the procession started for the cemetery, its mood changed completely. The church bells rang out joyfully and the crowd's song was a triumphant shout. When water had been dipped out of the grave and the coffin lowered, everyone came forward and threw in handfuls of earth until the ground was level and then mounded it with rocks.

My heart ached for the poor husband while this was being done. He walked off, laid his head on the top rail of a fence and sobbed bitterly. The rule was that a man could marry again in forty days. Mr. Malutin gave away all three children and in just forty-one days he was remarried. I resolved not to waste sympathy on widowers in this village.

Kodiak, Wood Island and Seward

By the end of my second winter in Afognak, arrangements for the new Nelson school were under way. There were good businessmen in Afognak, capable of fulfilling the bonding requirements mandated by the new law; they had merely lacked understanding of the law the previous year.

A new building for several teachers was to be constructed during the summer. The community asked me to stay but I wanted to go to a remote place that had no school and start one there. After I sent my request to Washington I was assigned to a remote reindeer station at Reindeer Bay on Lake Iliamna, with time for a vacation and visits in Kodiak and Wood Island before setting out.

I had found, during my teaching experience in other places, that once people had a good school they would always demand a good school, so I was not worried about future schooling in Afognak. Furthermore other promising developments were afoot. The saloon was to be closed down. It should never have been there in the first place because the island was a government reserve, where a saloon was illegal. I had been in correspondence with influential government people about Afognak's needs and wishes, and now a sawmill and fish hatchery were prospects.

I would carry away with me many valuable lessons gleaned

from these primitive people and memories of many loving deeds on the part of an affectionate, grateful population. My central object had been to create in them a thirst for something better than they had previously known and launch them on the voyage to achieving their desires.

Before taking up my new assignment I planned to visit Kodiak, to the south of Afognak, then spend a few weeks on Wood Island, which was within sight of the town of Kodiak, across a strait.

Kodiak was the metropolis of all that part of the country: the outfitting station for visiting hunters and for prospectors going in all directions to the other islands, and westward into the interior. The U.S. commissioner, judge and marshal were stationed here; also the postmaster; an agent of the experimental agricultural station; and the agent of the Alaska Commercial Company, the major trading organization, along with the company's manager, bookkeepers and clerks. It had a resident physician and a dentist and a graded Nelson school requiring several teachers. That pretty well accounted for the permanent American residents. The rest of the people were part native Alaskans and part Russian, with inclusions of other Caucasians deriving from every part of Europe. In appearance, dress and manners they were white citizens and so stood in law.

I received a welcome at the wharf from friends I had never met but who knew of me. In Alaska everyone was your friend and interested in you, and I was interested in everyone. Among people who were away from much of civilization, and perhaps isolated for periods of the year, stronger friendships could form in a month than would develop in years where there was much that was distracting and artificial.

Kodiak Island is a hundred miles long and fifty wide, with a few smaller settlements along its coast. At this time, in

1906, its interior had not yet been explored, but from the summits that had been scaled it appeared to be an endless succession of snow-covered peaks and snow-packed high valleys as far as the eye could see.

I stayed with the family of the manager of the Alaska Commercial Company, the Gosses. Kodiak had been the first Russian capital before Sitka, and their home had been the mansion of the governor general, Alexander Baranov. The ridge of the house was crowned by a bust of Peter the Great. I overheard the manager say to a carpenter who was repairing the roof, "And you may as well paint Peter while you are up there."

Many other old buildings were standing. The most remarkable, I thought, was the warehouse at the wharf, which had taken twenty years to build. The logs were mammoth and must have been brought from a great distance, perhaps British Columbia or even farther south, because no trees in southern Alaska approached that size. The vast, gloomy building was always dark and chilly even in summer, purposely so because it had been the storing place for furs.

While I was in Kodiak, Miss Vonderfour, headmistress of the Czarina's boarding school for girls, was dismissed and recalled to Russia by the Czarina. It was said that previously she had been employed by the Czarina as a governess and had lived at court. She spoke English well, and the rumor was that she allowed her pupils in Kodiak to speak it and that she taught them about America, and that priests in Kodiak complained of this to authorities in Russia.

After Miss Vonderfour's dismissal, she invited me and my friend Mrs. MacDonald to visit her for an afternoon, bringing our thimble work. She was living temporarily in two scantily equipped rooms of an empty house. She served us beautifully prepared refreshments of orange juice and small round cakes.

She was sad and felt wronged and was hoping to find work in Alaska, feeling that it was safer than for her to return to Russia.

The experimental station at Kodiak was operated by a man from the Kansas state agricultural school. One of his principal projects was to introduce Galloway cows and acclimatize them. These black, stockily built, shaggy-haired cattle could, at a distance, easily be mistaken for buffalo. A few years previously Fry Bruhm and Company had sent hundreds of sheep to Kodiak Island with the object of planting a herd. By error, they were landed in the town of Kodiak, many miles from where they were to be kept, and no way to get them there but in boats. They were landed in a blizzard, became panic-stricken and ran off in all directions. Every one of them was said to have perished in the storm. For years afterward natives in Kodiak had plenty of good woollen yarn, for they were permitted to shear the frozen carcasses. They cleaned, carded and spun the wool with the crudest of implements.

Bear hunters came to Kodiak from all over the world. Another guest at the Gosses' house while I was there was Captain Floyd Harris, a soldier and scholar who was an American military attaché. In a London furrier's shop he had seen an immense brown bear skin and was told it was that of a Kodiak bear. Although he had been in many parts of the world he had never heard of Kodiak. He resolved to hunt such a bear himself. With Old Fred, the best bear hunter on the island, he spent a couple of weeks in the wild and came back with four huge pelts. Then he regaled us with tales of court life in the European capitals.

The sky over Kodiak was sometimes so blue that it lost its ethereal quality and became a canopy of rich violet velvet. Wild roses were everywhere, each blossom as large as the top of a coffee cup. A hundred and fifty kinds of wildflowers had been found within a short distance of the town, and their blues, reds, oranges, purples and pinks were as brilliant as though they had been dyed. Berries were equally brilliant. A high hill behind the town, where we often hiked and picnicked, was riven from base to summit by a deep fissure, cleft suddenly by a terrifying earthquake that had occurred a hundred years previously. People in Kodiak were still talking about that experience, as described to them by grandparents.

Mrs. MacDonald, my good friend from the Russian village in Afognak, had come to Kodiak while I was there to visit her father, an Englishman who was connected with the Alaska Commercial Company. She took me to see a remarkable Russian woman, 104 years old, who had been a small child at the time of the earthquake. The dear old lady had one finger wrapped in a little rag. She apologized, saying she had hurt it cutting kindling. Until she was a hundred, she roamed the woods, sometimes staying all day, coming home at nightfall with a basket of berries and an apron full of mushrooms.

With Mrs. MacDonald as interpreter, the old woman told us in Russian of the monk Gregory. Mr. Goss, my host, and his wife were with us. Mr. Goss spoke Russian and understood it well. He was much better able than I to judge whether what the old lady said was authentic; he said that she was reliable and that the story she told was accepted as factual. Everyone in Kodiak and Afognak knew this story, but the old woman was the only person still alive who had heard it herself from followers of the monk.

Gregory came from Russia and was said to be the first to carry the news of the Gospel to Alaska. For many, many years he lived on Kodiak Island, dressed always in a single garment made of the skin of an animal. He wore heavy chains about his waist and on each arm, and on his legs was an iron weight, which was pointed out to visitors in the Kodiak church. He ate the plainest food, never enough to satisfy his hunger. Many days he fasted and sometimes fainted. He lived in a barabara, a crude underground hut, and slept on a stone bed with a stone for a pillow. Summer or winter he never wore shoes.

The last several years of his life were spent on Spruce Island. Three days before his death he called some of his followers on that island to his home. He had built a little temple of earth; beneath it, he told them, he would dig his own grave. He instructed them not to go to Kodiak when he died and to tell no one there he was going to be buried. Above all, he forbade them to touch his clothing but to bury him just as they found him, simply lay him in the ground and cover him with soil he had prepared. He gave them papers to take to Kodiak after his burial, some of which were to be kept there and others sent to Russia.

The men saw no more of him for three days, but at the end of that time they saw a light burning outside his barabara in a stone filled with whale oil and a rag for a wick. When they saw him lying dead in the barabara they were frightened and ran down to the shore to go to Kodiak for help. But the sea, which had been calm, rolled and frothed so violently it was impossible for their bidarkas to put out. In fear the men huddled in their own barabaras. Finally they decided they had better heed the monk's commands, so they crept again to his barabara, carried the body to the little earth chapel and buried him exactly as he had commanded. No sooner had they finished than the storm ceased and the sea became as gentle as a pond in June.

Among the papers Gregory had given the men were instructions that he was to be taken from his grave after one hundred years. He predicted that the grave would break open in the shape of a cross, and that his body would be like stone and would heal the sick. He also wrote that if those who had faith came to his grave while he lay buried and took a bit of earth from it, they would be healed.

At the time I was there, about a hundred years had passed and the grave had not broken open, but the natives said he had made other prophecies that had come true about the strange and different people who were to come among them and the strange machines they would use. When people used lights that came and went in a flash, he said, the end of the world was near.

At intervals of ten years, ever since his burial, delegations of priests and monks had come to Alaska from Russia and quietly visited the grave. The most recent delegation had come in about 1890. Since then Russia had not sent anyone. The natives had been taught all their lives to watch for the opening of the grave, and were curious to see what would be found.*

When Bishop Innocent visited me on Afognak I asked him about the story, which was first told to me there, and asked him whether he believed a monk would be a saint if his body turned to stone. Yes, he said, he believed it. If a body did not decay and was like marble when they dug it up in a hundred years, it had great healing power. Such a saint, he said, had recently been discovered in Russia and placed in a gold coffin in one of the cathedrals, and people who came to it were healed. He added that saints had been good people on earth.

I was surprised that Bishop Innocent encouraged the superstitions about Gregory. Mrs. MacDonald, who was an educated and intelligent woman, had been taught all her life to watch for the opening of the grave, and she asked me what I thought. What could I say? I told her I did not know anything about it, but I asked her what she thought about the strict orders not to change his clothes, to lay him right on the earth and

*See "Who Was Gregory?" p. 243.

then to cover him with the earth he had ready. Had it occurred to any of them that chemicals might have been used? She said they had never thought of that.

On Wood Island, where I went next, I felt quite at home because the population was much like Afognak's. The center of island life was the Baptist mission, with an orphanage and school. The native folk lived in a settlement to one side and those who called themselves Russian to the other, both at quite a distance from the mission buildings.

This was the most beautiful place I had seen yet; surely, I thought, the most naturally beautiful spot on earth. It was so lovely I was almost tempted, although not seriously, when the mission superintendent asked me to stay and teach at the school. Two other schools in the vicinity made overtures, and a delegation of three men from Afognak arrived to try again to persuade me to take charge of the new Nelson school there. All these positions were at better salaries than I was to receive in the remote interior. But the people out there by themselves, groping for the light, appealed to me. So I kept to my determination to go. I had studied some anthropology and so could go about the work scientifically. In nine cases out of ten, I thought, those people would get some one to work in that uncivilized place who did not understand the development of a race or of a child.

The first leg of my trip to the interior was by boat to Seward. The ladies of Kodiak and Wood Island made up a "sunshine bag" for me and I was advised to open up one package a day on my journey, as long as they lasted. A kind thought.

On the steamer to Seward I was unable to hold up my head for two days. The *Dora*'s decks were deserted, so continuously and sickeningly did the ship roll, and from the moment the voyage began I had been in my berth. The third day I felt better but still could not get up. The sunshine bag was in my stateroom. I looked at the many packages and decided there would never be a time when I was in worse need of comfort. So I opened the whole job lot and had it over. I read all the Christmas letters too. I could read them again at Christmas.

The previous time I had seen Seward there was no town, only a few houses and a dream. In the two years since, Seward had become a boomtown. A company had sold stock in the States to promote a railroad joining the Pacific Coast with the Arctic Circle. The officers of the company arrived first and built a row of expensive, splendid bungalows, dubbed "Swell Head Row." Some excellent people lived in the row but it was clear that most of them had never lived on a frontier before. Instead of wearing good stout boots and outing suits they meandered among stumps and briars in black silk and dressy hats, carrying calling-card cases. Their tea parties and hobbies of embroidering and photography were sources of anxiety to them. But I reflected that if they were writing their thoughts about me, I might be quite as ludicrous.

The railroad depot and offices were imposing. Aside from the dwellings for people connected with the railroad, other houses were log cabins and these were rapidly multiplying too. I had a friend, a graduate of an Eastern university whose husband was an attorney, whose home was a one-room log cabin. They thought it wiser to buy a little plot of ground than to pay exorbitant rents and planned to live in their cabin until they were sure the boom would last. The tiny lot on which they built cost them six hundred dollars.

Their one room was a study in economy, yet at the same time refined. It was a revelation to me to see how comfortably and cosily they lived in a very small house. Along one wall was a black mantlepiece, seven feet long, hung with a brown and green curtain, and behind it a good bed, all made up and buttoned to the wall. Behind a screen in one corner was a cute little cooking range. In another curtained alcove was a dresser, a dressing table, clothes press and washstand. Out in the room was a china closet containing beautiful china, a little square dining table, four dining chairs, a couch and a couple of easy chairs.

I stayed at the home of one of the missionaries. The missions in Seward were centers for social life, unlike old missions. One woman who called on me there was Mrs. Raville, the daughter of Mrs. Lowell, a woman of native and Russian descent who had formerly owned the whole site of Seward. She did not realize the value of her possession and sold it all, except for rights to a few blocks of land, for a few thousand dollars, which looked like a fortune to her. The transaction was perfectly legal, her daughter said, but enormous wealth was being garnered by others from this poor native woman's legacy.

Mrs. Raville told me something of her mother's life. Her husband, Mrs. Raville's father, was Frank Lowell, a first cousin to James Russell Lowell. He had come from New England, I took it, in the early days of American possession of Alaska, married, settled down and had five children. But then he tired of living in the great lonesome Kenai peninsula, boarded a boat and left his family. Mrs. Raville, the eldest child, was still a little girl. As soon as she and a brother who was next oldest were able to, they set trap lines, wading through the snow and buffeted by winds. Many a bear these children trapped and shot, and dragged home if they could. When a bear was too heavy, they skinned it where it was killed and took home the pelt. These were black bears; they never trapped a Kodiak bear.

The family's struggle for existence was pathetic, but somehow Mrs. Lowell succeeded with the children's help, and even managed to get her youngsters an education. Mrs. Raville went on to tell me that she had heard of her father lately. He was in Karluk on Kodiak Island. She showed me the photograph of herself she was planning to send him, a large cabinet photo of a tall, graceful young girl in her graduation dress. She longed to see him. "After all, he is my father, and if he only cared for me I would be glad to love him." This is surely a childlike race, so forgiving.

A couple of years later, when I was teaching on Wood Island, four ladies from Boston came to visit their friend, the new superintendent's wife. When I heard that one of them was the widow of a Judge Lowell, I pointed out to her three young grandchildren of Frank Lowell who were living at the mission and told her their family history. Her husband too had been a cousin of James Russell Lowell. She figured out the family connection of the children to her late husband. This kind and intelligent woman took an affectionate and practical interest in these three little kinfolk. They found a good friend in her. She was confident enough of her position in life to do as she thought right.

Winters were so bitter in Seward the schools were being kept open all summer and closed during January, February and March. But in the summer, when I was there, wild food was abundant. One morning when the wife of the missionary at whose home I was staying wanted some currants, she sent off her husband with a large water pail. In two hours he was back with the pail filled. The bay teemed with big silver and king salmon. Grayling trout were found throughout Alaska, but at Seward they were unusually large.

I had waited eleven days in Seward before the *Dora* returned to take me on the next leg of my trip, a one-day journey into Cook Inlet, on the opposite side of the Kenai peninsula.

Wild-goose Chase into the Interior

My new appointment was supposed to be to a reindeer station some twenty-four miles beyond the village of Iliamna, which in turn was over the mountains from Iliamna Bay. The *Dora* anchored many miles offshore from a rendezvous place named A.C. Point. This time I did climb down the ship's rickety rope ladder. Although I was no longer immobilized by terror, the maneuver was still a horror to me.

My instructions had been to take with me all the food I would need for a year. Accordingly, I had outfitted myself in Seward at my own expense. Freight transport was also at my own expense because only my personal traveling costs were paid, with a bare allowance of 350 pounds of baggage. My food supplies and chattels, like me, were lowered miles out at sea, then rowed to the Point. That ended the responsibility of the steamer company.

The A.C. Point was a desolate shore in a sort of alcove at the foot of bluffs and mountains. It boasted one surprisingly large building and a single cabin. The large building had been constructed as a station and warehouse by a company formed to lay a railroad. The first use of the capital raised had been to erect the building I now saw. When the enterprise failed for lack of further capital, the big building and the cabin had been abandoned and were now used as common property by trappers, prospectors, traders and other travelers when they disembarked from the *Dora* or were awaiting its arrival.

My instructions specified that the superintendent of the reindeer station would be at the Point to meet me. He was to have a boat ready at the Point to take me to the head of Iliamna Bay, and a horse ready there to take me across the mountains to Iliamna village, and from there I was to travel another thirty miles to the station by water on Lake Iliamna. So I had landed at the Point in expectation of being met by a responsible person who would provide transportation. The officials in Washington and on a missionary board in New York who had cooperated in making arrangements were confident their instructions on my behalf were being carried out.

I assumed that the superintendent of a reindeer station would be a manly sort of man. I suppose my subconscious had also clothed him in some of the attributes of a school superintendent. To my surprise, a bleary little fellow who had rudely evaded meeting my eyes was pointed out as the superintendent. I think he was a Laplander. He pointedly continued to ignore me.

Fortunately, a number of gentlemen were standing about on the Point. I inquired of them where I could find someone to carry my outfit to safety from the incoming tide. They cheerfully assured me my goods would be taken care of, and forthwith every coat came off and they lugged all my freight into the warehouse, quite a distance. The reindeer superintendent stood sullenly by, never moving a muscle to help.

An offer to pay them would have displeased the men who aided me, but I had brought with me a large watermelon. Some had not tasted melon for a long time and so, along with my thanks, this pleased them. They gave me the key to the cabin and laid plenty of wood beside the little stove. With my bedding roll and travel hamper of food, I would be comfortable for the night.

Just before I entered the cabin, the superintendent finally spoke to me. He informed me they did not need me. They didn't want me to teach at the reindeer station. He already had a teacher coming, he said, and he had expected her on this boat but she hadn't arrived. That simplified matters; at least now I had my bearings. I asked him if he had a horse for me at the head of the bay and he said he had not, and there was no way for me to get to Iliamna village and no way for me to get from there to the reindeer station.

Early the next morning, about four o'clock, a group of boats started off from the Point. I was kindly invited by two men to enter their boat. Since the *Dora* had sailed away, and since I could hardly just remain in that cabin on the shore, I accepted the ride, leaving my freight in the Point warehouse. The tide was with us, so we arrived at the head of the bay in good time, still early in the morning. The two gentlemen who had brought me along introduced me to a scholarly white-haired old gentleman who for the present was living in one of the two cabins at the head of the bay. He told them to take me to his cabin while he went on ahead to make a fire. He sliced ham and made hot cakes and bade me eat because I had a long, hard journey ahead. The reindeer superintendent had come up in another boat but he was so intoxicated that he was laid out in the other cabin.

About a half mile south of these two cabins were a store-house and cabin used by traders of Iliamna village. My two boat companions and my new benefactor consulted and decided I should have a guide. They found one at the traders' storehouse, and assured me he was perfectly reliable, so off he and I started, on foot.

The trail over the mountains to the village was only twelve

miles as a straight survey line goes, but that did not include windings around the mountains nor the ups and downs. The scenery was magnificent and the day perfect. I had lived in the Rocky Mountains and crossed the continent several times, but never before had I been in such wild grandeur of chasms, valleys and mountain peaks. Sometimes we would be tramping along the edge of a mountain, looking down hundreds of feet into a valley cut by streams from the glacial ice fields and melting mountain snows. Then we would dip down into a valley where grass was higher than our heads and fireweed blazed everywhere. Sometimes a valley merged into a bare clay area where fresh tracks of bears were printed.

But this trip was not all joy. We had to cross many glacial streams, which did not look deep but were swift and deeper than they appeared. It was all I could do to hold my footing on the slippery rocks. Once I fell on my face and would surely have drowned if the guide had not rescued me. The biggest stream, the Chinkelyes River, was about forty feet wide and quite as deep as I could wade but fortunately was not as swift as the smaller streams or I could never have forded it. The water was ice-cold. Although I wore waterproof, knee-high boots, my feet were wet and ached dreadfully. Toward night I was walking very slowly and I knew that if a bear crossed our tracks I could not run one step. But no doubt the bears were no more eager to meet us than we to meet them, for a fresh track now and again was all we saw.

When we finally reached the village, the only place for me to go was to a store, a two-room building, one room for the store and one for living. In this humble abode was the truest hospitality.

Olga, the wife of Pete Anderson, the storekeeper, was predominantly Russian but could speak English. She got warm water in a large basin, sat down at my feet without a word and

Hannah's friend in need, Agafia Anderson—nicknamed Olga—with her children Michael and Maud. The name of the child in the center is not known. *James Carter collection, Alaska State Historical Library*

took off my boots, tears of sympathy rolling down her face. I was too heartsick for tears. My feet were blue-black and when the blood began to circulate again, it oozed out all around my toenails.

The illustrious Reindeer Man got his meal at the store. When he looked into the living room he stood and jeered at Olga helping me. Then all my Irish spunk came to my aid and by the time I was through with my say he was quite sober. At any rate, when he slunk away he looked abashed and as if an American woman was a quantity to be reckoned with.

There was no place in Iliamna village for me to sleep, so when the store closed for the night Mr. Anderson brought a narrow mattress and spread it on the store counter. There I slept for ten nights in prolonged pain from my feet.

When I was rested enough in a day or two to take my bearings, some of the white men and the better class of natives helped me prepare a good map of Iliamna Lake and locate every village in its vicinity, with notes about the population of each. There were no children at the Reindeer Station! Clearly, the logical place for a school was in Iliamna village instead.

People there were wild to have me stay. Several men offered to move out of their houses so they could be used for a school. Zackar, the chief of an outlying village, Nondalton, and a delegation of his men arrived and pleaded with me not to leave the country. They wanted a school so badly.

I had authority to erect one or two buildings at the reindeer station, but no authority to spend any money in Iliamna, Nondalton or anywhere else. I concluded the situation was too serious for me to meddle with it on my own and decided I would have to lay the matter before the department in Washington.

I told the people I must leave Iliamna but promised I would return sometime. When I gave my promise I could not see how to fulfill it but was determined that, if I lived, that promise would be kept.

For my trip back to A.C. Point I asked the Iliamna village

chief, Kusma Rickteroff, to secure me a good woman to come along and wait with me until the *Dora* returned, and asked for his assurance that he himself would come to the Point at that time and take her safely back home. I would compensate her for her time.

They debated as to who should go, and decided on a young woman named Thedoska Rickteroff who spoke good English. She had a two-year-old daughter, Wassalissa, whose white father was dead. I promised, for my part, to take good care of mother and child.

We had three horses: one for myself, one for Thedoska and Wassalissa and a pony to carry my hamper. Two white men and seven native men came with us afoot. By this time the bears were so thick that the men all carried guns.

The streams were not nearly as deep or strong as before, for the snow melt was about exhausted. The scenery was blurred nearly the entire trip because the rain came in torrents, but in my slicker and sou'wester I was warm and dry. Once, on the edge of a high mountain ridge, I came near pitying myself in my disappointment. Of all moods, I think self-pity the most harmful. To combat it, I turned partly around on my horse and took in the scene. Just then the clouds shifted and the sun glinted through for a few minutes. Farthest back in the line came the seven short, heavyset Kenais, each shouldering a gun; then the pony with the hamper; next Thedoska and Wassalissa, and the two white men alongside our horses. It was a comical sight, and if I could have observed myself along with the rest of the crowd, it would have been more so.

I comforted myself that when I reached the cabin at A.C. Point I would cartoon the whole outfit, for I had paper and watercolors in the hamper on the pony. Later, I did indeed cartoon the procession, but when the picture was finished it did not look as comical as I had imagined it would. The background of mountains, the sky with its overhanging mist clouds and the sunshine rifting through were too majestic for our ridiculous parade to count for much. We were atoms, hardly worth notice in the grand vastness of mountain, valley and sky.

The horses knew the route perfectly well. The trails were narrow along the edges of mountain gorges, and although the horses stumbled sometimes they were steady in the dangerous spots. Because of the storm, we were a long day coming over the trail and then another day in the boats to reach the Point. For our overnight stay before taking the boats, Thedoska, the baby and I stayed in the cabin at the head of the bay, where we cooked our meals and slept.

We reached the Point about eight days before the *Dora* was due. In my steamer trunk in the warehouse I found material for Thedoska to make Wassalissa a couple of pretty little dresses and two waists for herself, and she was happy and busy fashioning finery. As soon as she finished a new waist of pretty material for herself, she slept in it!

I had a good telescope organ in my freight, and on the Sunday during our wait I asked the men who were then at the Point, also waiting for the *Dora*'s arrival, if they would like to hold a short service with the organ music and my hymnbooks. They sang and sang, choosing their favorite hymns. Some said they had not heard those songs since they were lads.

That day one of the men wanted to buy my year's supply of food just as it was. I wanted to sell it, but thought it proper to wait until Monday to transact business. Quite a discussion went on, I was told, about whether I was justified in not selling my goods on Sunday. Some thought I was, others that it was a foolish sentiment. On Monday I sold the things and received my money. The next day, Tuesday as we all thought, some new people came over the trail and we discovered from them that we were a day ahead in the time. There, I had sold my goods on Sunday after all! A joke enjoyed by all.

The Iliamna chief arrived just as the *Dora* was rounding a distant island and its smoke could first be seen. I handed Thedoska and Wassalissa over to him. In about an hour the steamer's whistle would be heard; then in about another hour its boats would reach the Point to take us off.

During that interval some Eskimos arrived to see me. They had heard a teacher was at the Point and that she was going away. They could not speak English but the Iliamna chief could partly understand them. The Eskimos said they had come to see me because they wanted to learn. I gave the young man among them a magazine, supposing he would look at the pictures, but he paid them no attention. Instead he pointed to the letters and made me understand he wanted to know what they were. As he indicated each letter I gave him the sound, and I think he got just a little insight into the mystery of reading, for he seemed delighted. With the chief as interpreter, I conveyed that I would tell their wish to the proper persons and sometime, I was sure, a teacher would come to them.

All the boys from Iliamna village also came down to the Point. One did the talking for the group. They wanted to know when I would come back and asked me not to forget. I told them I would not forget but I could not say when it would be.

On the return steamer trip I again had to sojourn in Seward. Another transformation! Many of the railroad officials and their families had left abruptly. Funds for the project had given out and no more were in sight for the present. Seward was such an expensive place to live, they had to have a steady income or depart; I heard that some who were leaving had none too much money to get back to Seattle.

From Seward I cabled to Washington an outline of the situation I had found and asked what I should do. Word clicked back over the wires in the air and under the sea that I should write fully of the circumstances, and meanwhile go to Unga and take charge of its school. Unga was hundreds of miles to the west but on the direct steamship route.

We had a calm voyage from Seward to Kodiak, where the *Dora* stopped on its way westward to Unga. The superintendent of the Wood Island school happened to be in Kodiak awaiting the *Dora*'s arrival. Of course he was surprised to see me. He said I should not go on to Unga. Wood Island school had been placed under the Nelson law, but the principal teacher who had been elected from among applications sent in for the position had not arrived. He said that therefore I should take the position. If the applicant who had been chosen did turn up, I could instead have a position in the island's mission until spring.

I did not feel drawn toward Unga. In addition I was tired and did not feel well able to undertake another long journey. I would have decided to stay on Wood Island in the first place if my sympathy had not been won by the people without a school in the interior. Word of my swift change in plans had to go by letter from Kodiak to Seward, by cable from Seward to Seattle, then by wire to Washington. I simply stated that I had accepted the school at Wood Island.

In the meantime, while my message was starting on its way, my baggage was hastily taken off the *Dora* at two in the morning and promptly carried to Wood Island by rowboat. It turned out that the principal teacher who had been expected had not received word that he had the position. The letter to him was returned to Wood Island owing to some mix-up in the address.

After the full particulars of my wild-goose chase reached

Washington, letters from the various officials who had sent me expressed deep regret that I had been compelled to endure the hardships. The Reindeer Man was to be investigated. The disappointment of the children in Iliamna was often on my mind. I told myself that these things take time but that everything takes place in due season.

Life on Wood Island

In the days of Russian rule, Wood Island had for a time been a commercial ice-producing and -shipping center, its blocks of ice distributed to many parts of the world. A chain of three lakes, with dams between them, supplied the ice. Water from the higher lakes was turned into Lower Lake, then the dam was closed, the next lake was filled and its dam closed, and then the last. The lakes could be harvested and then flooded again at will in this fashion. The buildings associated with this work had vanished, but their log foundations, still perfectly preserved, showed that they must have been enormous. A net of corduroy roads, still in use, had been constructed for teams hauling the ice.

Later the North American Alaskan Company had a station on the island for many years. When it was abandoned its imposing, white-painted buildings were left standing and some were used by the mission.

The mission, founded in the late 1870s, was supported and supplied with workers by a women's Baptist missionary society, with its membership largely in New England. This was now the island's chief establishment. Facing Kodiak across a narrow water, it was known as the Kodiak Baptist Orphanage. It stood on the shore of Lower Lake in which the buildings, shining through spruce boughs, were reflected as perfectly as if they were seen through a clear glass. They included a picturesque chapel, a girls' dormitory and a main building that housed the boys' dormitory, apartments for the superintendent and teachers, dining rooms, assembly hall and kitchen.

The orphanage accommodated fifty children, not all of them orphans. Any destitute children were admitted, and although the orphanage was loath to admit others, all but the most prosperous native families sought admission for their children of school age. I believe the presence of these more fortunate children, as far as they could be accommodated, was helpful in building up a good school community. As the mission home for the children was conducted on the plan of an admirable Christian home, the children were loving, docile and easily managed. Most children enrolled in Wood Island School lived at the home. The few who did not were mostly

The Baptist mission buildings at Wood Island as they looked inundated with ash from the 1912 Katmai volcanic eruption. *Hannah Breece collection*

in the lower grades. Until the Nelson Law provided for the school to become the responsibility of the community as a whole, the superintendent of the mission had managed it.

The school building, with its large windows framing the ocean, was set so near the sea that the tide partly washed under it. It was charming; indoor window boxes were filled with pansies that climbed far up the windows, and nasturtiums that climbed anywhere one trailed a string.

On mild days when there was sunshine I took the pupils out onto a sunny bluff for the day. It was an ideal place to teach geography. And on some of the precious sunny days we went to a sand field to measure acres and rods. The children loved to trace maps of the world there and hear stories of the people in strange countries.

To the west, on Kodiak Island, stood Old Barometer. Anyone planning a walk, a picnic or a fishing or berrying expedition the next day scanned Old Barometer's white head the evening before. If night fell on its clear-cut outline, all was well. But if a misty veil hung over its cap or a fluffy cloud above it, the gala must be postponed. Old Barometer never failed.

One summer evening Mike Chabitnoy, one of my pupils, came running to the school and urged us to see what they had on the beach. It was a shark larger around than a barrel and about ten feet long, lubbered in fat. When the audience arrived the boys put on their performance. One of them jumped upon the thickest part of the body and out flew a large salmon from its open mouth. Another and another jump until five large, perfectly whole fish had leaped forth amid screams of laughter from the children. They immediately named the shark Jonah.

The boys had been in their dory on the way home from cutting wood on another island, so they had a rope and an ax. When this creature swam up to their boat one boy knocked it on the head with the ax and another lassoed it. They dragged it to shore as the tide was going out and simply held it from slipping back until waves touched it no more. Mike said that when it was firmly beached they had to kill it some more; I suppose it had been stunned.

If the children needed sponges, they found them on the beach, splendid specimens but not abundant enough for commercialization. After a storm my pupils and I often walked along the shore at low tide to see how many different kinds of sea flowers we could find. The oysters resembled those to be found in Delaware Bay, but in these northern oysters the mother-of-pearl lining was more irridescent. The children gathered sea urchins to eat, as well as oysters.

One day the boys came trailing an immense octopus on a pole and put it into a tub in the hall for nature study. That was one occasion when I shrank from being close to nature's heart. The natives cleaned octopus legs and made a sort of tripe with them.

Dried fish served as the candles on the first Christmas trees people had on Wood Island years before. Natives had always used dried candlefish, a sort of oily smelt, for candlelight. To catch them, the children thrust their hands down in the sand just after the tide had gone out. Fresh, they were delicious when fried brown. One night the school went down to the ocean to watch the lights on the water. There must be millions and millions of phosphorescent creatures in the North Pacific, leaping about in dazzling displays of color and brilliance.

The Japanese cook at the mission, Charlie Cook, as the children named him, appreciated the halibut the large boys caught, but only if they were large; small ones, he said, were too watery. Children in a place like Wood Island are raised on the water. In the Lower Lake were several boats, and when they were not in school the boys from six to eight years old almost lived in them.

Even though it rained so much of the time that we hardly noticed it, Wood Island in summer was beautiful beyond compare. Much of it was covered with virgin spruce forests. I counted the rings on a stump and it had taken that tree four hundred years to get ready for two men to fell in less than two hours. It was probably five feet in diameter and had been proportionately tall. In the forests branches and twigs of dead trees were covered with heavy moss cushions and limbs ended in great emerald balls. Every dead log and old stump was a thing of beauty. To lift one of the hoods from a stump was to hold in one's hands a basket so finely woven and richly tinted that the soul cried "Marvelous!" Ferns resembled tropical growths; flowers and berries were everywhere; and from growing trees air moss swayed in the breezes.

People were resourceful in using what nature afforded them. One morning I passed by Old Nicholai Luke's and saw the intestine of a bear that had been cleaned and scraped until it was a transparent white, and then blown full of air and stretched out to dry. He told me he would fill it with melted seal oil, then coil it before the oil hardened and chop off pieces as needed through the winter.

To me, the most surprising person on the island was Nicholai Pavlof. He was the son of the last Russian vice-governor of Alaska and was born in the capital city, Sitka. When he was a youth he was sent to San Francisco to be educated in English, then to school in Russia and then to France for two years. His two daughters, Mary and Annie, bright and beautiful girls, were in the grades I taught. His cottage was on the edge of a deep woods, facing toward the sea. He had built a walk in the woods with a swinging bridge over a tiny ravine. The bridge's sides were woven of saplings and the roof was formed of thick branches of spruce. The ascent to it was made easy by broad stone steps here and there. This charming walk led to a south-slope flower garden. A bit farther on were strawberry and raspberry patches, the raspberries trained into arbors. Then came the garden where he raised cabbage, lettuce, carrots, celery, turnips and parsnips. Down the hill he kept chickens, geese and pigs. His several cows were pastured in various places, fenced so the animals would not stray into swamps and sinkholes. At the extreme south, on a high, grassy bluff, were his large potato garden and a hay field to fill his silo.

His place gave a fair picture of the household economy of the most prosperous native homes. At the other extreme were one-room cottages where the only occupations of the householders were hunting and fishing. Such a room contained a small cookstove, a small wooden table, one or two wooden chairs, some chests, a trunk or two and a board bench with bedding. All houses were well kept and clean.

Many had delightful little luxuries. One week when I went calling, several ladies were preserving wild rose petals or, as we would say, candying them. They were pretty and dainty served on white plates. Mrs. Aggian, after pouring me a fragrant cup of tea, added a slice of lemon on which she laid the rose petals, then put two lumps of sugar on the saucer. Sugar never went into the tea; one took a sip of tea, then a bite of sugar.

Most families kept gardens on a side of the island where the land was cleared and the soil fertile. At this site there had once been a settlement large enough to qualify as a town in these parts, with many fine gardens, for Russians know how to farm. But in the 1850s a smallpox epidemic depopulated the town; nothing remained but here and there a tumbledown chimney and old foundation logs.

In winter Wood Island changed dramatically. The winds howled from north and south and counter-howled from east and west. When a storm ceased, the quiet of the forests was broken by the dripping of water as ice fingers on rocks and spruce loosed their grasp. Then above the *drip, drip* could be heard the gurgle of water in rills and streams. So the winters passed: storms of wind, snow and sleet, alternating with thaws and sunshine, but always ice on the lakes and snow on the ground.

At the end of my first winter I agreed to stay on another year. The superintendent, Mr. E. P. Coe, convinced me it would be a detriment for the children to change teachers in just one year. His wife, a dear friend of mine, argued that I might do more good training these boys and girls who would go all over Alaska than if I took another school. I had faith in her judgment, but I was not entirely happy to accept, re- membering my promise in Iliamna, but could only continue hoping a way to get there would open somehow, some time.

During the summer a rich woman from Seattle visited the mission while she was spending a month in Kodiak. We had a vague dream that she would notice how much a hospital was needed, or even an infirmary. We entertained her as best we could so her visit would be memorable. And she did present a gift to the orphanage. She sent over from Kodiak two pounds of stick candy! Then she had a meeting with two prospectors who beguiled her into putting twelve hundred dollars into a gold prospect. Upon hearing this, everyone on Wood Island just smiled at her innocence.

Later on when we learned she had lost the money, I would normally have been sympathetic, but remembering something she had told me I felt no pity. She said she had once promised herself how much good she would do for others if she had fifty thousand dollars. But when she had it, it made her so unhappy to use it. Now, she told me, she could not be comfortable using some of her money for others until she had a hundred thousand dollars. I told her I did not envy her. I would rather be in my place, poor but feeling rich, than in her place, rich but feeling poor.

During the summer the mission's assistant superintendent, Mr. George Hill, and its doctor had a romantic wedding. The doctor thought it would be unique to spend a honeymoon week in an ancient barabara; she was a Chicago woman and I suppose her friends there would appreciate her account.

A squad of boys, supervised by the bridegroom, were cutting hay on the western part of Kodiak Island, and this circumstance afforded a good excuse for the barabara honeymoon because a scow and provisions had to be taken to them. Some of the rest of us tagged along for the day.

At some remote time a village had been at the site. The ancient dwellings looked like rounded mounds of sod with a rude sliding door and a rough casement peeking from the front of the sod. Only a few barabaras could still be used. To enter we had to crawl about three feet down on hands and knees. The ceilings were just high enough in the center for a person to stand upright. A hole in the roofs allowed smoke to escape. Ceilings and sides were lined with rough timber. The doctor stayed several days, and at least the beauty outside compensated for the wretched abode. I doubt that she stayed in the barabara much of the time.

A clear little river flowed through the valley where the hay-making was going on. It was a seething, living mass of silver salmon, so packed together they were swimming atop each other. The boys made a fire and hung a dinner kettle over it to boil, then stood on a plank bridge, stooped over and lifted out two large fish, dressed them, cut them into three-inch slices and dropped them into the salted water just as it began to bubble.

Part of our trip to the barabaras was on the open sea, and on our way back we encountered killer whales, the first I had seen. They resembled great monsters, jumping in the water as if Lucifer Himself had been let loose. Three bidarkas, boats made of skins with little round hatches for the paddlers, passed us. They were rounding up a shark of a kind different from the one the schoolboys brought to the beach. This one was about twenty feet long and perfectly round, probably a foot in diameter, somewhat resembling an immense serpent. The natives hunted them for the oil; if they ate the meat they did not say so.

There had never been as many killer whales in the island waters as there were that fall, folks said. They were there to kill whales and the whales were there because of great schools of sea food. In high tide the killer whales came so near the shore it was thought dangerous for the children to play close to the water. Because of the presence of the killer whales, people on Wood Island were having a difficult time getting a whale for themselves. The whales not attacked by the killer whales were frightened away.

If the community did not succeed in getting a whale, the people, rich and poor, would have a difficult winter. They were superstitious about the whale hunt. While the men were on the water, women were forbidden to cast their eyes toward the sea, so every woman had to stay closely indoors. If a whale was wounded and a woman looked at it, they believed, one of the hunters was sure to be killed and the whale itself would escape. They also believed that when the men started out, a tiny man no bigger than a finger ran on top of the water after the bidarkas. If he caught up to one and climbed on it, the man in that bidarka would surely be killed. He had better turn back instead. So all the men paddled as fast as they could to escape the little man.

When a whale hunt was successful, people flocked to the shore, back and forth, back and forth, carrying large pieces of meat. Each family put a barrel of meat in brine and dried what they needed besides, and rendered the blubber for winter lard. The Russians used it in pies and cakes and to deep-fry doughnuts and other foods. The Aleuts fried fish and hotcakes in it.

I found whale meat much like beef steak in taste but as tender as calf's liver. The blubber was like beef bone marrow, but firmer. Sometimes a seal steak was sent in to us; it smelled like chicken while it was cooking but tasted like veal.

One day in fall, a pupil called my attention to the beach and the whole school went out to see the sight. A calf had died the day before and its carcass had been thrown in the water. Any dead animal returned in the tide, day after day, then disappeared. Hopping about the calf and feeding on it were a motley horde of seagulls, crows, ravens, one big hawk and an eagle, all at peace among themselves.

That second winter on Wood Island, a little before Christmas, I had a horrible experience. I had been working alone at a desk in an abandoned North American Alaskan Company house across the lake from the mission. All afternoon I had heard the shouts and laughter of skating children without being conscious of them until quiet set in, when I realized

with a start how late and dark it had become and that the supper bell must have rung.

The lake ice was thick, and since going across it was the
shortcut there was not even a trail in the snow around the
lake. I had crossed the ice every day in winter as a matter of
course. But this time, as I stepped on the edge, I was overcome with terror. I tried to suppress it and start again but was
possessed by fear. Trembling, I called out to Aleck, a large
boy who still lingered in the distance. He and his small brother
were the only people still at the lake. Aleck skated to me and
said, "Why, we have hauled loads of wood all day on the ice
with a two-horse team. Just start and walk over."

I also thought my fear was foolishness but no sooner had
taken a step or two until I had to hurry back. Aleck called his
little brother as a joke and told him to walk beside me. I
laughed too and took the little fellow's hand but again I re-
coiled. Aleck, now realizing I was genuinely frightened, sent
his little brother home and led me by the hand. We had not
gone a rod when I sank into the water with Aleck still holding
my hand. He had a good footing on the ice, but I had gone into
a hole.

The water was so deep I had no footing on the lake bottom.
I told Aleck to hold me up and not let go. My clothing was
heavy but I was thoroughly chilled and my feet cramping. Just
then a native boy visiting from Eagle Harbor on Kodiak Island
crossed the ice and Aleck hailed him. Each took me under an
arm but I was helpless and thought I would sink before they
could save me. Luckily they were both large and strong and
managed to haul me out.

That night when the reaction took place, I think I came
close to dying from failure of my heart. But I was given good
care and in a few days was all right except for nervousness

about crossing the ice. I could never again make myself cross that frozen lake, and if a bit of ice crackled under my feet I went all to pieces. At night I would wake from nightmares that I was struggling in the water. But had I not been warned by fear, or had I crossed alone in spite of the fear, no trace of me would have been found. That night a storm set in which would have frozen the hole solidly and covered it with snow. At the time I came along the hole was glazed just enough to be hidden. A new pupil had sawed the hole to dip water for cleaning the schoolroom. He had cut it larger than necessary and also had neglected to stand a pole in the opening, the customary safety precaution.

Wood Island had so many workers to help with children and schooling: the mission superintendent and his wife; the assistant superintendent and his wife, the doctor; a boys' matron; a girls' matron; and the Japanese cook. It would not be difficult to get a replacement for me in this lovely place. I knew I could use my time to better advantage among people to whom no help had come.

Mr. Harlan Updegraff, who was now chief of the department in place of Dr. Jackson, sent me word that as a result of Washington's investigation, the Reindeer superintendent had been relieved of his position. Iliamna was to have a new school. I had been appointed to Nushegak, an Eskimo village on the Bering Sea. When this message reached me, a new superintendent was expected at the mission. He arrived while I was in Kodiak mailing word of my acceptance of the Nushegak post to the cable office in Seward. The new superintendent, the Rev. G. A. Learn, was upset at this news and extremely insistent that I stay because he was new to the work. In Kodiak and Wood Island it seemed that everyone I knew disapproved of my decision. What to do? I had made good in this part of the country for several years and made many friends. Knowing this society as I did, I knew that to go obstinately against such concerted wishes would annul friendships and much of the good I had been able to accomplish as well. Besides, an old Book tells that in the multitude of counselors there is wisdom.

So at my direction, the postmaster withdrew my acceptance of Nushegak from the mail. One year's unexpected emergency service in Wood Island had now expanded into three years. What it meant, I did not know except "I will work and wait."

It was a sad winter for our island and others. Whooping cough was often a fatal disease, with no chance for recovery if pneumonia set in. On Wood Island eight children at the mission died from it, as did every baby outside the mission. Father Petellin wrote me a pathetic letter from Afognak. He said their hearts were broken. All the babies had been buried.

The children had loved the former superintendent and everyone had been sad at his departure, which was necessary because of his wife's health and their children's education. But the new superintendent took the children to his heart and they readily transferred their affection to him. Children are quick to read those who are to care for them. He won everyone's respect and admiration during the whooping cough epidemic. All the workers at the mission nursed the sick, but he bore the brunt and was most self-sacrificing. His wife was a most interesting woman. She was born in China, crossed the Pacific a number of times, and had formerly taught Greek near Boston.

One spring day after the epidemic had run its course, the mission had its annual Sunday school picnic on Forget-me-not

Island, which was just a bit offshore. Its miniature hills were wooded and its rolling little valleys were basins of English forget-me-nots growing about a foot high and blooming so luxuriantly that the ground was blue the summer long. I noticed that a crowd of little girls had strayed from the picnic and were busy at work on the beach. There lay a little black pig, dead. It was cool and sprayed with salt water, so in perfect condition. The little girls were playing funeral. They had twined forget-me-not wreaths for the pig's neck and feet and were now covering it over with flowers. They came away with me and I think soon forgot about the "pig baby."

When the spring freshets came to Wood Island, the dams between the lakes broke open and Lower Lake spread far over the flats. To get between the schoolhouse and the mission, where I lived, meant taking a detour of two or three miles or else crossing the lake's flume, a deep, narrow channel flowing to the sea. The boys had laid a log over the flume for a bridge, fixing it firmly in the banks. The log was about a foot in diameter, and the pupils walked safely over it, as did I. The swift channel it bridged was about twenty feet wide.

One night I worked at the school later than I intended and it was dark before I noticed, just as happened the dreadful night I fell through the ice. Rain was pouring and the wind roaring. I lit my lantern and started home by the long, roundabout way, but after a short distance I heard the bellowing of an animal coming toward me at a gallop. I knew about this bad-tempered creature. He was not one of the native Russian cattle but an animal imported from the States. I could have run to a nearby house but did not have the presence of mind. Instead I ran to the flume. But I was nervous from fright and running, and at about the center of the bridge my lantern light shifted and in my confusion I lost my footing and pitched headlong into the swift current. I grabbed at a floating log that had lodged in the bank.

Somehow I scrambled up on the lodged log. My skirts bound around my feet so I could not move, the water was halfway over the sides of the log, my lantern was gone and I was in utter darkness. But so far, so good. What had happened to my dignity? The fix I was in was so ridiculous I laughed. Then I began to shout. I was out of earshot of the mission but two native houses were close by. Old Luke came to his window, peered out, then walked away. He said afterward he thought he heard someone call but decided it was the storm.

The water tearing down the flume under the bridge was rising and I feared my log might float off under the bridge to the ocean and me with it. So I called louder and louder. I heard Annie Ballagnogoff call to her husband, and I will never forget that high, screechy little voice: "Oh, Wassillie, come here! Someone is drowning and it is the teacher!"

"No," I called as she ran to me, "I'm not drowning but tell Wassillie to come and help me!" In a moment they both came with lanterns. Wassillie was wearing his rubber wading clothes and a slicker, so he held to my log and moved along it to me. The water was about five feet deep but he was tall and strong. He soon had me untangled and helped me crawl to the side of the flume where I had started. Then the three of us made a beeline to the nearest shelter in an empty building. Wassillie made a fire and went to the mission to tell them I would not come that night. Annie saw to it that I was warm and comfortable.

The next day I went to school as usual but everyone acted as if I had been raised from the dead. They knew as well as I that had I plunged off the ocean side of the bridge, nothing could have saved me. I reproached myself for my folly and promised to keep better track of the time when I was at work.

When the school term ended I received what I had been awaiting for three years: an appointment to Iliamna! A school had been built there, along with a home for the teacher.

After I resigned from Wood Island, the community school board met and re-elected me for the next year, and once again the superintendent was insistent. But this time nothing would stop me. I would just get ready and go. And this time my friends accepted my decision.

So once again I embarked on the *Dora* for Seward, and once again had a ten-day wait there. The days of elegant society were suspended and the pretentious bungalows vacated because the railroad project once again had been suspended awaiting further funds. My dear friend, the wife of the U.S. marshal, and her family were living free in one of these fine furnished homes at the request of the owner, to protect it. They had me stay with them.

Although the lavish tea parties were no more, a grander gathering was about to occur. The National Editors Association, which was meeting in Seattle, was coming to Seward on an excursion. The Chamber of Commerce arranged to take the group to Turnagain Arm, which was as far as the railroad had gotten. This curiously named place was an estuary at the head of Cook Inlet. Captain Cook, the explorer, thought he had found a navigable way through the North American continent, but when he reached the head of the inlet, where it divides into two arms, the call came to his crew, "Turn again!"

I received an invitation to accompany the group of several hundred visitors on the rail trip. We went in open cars on a perfect day. The ladies of Seward provided an excellent lunch

Seward's main street, ca. 1913. *Seward Community Library, Sylvia Sexton collection*

for the whole party. The railroad had been built along the old prospectors' trail, but construction included several long tunnels through mountains, which had cost millions.

Opposite one of the glaciers, separated from us only by a deep canyon where masses of ice had crashed for ages past, the cars stopped and we got out. All the passengers, old men and young men, and women too, forgot for an hour that they were grown up. We turned into a crowd of boys and girls snowballing one another. Such dodging and running, such screams of laughter! Then a short walk took us again into summertime, and the crowd returned to the cars with arms full of ex-

quisite wildflowers. As we were steaming across a level of
high grass an immense moose came trotting directly toward
the train without seeming to notice it until there was a great
shout from every throat aboard. Then the magnificent creature raised its head, gazed intently for a moment, appeared to
decide we were not part of the landscape, wheeled about and
vanished into a clump of trees in the distance. We skirted a
fourteen-mile-long lake reflecting mountains beyond our
sight. Wild fowl skimmed its surface and songbirds caroled
above. We passed more gigantic rivers of ice and snow, a
powerful glacial waterfall and broken ice blocks in chasms,
blue, green and white, like walls of gems. In Cook Inlet we
saw the mad rush of the sea hemmed in by mountains. The
bores of the incoming tide leapt in the air. The tide normally
rises and falls thirty feet in six hours, making it the second
highest tide in the world, exceeded only by the Bay of
Fundy's. The tides of Cook Inlet, where the *Dora* so regularly
ventured, made navigation dangerous for many miles there.

We halted in extensive, parklike country and lunch was
served, but the best feasts were the after-dinner speeches
made by editors and publishers from all over the country and
some from foreign lands as well. In all that mass there was
only one woman editor to respond. She was Mrs. Cornelia
Jewett, and she made an address that equalled any given that
day. While Mrs. Jewett was in Seward I became quite well acquainted with her and was so proud to have had contact with
a woman who was such a power for good.

On our return to Seward at day's end a reception and mass
meeting were held in the town hall, and there it was stated
that Resurrection Bay, Seward's bay, was capable of harbor-
ing within its bounds all the fleets of the world.

Just as the late summer sunset touched Resurrection Bay
with an orange glory, the *Dora* steamed in, to carry me off

again to A.C. Point, or rather to the ship's anchorage miles off the Point.

Down the awful rope ladder I went again. I suppose I did cut a figure, and someone on the *Dora* took a snapshot of the descent to send to Mrs. Jewett. Unbeknown to me, she had asked for it.

Hannah making a dreaded descent on the *Dora*'s rope ladder. This is probably the snapshot taken at Cornelia Jewett's request without Hannah's knowledge. *Hannah Breece collection*

Back to Iliamna

My journey was easy in comparison with the time I was left in the lurch by the Reindeer Man. The U.S. commissioner for the area, Mr. John F. McLean, had been instructed to pay any reasonable sum for a good guide and to order transportation as comfortable as the country and conditions permitted. So at A.C. Point a boat was on hand to take me and my baggage to the head of Iliamna Bay, where Mr. Wilhelm Nielsen, a Dane, awaited me with his horse, Old Dick. He was to walk, I was to ride and my baggage would follow. Uncle Sam was charged more than twenty-nine dollars for these arrangements. I thought that was a lot.

There was only one hitch. Apparently as an afterthought by Mr. McLean, a message arrived at the Point at the same time I did, directing that the horse should have a saddle. For Mr. Nielsen to get one would mean a day's delay. So I said a folded blanket would do, with ropes fashioned into stirrups. The improvised rig had no reins, but Old Dick's mane was long and thick and I reckoned I could grab it if he tried to run away. The horse had a bridle though it lacked a leading string, and I directed Mr. Nielsen to walk at his head and hold the bridle.

The trail had been cut around some of the more dangerous parts, branches had been trimmed, logs removed, and rude bridges crossed the smaller streams. From time to time Mr.

Nielsen let go of the bridle to light his pipe or rest his arm, and I became tired of reminding him to hold on. During one of these careless intervals I urged Old Dick down a stream bank, damp and sleek. The foot of the bank, it turned out, was a drinking and wallowing hole for bears. The odor was over-powering; there were fresh tracks too, although no sign of an actual bear other than a shaking of the underbrush as one ran away. Without warning, the terror-stricken horse abruptly backed up. It was all I could do not to tumble over his head. At the top he dashed on for a rod or two, then gave one spring across a narrow but deep ravine. When he landed, it seemed to me he had all four of his feet in the same spot. I almost slid off at the side but grabbed his mane and stayed on somehow. My feet were in the rope stirrups and falling would have been serious. The ravine was not more than eight feet wide, but while we were over it I would have made an affidavit that it was as broad as the English Channel.

Mr. Nielsen was badly frightened. He had to run some distance to find a place where he could cross the ravine. I did not have to say another word about holding the bridle.

When I arrived in Iliamna, most of the village people were off at their summer fishing camp about six miles away. But those at home gave me a happy welcome, as if they had known me always.

Of course I promptly inspected the schoolhouse and found that its commodious one room contained modern desks and seats for pupils and teacher but no other equipment. However, it had ample space for the extras in my freight and I had authorization to buy or have made whatever was lacking. The teacher's house was comfortably furnished and well equipped with cooking utensils and dishes.

Both buildings were constructed of huge logs, at great cost.

It was odd how they had been located. They were considerably more distant from the village than they need have been. The obvious advantage was the grandeur of the site, on the brow of a hill that sloped to a broad, deep river some five hundred feet below. The treeless slope was a gorgeous blaze of fireweed and other scarlet-leaved plants. So both buildings not only enjoyed unimpeded, magnificent views, but were proudly in view themselves to anyone for miles around.

The disadvantage, besides isolation, was that the site was unprotected from the fierce wind. Worse, the trail between the cottage and school, about a hundred feet long, was peculiar. It was steep, and also ran along a part of the slope so precipitous that there was hardly sufficient room for a narrow walkway in front of the schoolhouse door. Since there was plenty of level space behind the school, I marveled that the building had not been set at least a few feet farther back or else that its door had not been situated at the back or along a side.

Well, it was awkward but I could manage. And I was content. If I had wanted a school where a teacher was sorely needed and where it would be hard to place a good one, I had certainly found it.

One trail that led to the scattered cabins of the village wandered down along the river. The other trail, along the hill, cut through a thick forest before it entered the village. The government building and the Russian church were situated on a bench of the same hill as the school, but were even more distant from the school than the village. Standing a little apart from the village was the store of the Alaska Company, its warehouse and the home of its manager. Dotted all among the cabins and in some cases beyond the settlement were fish caches: log buildings raised on stilts some twelve feet high. When a cache's door was padlocked, its ladder was removed. This is where families kept their winter stores of food.

The most important building in the village, and indeed in all the country round about, was the home of Old William Rickteroff, the reader of the church. He stood in place of a priest. The priest was supposed to come once every three years, but at this time had not turned up for the past five. I came to think of William's home as the Metropolis. It was in the central part of the village and stood out conspicuously because of its size and neat, well-kept appearance. It was the center of all social life. Every Sunday night dances were held there. It was the assembly room for any other public gatherings. Like the other houses, its living space consisted of only one room, but William's room was huge, scrupulously clean and had a notably smooth, hard floor. Its dining table, as in

Iliamna village. The church is at top right. The buildings on stilts are fish caches. The isolated school and teacher's cottage, not shown, lie beyond the wooded hill at the left. *Hannah Breece collection*

other Iliamna homes, was only about six inches high, more a platform than a table. It was the custom to sit on the floor around it. Along the walls were narrow beds that served for seating during gatherings.

Old William was merely middle-aged, with a long, iron-gray beard. The really aged member of his family was Old Darla, said to be more than a hundred and she looked even older. But she was forever busy; seated on the floor she diligently sewed fur clothing, boots of sealskin for cold weather and boots of dried fish skin for wet weather, for the whole family. William's wife, Maria, and married daughter, Mary, were constantly busy too, making pretty, elaborately beaded moccasins. William and his wife looked to be nearly pure Russian. Their older son, William Mike, was a handsome young man; the other son, Stephen, was crippled and much petted. Little Paraskovia, about eight, completed the family.

Another very important house belonged to Epheme Rickteroff, the wise man. The wise man of a village was invariably blind, and so it was with Epheme, although one never would have guessed it to watch him. He was tall with shining black hair, a long black beard and a complexion that was almost too pale. Epheme spoke excellent English and was a philosopher. If life had afforded him different opportunities, I think Epheme would have been widely recognized as a great man. He was the judge in all cases of difficulty, and his decisions were accepted as final. He and his wife, Agafia, a handsome, intelligent woman, had a son and two daughters ranging in age from eighteen to seven. His house, although much smaller than Old William's, was arranged similarly. Epheme, Old William and Kusma, the village chief, were brothers. When they deliberated together at Epheme's house, or when other men were in conference with Epheme, the narrow wall beds were used like sofas, with the men reclining upon them.

The blind sage of Iliamna, Epheme Rickteroff, with his wife, Agafia, and their daughter, Vera. *By permission of Mrs. Ray F. Schaleben*

Old Matrona was another person of special importance. She was the Dorcas of the village. Wherever there was sickness or sorrow, there one could find her. She sewed for the needy and took care of wayward children. She was tall and

slender with smooth black hair and little black eyes but a
rather light complexion, and was always neat in a calico dress.
Her home was poorly equipped but she was raising two orphans: a poor little humpbacked girl and a boy who had now
become old enough to help her. Old Matrona was to become
a great help to me in school, assisting with the small children
when my attention was concentrated on older pupils. Whenever she could, she stayed at school all day.

Altogether the village consisted of about 150 souls, including four Danes, one German, one Swede, one Frenchman and
four American men. Three Danes and the German were married to native women. In addition were varying numbers of
transients: traders and prospectors coming through or waiting
out bad winter weather.

The native people were not Aleutian like the population of
Afognak. They were Kenais. Although others considered
them Indians, Kenais themselves claimed they were an entirely separate people, distinct from all others. As I got to
know them, I fancied they were somewhat like the Karen
mountain people of southeast Asia, a race I had studied in
anthropology classes in Chicago. At a time long ago, people
in Iliamna said, the Alaskan Kenais had divided into two
groups, and the villagers were descended from one of those
groups.

Before the Russians came, none of the various peoples of
Alaska had been subjugated by outsiders, nor apparently by
each other, although warfare among them was common. They
were independent and free. Of all the peoples the Russians encountered, the Kenais were the most difficult to subdue. They
refused to defer to Russian soldiers and priests or to be pacified
with trinkets, beads and brightly colored cloth. So the Russians
resorted to a brutal strategy. At any rate, this is the story told
me in Iliamna; people there all believed it absolutely.

The Russian soldiers built a huge log house and partitioned off a large room along one side. The two doors into this room were not opposite, one being at the corner farthest from the other. A second room, equally long but narrow, paralleled the large room, again with its doors offset and with its outside entrance through a vestibule set at a corner without a view to the interior of the narrow room. So in effect, the building contained a sort of interior maze. The Kenais had no idea of its purpose but were suspicious of it.

One day the soldiers forced all the men and large boys into a work party outside the village. The soldiers remaining in the settlement drove all the women and children into the large room and penned them in. When the men and boys returned at night they could catch no sight of their families but could hear cries from inside the big building. The Russians told the men and boys they could go in to their families, but the men feared treachery and at first refused.

Finally, however, concern for their children, wives and mothers overcame their fear. They were permitted to enter the narrow room one at a time. As far as those outside could see, each entered in safety; as far as the women and children could see, nobody entered at all. Beyond the vestibule, and out of everybody's sight, stood a Russian soldier with a club of the kind the Kenais themselves used in warfare, made of the thigh bone of a moose. As each man or large boy entered, he was swiftly and silently killed with a blow to his skull. After all the Kenai grown males had been murdered, the women and children were set at liberty.

The Russian men married the native women, whose families took Russian names. They were obliged to adopt the Russians' religion, which came to appeal to them as they enjoyed elaborate ceremony and form. A soldier named Rickteroff had been a high officer. Many of the families bore his name, and these took pride in being from a bright lineage, although they also continued to think of themselves as Kenais. Villagers named Rickteroff, like Old William, Epheme, Kusma and their families, did indeed tend to be outstandingly intelligent and capable. Nevertheless, Iliamna people did not care for Russian ways as wholeheartedly as did Aleuts on the coast. In this settlement were no pictures of the Czar and Czarina. Nor did the Kenais like the Aleuts.

No caste lines in this village conferred status; perhaps that was because all were of mixed blood, although, it seemed obvious, mixed in greater and lesser degrees. Those more purely Kenai were usually, although not always, shorter, stockier and physically very powerful. A striking difference from Afognak was that families of white men who had married natives did not enjoy high status. Perhaps this was because, in Iliamna, a white man who married an uneducated native woman did not bring his wife up to his standards but instead almost invariably descended into native ways himself. It seemed to me that the community lost respect for European or American men who stooped to native standards of living. But in any case, at this time sentiment concerning intermarriage was rapidly changing in Alaska. Where formerly it had been not only countenanced but encouraged, now it was not.

Nor did Iliamna have caste lines drawn by wealth. Everybody in Iliamna was poor. These were the poorest people I had ever encountered. Like people on the coast, the Kenais had been comparatively rich during "sea otter days." After hunting had driven these animals almost to extinction, they were protected and trade in their furs was outlawed. The loss of sea otter wealth threw Iliamna's people into poverty and made them almost totally dependent on fish.

The year's economic cycle began in summer, when people moved out of the village into two fishing camps opposite each other at the mouth of the Iliamna River where it emptied into the lake, six miles downstream from the village. Kusma, the chief, lived in the larger camp on the south bank and his assistant, the second chief, in the camp on the north bank. In camp they lived in tents or other makeshift shelters and worked very hard from early morning to late at night catching, preparing and making bundles of fish. The preparations were done meticulously; no pains were spared.

For *bolika,* smoked salmon, the best salmon were cleaned and then the bones were stripped and the skin removed. The skin was dried and made into boots for wet places; the bones were dried and used as an article of commerce, dog food. With a sharp knife they would split the flesh of the fish down the center but leave on the tail to hold the two pieces together. They would put the split fish into a pickle of brown sugar and salt for a day or two, then hang them in the fish house to be smoked. Traders paid about fifteen cents for half a smoked fish. Before coming to Alaska I had bought it in the Seattle markets for thirty cents a pound. People reserved enough *bolika* for their own winter use.

Eukala, dried salmon, did not require quite as much work because it was not skinned and only the backbone was stripped out. Traders bought it in bundles of a hundred fish for six to ten dollars a bundle. For its own use, each family would put down a barrel of salted dried salmon and bury a good supply for its dogs.

When fishing season ended in early September, the village returned to life. People picked great quantities of wild cranberries to cover with water and freeze in blocks for winter use. For about two weeks most men went off to hunt bears, and many women departed each day to snare squirrels. (Most other kinds of game had been hunted out and depopulated in the vicinity of the village.) These were not articles for trade.

The villagers killed only enough bears and squirrels for furs and fresh meat for themselves.

I was given some nice steak from a young black bear. It came from the bear's right side. Nobody would think of eating meat from a bear's left side. They said, suppose the bear had eaten a man or woman; the person's blood would be sent through the left side of the bear. To make a mistake and eat from the wrong side could be the greatest misfortune.

School started at the time of the squirrel and bear hunts.

11

School in Iliamna

Early in the school year I made a serious mistake in my treatment of Pete Rickteroff, the nine-year-old son of Kusma, the chief. Pete would not stay at his own desk. He kept slipping over to his cousin, Paraskovia, the little daughter of Old William, the reader, and kept her from doing her own lesson. I reproved him time and again but still he darted off whenever he pleased. You see, he was going by the new method, but I was not quite ready for that and neither were the pupils. One morning, exasperated, I took him by the hand and led him back, and since he could as yet understand little English, I gave him to understand through gestures that he would be punished if he did not obey.

That noon Pete did not return to school. At about three o'clock I heard the church bells ring and horns toot, and sent to the village to learn what was wrong. Pete had not come home at noon and someone reported that he had been seen running to the woods. Everybody went on the hunt for Pete, and everybody was frightened because he could have been attacked by a bear. He had become lost and was wandering in circles, and was found after about an hour's search.

His father brought him back to school the next day and told me I had done right to try to make Pete obey; he assured me the little boy would not run away again. But little Pete had taught me an important lesson. I resolved never to frighten another child with threat of punishment. Primitive people are never severe with their children.

Women in Iliamna did not understand that there was a connection between hygiene and health, and one of my important duties as a teacher here was to improve their standards of household sanitation, especially in the preparation of food and care of the children. I had food authorization enough to provide one dinner a week for mothers and children and used these weekly events not only as schoolroom parties but as occasions for morning cooking and hygiene classes for the mothers and older schoolgirls. On other mornings, mothers who wished could come for sewing.

The mothers enjoyed all this and hated to miss cooking and sewing sessions, so whenever I visited a home and found it filthy and unkempt I told the mother she could not come to school until it was clean. She would hustle about and wash and scrub for a day or two, then return. As far as I could tell, they did not resent my interference.

One young mother who brought her baby boy to school every morning did not bathe him, I was sure, because he and his clothing were both unbelievably dirty. After eyeing the youngster dubiously for some time, I got ready for a grand lesson.

I procured a wooden cracker box and had the boys reinforce it and put good strong handles through the ends. Then I asked the older girls to take as their project the creation of a nice little bed. They were delighted with this assignment. Under direction they made a little mattress filled with dry moss and a tiny pillow filled with eiderdown. They made little sheets and pillow slips and blankets of outing flannel. Then I had a carpenter come and suspend the bed from the ceiling securely with strong ropes. I told the boys to put a kettle of water on the stove, then prepared warm bathwater in a tub, with soap and towels near.

I then asked the mother to undress the boy and wash him. She was furious and insisted it would kill the baby if I made her put him in water. There was no point of contact between my words and her conceptions and no way to bridge them with more words. The only recourse was an object lesson. So I took the baby and, in spite of her efforts to stop me, removed his filthy rags and put him in the tub and he had the washing of his life. He was a sturdy six-month-old and kicked and crowed while he was bathed. Then the girls helped and together we dressed him in new, clean clothes. The old ones went into the fire. When it was all over, and the mother saw her child so clean and comfortable, lying there in his little white bed, she thanked me over and over in Russian, *"Spaseba! Spaseba!"*

This baby had a white father, a Scandinavian, and with his blue eyes and golden curls looked like a small edition of his father; but the white fathers here took no hand at all in raising their children until they were of school age, and provided no help and exerted no influence in the way their wives ran the homes.

I have always been careful when working among inferior races to convey to them that I have their interests at heart and love and respect them as people, but that I do not come among them to sink to their level but to uplift them. If this standard is not adhered to, little can be done to improve their lives. I am superior to an uneducated native woman and give her to understand that I realize it. She knows it herself. But I want them to realize I have faith that the ability is within them to improve themselves and their lives and their children's lives. They are more uncivilized in many ways than I may say here. But I want to draw a line between "whitizing" and civilizing them.

The object lesson in child cleanliness worked. Soon, at the mothers' own requests, the village had two other clean and pretty suspended beds. At this time the village had only those three babies. The widespread whooping cough epidemic had carried off the infants and almost all the little ones the previous winter.

The nearest doctor was stationed at Koggiung, about 120 miles to the south. Washington tried to equip teachers with knowledge of simple remedies and provided us with good medical kits. I could handle such things as broken bones if the break was a clean one, and skin infections and cuts, bring comfort for colds and some pains, and teach some disease-preventive measures. My chief medical guide was a book, compiled for the War Department by Dr. Krulish, describing many of the diseases prevalent among natives and advising on treatment.

A newly born infant died during my first winter in Iliamna. Its mother was dying of tuberculosis and the child lived only a few months. I did not give it any medicine because it was so young, and I did not know what to give it anyway. It just rolled its eyes up and drew back its little head, and I thought that perhaps it had tubercular brain trouble.

The father was of the old school; that is, just about the only person in the village who would not even try to shake off superstitions. When the baby died, he had much to say about whose fault it was and decided to lay it at my door. I went to Epheme, the wise man, and told him the father was very angry with me and why. Epheme thought a few minutes, then said, "Don't worry. I will speak to him. I will tell him to shut up. This is the Lord's business."

I heard no more accusations, but that was not quite the end of the matter. The next day I went to the family's very small cabin. The mother lay in bed, almost gone, coughing incessantly. The one other child, a daughter of fifteen, sat on the floor at the low table with her father, who held the dead baby in his arm, as though to eat, while he poured tea and dispensed pilot bread with his other hand.

All the village had been eating in the house with the dead child at the table. I talked kindly to the father, for he understood English, and told him he had better have the funeral that day. He did not and next day I found him still dispensing food with the little corpse in his arm. Pitiful as it was, this would not do. I told him that if the funeral were not held within three hours, the commissioner would have to be told and the father must answer to him. The baby was buried within that time. It was the only incident of the kind that occurred in the three years I was at Iliamna.

The cemetery in Iliamna village. Russian Orthodox crosses have three crosspieces, the bottom one slanted. The gable and spirelike forms are optional elaborations. *Hannah Breece collection*

The schoolhouse was so large that it was possible to equip it for many different purposes. I was told there was a fine large cooking range at the reindeer station that was not in use, and I sent for it. It came at once by reindeer sledge. Beside it the village carpenter built a large cupboard to hold dishes, cooking utensils and groceries. Two big dining tables covered with white oilcloth were placed on the other side of the range. There was plenty of soap and water and a good place to wash hands, and good arrangements for dishwashing, an example that was certainly needed. I had a large screen made to divide off the kitchen from the rest of the schoolroom, but often the screen was set aside so the whole school could watch the morning cooking and hygiene lesson. We used only such foods as were within the possibilities of the villagers' own homes.

Two mothers or big girls were appointed at each dinner to wait on table, and two to wash dishes. The mothers and pupils learned at the dinners to pass food from one to the other and practice other niceties of table manners and table setting. This was a kind of game.

The sewing area was at the other end of the room. It had benches, a large table for cutting and even a sewing machine set in front of a window. Washington had seen to it that we were furnished with bolts of outing flannel, Indian lawn, bleached and unbleached muslin, blue denim, gingham and sewing accessories.

The women were good seamstresses and it was fascinating to see them improvise fine thread when they wanted it. They would take a spool of Number 50 and put the end of the thread between their teeth. Using their hands, they untwisted the thick thread as it came off the spool and rewound it as fine thread on an empty spool. They were accustomed to making their own sinew thread for sewing furs and skins, making the most beautiful skeins from sinews obtained from the reindeer station.

Every mother sewed for her children: jumpers and shirts for the boys; dresses, aprons and underwear for the girls. Each garment was labeled with the name of the person to wear it, whether children, other family members or friends, and as fast as it was finished, it was folded and put away to save as a present for the Christmas tree.

At Thanksgiving, when the early winter blizzards had abated to be replaced by bitter but stilly cold, we held a big community dinner. The boys decorated the schoolroom with red, white and blue bunting and small American flags I had brought in my freight, as well as large American flags supplied from Washington. The girls made paper roses for the tables— rather strange bouquets, but it all looked pretty. For several days beforehand both boys and girls cooked. They prepared biscuits, baked beans, rice and great pans of plain cake iced with pink sugar. A young man who had been brought up in an eastern American city and was now working at the trading company's establishment used the kitchen in my house to bake many pies of canned pumpkin and raisins. On Thanksgiving morning the larger girls made a big supply of *peruk,* Russian fish pie, and also thawed and warmed the other food.

Everybody in the village came to the party: pupils, the other natives, the whites who lived in Iliamna and a number of prospectors. To my delight, a white woman I had heard of but not yet met, came too. She and her husband had taken up a grubstake about forty-five miles to the west, on behalf of a Seattle gold-mining company. Investors in such companies outfitted prospectors; the claims they registered were the property of the stockholders. I had no faith in a hoped-for gold mine but was glad a woman prospector had turned up.

The white men had prepared for the feast by rehearsing

songs accompanied on my organ. They opened the hour-long service. Then the Thanksgiving proclamations of both the Governor of Alaska and the president were read and interpreted. Hymns of thanksgiving and patriotic songs followed. At the feast the white men served and the visiting lady and I sat with the native people, more because it pleased them than that we wanted to be waited on.

When everyone had eaten to heart's content, folk were told to take home the food left. They chose to combine it and that evening had a village party at Old William's house. I too had a second festivity at my cottage, as good a Thanksgiving dinner as the country could afford, attended by the white transients.

We had Christmas festivities too, of course, but the Thanksgiving feast was the big school event of the year.

Although everyone in Iliamna was poor, poverty did have its gradations. Children of widows or those who had lost both parents lived any way they could manage. I had noticed that these were among the hardest-working and best pupils because they were accustomed to such struggle for existence. In summer, families with fishing seines employed them and gave them a meager supply of dried salmon as payment. They got just enough to keep them alive, never enough to sell. They had no way to raise money for a seine of their own.

After I reported this situation to Washington I was authorized to buy materials for an industrial project to be undertaken by these schoolchildren. To assure that the work was done right I got an old Norwegian fisherman to oversee the seine weaving and knotting and the attaching of corks and leads. The pupils made the best seine ever seen in the village, and it was theirs.

This was in accord with government education policy, which was to train and teach these folks so they might live an

Christmas Eve, 1909, in the Iliamna schoolhouse. *Hannah Breece collection*

intelligent, useful and happy life in their own environment. The department in Washington did not want to make them dissatisfied with what they had, or urge them to go into a strange country where they would be entirely out of place and probably unhappy.

My most unusual pupils were six young men apprenticed at the reindeer station, which had been set up by the government to experiment with reindeer as a replacement for diminishing caribou herds. These youths were entitled by the government to two months' schooling a year. They came to

Eskimo reindeer apprentice with his outfit for school. The Iliamna schoolhouse is at right, the teacher's cottage at center, and at far left is the reindeer apprentices' school cabin. *By permission of Mrs. Ray F. Schaleben*

us two at a time. They brought their own food and lived in a small, comfortable cabin built for them near the schoolhouse. I sent books and writing materials back with the first pair so they could teach the third pair what they had learned and give them a good start before they reached us. The third pair, with that good start, took back more advanced work to teach the others. They were bright and diligent and eager to teach each other, so they advanced almost as much as pupils able to attend school all winter.

12

Surviving in the Cold

Lake Iliamna, seventy-eight miles long and more than a thousand feet deep, is the largest lake in Alaska. In Kenai, *Iliamna* means "mother of winds," a name it deserves.* North winds have an unimpeded sweep from the Arctic Ocean. West winds have a pathway up the great Kvichak River, the lake's outlet into Bristol Bay of the Bering Sea. South and east winds sweep through the mountain divide from the Pacific.

The sky is thus one of the grandest studies of wind and cloud action on the face of the earth. Imagine the whole center of the sky covered with black, heavy mingling clouds. All four of the mighty ocean gales rush in and one cannot overcome the others. They collide and burst through the awesome mass of blackness. A huge wide-mouthed tunnel furrows through it, and the clouds scurry into its yawning mouth, boring downward from the black mass until they form a gigantic funnel-shaped snake that swoops about like a monster with its gaping jaws always open toward the face of the lake. From my cottage I had a clear view of such storms and was entranced by them for hours. One could not see the water in times like these, but the waves dashed and foam mounted on their crests.

*Actually, in Kenai the name means "islands lake." Hannah's version might have been a nick-name.—Ed.

Log buildings had to take into account such storms, to say nothing of bitter cold. People kept buildings well chinked with dry moss, and banked with earth and sod to a height of three feet above ground. Foundations were great logs, hewn on their upper sides, set in the ground as underflooring. Upon these, roughly sawed boards were laid crosswise, and on top of those, crosswise to the rough boards, was a layer of smoothly planed flooring. If the house was well chinked and well banked and sodded, feet would be warm as toast all winter provided they were cuddled in heavy woolen stockings and reindeer or seal mukluks.

Winter set in during the latter part of September with a succession of blizzards. As the snow accumulated, it soon reached a depth of six feet or more. I dressed for winter as the rest of the people did, never going for as much as a step outside without my parka, which was lined with squirrel skins and had a hood edged with fox to protect my face. Outdoors I wore at least two pairs of woolen stockings and pressed felt boots and never went as far as the village without fur boots as well. One of the women made me a beautiful pair, white and gray, trimmed in beaver.

At night the temperature in my cottage sometimes fell as low as forty-five degrees below zero. A mattress alone did not exclude such cold. Below my blankets was a big fur rug of bearskin, and on top of them a large squirrel-skin robe made by Epheme's wife, Agafia. Over that lay a spread of white canvas.

Getting up in the morning was not delightful, but I kept my parka and fur boots beside the bed and first thing slipped into them. Then I lit the two fires in my rooms, a quick operation since the fuel was all ready and a bit of kerosene or a lighted candle set the wood quickly ablaze.

Once the fires were going, I put on fur mittens and on the

coldest mornings took a warm iron in my hands, swung a lantern on my arm and set off in the dark for the schoolhouse along that abominable trail. With the bitter wind shrieking at me, this was an ordeal. There were times when I wept like a child and the warm iron in my hands seemed to do no good.

Once at the school, it did not take long to make good fires although it would be hours before the large space warmed up, which was why it was necessary to get the fires started so early. On my return to the cottage after this chore my house felt warm.

Several boys came to school before the other pupils and kept up the fires until school time and throughout the day. But they could not be depended on to get the fires going because the village was too far away. If I had not hustled out first, many a time we would not have been able to begin school until noon.

I did have one near neighbor, an aged Danish recluse who had been a cannery cook at Bristol Bay in his younger days and spent winters in Iliamna. The natives knew him as John the Cook. His cabin always stood silent, and frequently padlocked when he was off fishing, hunting or trapping. He was so withdrawn that I never got acquainted with him although he was my only close neighbor.

As winter wore on in my first year I became desperately hungry for bread, but it was no longer possible to set dough to rise because of the cold. Food in a skillet, if it was pushed to the back part of the range off the direct heat, would freeze solid. Even if I were to keep the oven going all night and lowered its door to use as a shelf, a bread sponge would be sure to freeze there, hard as an iceberg. Of course when the sun shone on the cottage, conditions inside were not like this, but that was much too short an interval for bread rising.

I had eaten pilot bread until I was tired of it. I had nothing but dehydrated potatoes, cabbage, spinach and celery and, of course, fish. I used powdered eggs and powdered milk. Although all these were excellent, I was so sick of eating soaked food, besides sitting down to it all alone. Obsessed by the thought of bread, I decided to try at any risk.

Before the house got too cold one evening, I made the soft sponge, mixing an extra-large batch because I was so hungry for it. Now what to do? My bread pan was a granite-enamel pail with a tight lid. I wrapped it in cloth so it looked like an old-fashioned bandbox ready for the train. Then I tucked the bundle in the foot of my bed and went off to sleep.

First thing when I woke in the morning I felt something squeezy at my feet. The bubbly, yeasty mass had pushed off the lid of the pail and oozed its way out. Fortunately it kept mostly within the bounds of the bread cloth, but I had to scrape the blankets at once or dough would have frozen to them. And what did remain in the pail and the cloth soon froze. The whole enterprise was a foolish mistake and pretty funny too when I could view it from a little distance. Needless to say, pilot bread suited me fine as winter bread from then on.

Almost every family in Iliamna kept a dog team and would have been helpless in winter without it. A team was a major expense. Six to nine trained dogs were worth about six hundred dollars, an enormous sum, and were costly to maintain because they had to be well fed.

The dogs were wolfish and belligerent creatures. They were much more attentive to race than the people were. The dogs belonging to white men did not attack white people but were aggressive toward natives and also to dogs belonging to natives. Those belonging to natives would attack white people and their dogs. Near the bottom of the village hill was a dog deadline, a territorial separation not created by people but by the dogs themselves. Woe to a dog from either clan that trespassed into the other clan's territory.

I had always gone about the village at will and the dogs did not seem to notice me. Dressed as I was, perhaps each dog clan thought I belonged to its owners' people. But I never went near dogs without carrying a stout stick, five or six feet long.

One Sunday forenoon I started to the church, wearing my parka and carrying the stick as usual. Mondilla Simeon's house was the first on the upper trail I was using, and one of his big malamutes lay near the trail. The village was apparently deserted, with nearly everyone already in church. I prudently considered backtracking instead of venturing so close to the malamute, but then noticed it was chained and felt perfectly safe. As I walked past it, the dog raised its head and stared at me. Then it gave a peculiar howl.

In no more than an instant, about a hundred dogs bounded to the spot from all directions, the whole clan of natives' dogs. They crowded and leaped all around me higher than my head, baring their teeth and snarling and howling. I screamed and wheeled around and around, waving my stick on every side to hold them at bay. All the time I was wheeling about I was also backing down the slippery hill. I knew that if I fell the dogs would tear me to pieces. They don't kill until the animal or person falls. Men on the trail with dog teams were deathly afraid of falling.

What with my screams and the dogs' blood-curdling racket, all this was very noisy. The store was right below me but there was neither door nor window on its upper side and the logs were thick. Just as I made my way to safety around the corner of the store, several men came running out. On hearing the dogs, they assumed they were threatening each other because natives from Nondalton had arrived the night before

Iliamna's church; the open shelter at left is the belfry. *Hannah Breece collection*

and their dogs were considered especially fierce. The men grabbed clubs and sent the animals back where they belonged.

What I wanted to know, but never found out, was what Mondilla's dog had called to the others with that peculiar howl, and how he got them to come so instantaneously.

During the winter I received news from Afognak. The new Nelson school there was successfully in operation. A salmon hatchery had already been established, I gathered that a sawmill was also being installed, and now there was even talk of building a cannery. Good for poor little Afognak!

But I received two pieces of bad news too. Miss Vonderfour, the headmistress of the Kodiak girls' school, who had fallen out of favor with the Czarina and been dismissed and recalled to Russia, had found employment for herself in Sitka translating into English old Russian documents in the archives there. She soon married another archivist who I assume was Russian too. After their marriage he took her out on the bay for a boat ride; she fell out of the boat and was drowned.

Mrs. MacDonald and Mrs. Pajoman both sent me word of a brief item in a Russian-language Alaskan newspaper. It reported that Bishop Innocent, after his recall, was being banished into exile for two years.

Getting and sending mail was an irregular business in Iliamna, especially mail that depended on steamer for part of its journey. At first thought it was a wonder we had any reliable communication with the outside world. In winter, when rivers and lake were frozen over, ice routes created a far-flung network of dogsled trails. Prospectors or traders planning to come in our direction picked up mail at the coast, while travelers through Iliamna who were heading toward the coast took our mail out. This was our opportunistic postal system for nine months of the year, and it worked some of the time.

13

Nondalton Fishing Camp

As soon as the topsoil around the Iliamna schoolhouse
thawed in the spring, I marked out a garden sixty feet
square. The sod was hard to cut but the women, with help
from the boys and girls and me, dug, chopped and turned it
over. The women and children went to the woods to get two
hundred long poles about five inches in diameter for a fence to
keep out the dogs.

They laughed while they planted because it seemed so out-
landish to bury seeds in dark, cold ground. I thought there
must once have been gardening because wherever Russians
went they brought gardens; also the cleared site at the school,
along with traces of old foundation logs, suggested that the
gardening might have been at that very spot. But if so, gardening had been forgotten.

We planted Russian and American turnips, lettuce,
radishes, beets, parsnips and flowers, setting them in borders
and rows. The agricultural station in Sitka sent the seeds, providing enough for many gardens. I offered a prize of a five-gallon can of Pearl kerosene for use in lamps and lanterns for
whoever raised the best crop. Four families made good-sized
gardens and fenced them. Some others planted a few seeds
less ambitiously. The prize was won by Epheme; ironically,

because lamplight was the last thing a blind man could enjoy, but of course his family could.

I had to leave Iliamna for the summer soon after the growing things began to sprout and flourish quickly in the long hours of sunlight. This was to fulfill my promise of three years before that I would come to Nondalton, in the remote Lake Clark country, if I could. Several times during the winter delegations from Nondalton had visited the school to observe what went on and remind me of my promise, and Washington had confirmed that I was assigned to Nondalton for eight to ten weeks.

Epheme and Kusma sent a committee to Zackar Evanoff, the Nondalton chief, requesting him to keep every dog chained during my time there, although I had no knowledge of this before I left. As far as arrangements for my travel, baggage transport and accommodations were concerned, I simply put myself in Zackar's hands, and splendidly capable hands they proved to be.

Moving me to Nondalton was a considerable enterprise. In order to accomplish much in only a ten-week session, I brought along every bit of equipment that could be useful, such as blackboard cloth, ample writing materials, schoolbooks, a good collection of pictures, my telescope organ, and song and hymn books. These last were not only for Sunday School. I had found that after pupils mastered the combination sounds of English speech, expression and reading could be taught in good part by singing. It always amazed me to find how quickly children learned vocabulary from songs, how tenaciously they retained it and how rapidly they matched up their sung vocabulary with written words.

Most men and boys in Nondalton could speak and understand English because each June and early July many went to

Bristol Bay on the Bering Sea to work in canneries, where knowledge of English speech was essential. But that did not mean they could read or write it, and few of the girls and women could even speak or understand it.

Among the sewing and other project equipment, I was bringing material for basketry because this generation of women had never used the native grasses, although they made splendid baskets of birch bark. It occurred to me that if they relearned basket weaving and liked the work, they had plenty of raw materials for it lying at hand. In addition I had medicines for distribution, food for myself and some for the needy. My own camping equipment consisted of a Yukon stove, cooking utensils, bags of bedding and a good canvas tent with mosquito netting. At Zackar's request I was bringing a large American flag. The people wanted a Fourth of July celebration, which they had never had, complete with rigging a flagpole and raising the flag.

Iliamna and Nondalton cooperated in organizing my journey. Men from Iliamna ferried me and all the paraphernalia down the river to the lake, cached the freight there and helped me set up my tent for the night. Then they returned home. Guides from Nondalton were already awaiting me, camped on the lake shore. I had unexpected companions on this overnight stay. The prospector couple working for the Seattle mining company who had come to the Thanksgiving dinner, were embarking on the lake from the same place at the same time as I, though for a different destination. Our tents were close together, pleasant for me, as I liked that young woman very much.

The next leg of my trip started early next morning. The lake was behaving at its best, not at all like the fierce and storm-racked mother of winds. Rowing along on its calm surface we passed islands as level as meadows, holding up majestic forests on parklike lawns sprinkled with flowers and ferns. Some islands were so large they appeared to be part of the mainland until our boats glided around them. Two or three mountains were thrown up in the midst of the water, but their tops were not above timberline so they were crowned with spruce, rounded and green.

Other islands were rocky with bluffs, where it was difficult to make a landing and where one had to scramble to reach high, mossy flats rough-hewn into the rock. These bare islands were nesting sites for gulls, and as we clambered over the rocks the birds hovered like thick clouds above us, rising, swooping low, screaming. Iliamna Lake was the major nesting place for gulls from all that part of the Pacific Coast. The birds did not eat fish but fed on berries. People came from far away to gather their eggs, which were delicious.

Where the nests had not been disturbed, each had three large blue-green spotted eggs. The gulls made no effort to hide them and hunters gathered eggs by the thousands. It seemed to me a pity there was not some limit or protection. I heard of one man putting away a hundred dozen for his dogs. Perhaps this was not as harmful as it seemed, because the gulls would not hatch their eggs unless three were in the nest. If one, two or all were taken, the mother bird replenished the nest with the required number and hatched out her three. But be that as it may, the guides did tell me the birds were fast thinning out.

Mallard ducks nested on the rock islands too. I saw mallard nests with ten or twelve eggs, but the mallards tried to conceal their nests. Swans skimmed the lake. More timid than other birds, they flew high in the air at the sight of a boat.

We left the lake for a portage of six miles along a most beautiful trail running partly over tundra and partly through thick forest. Pink, bell-like little blossoms looked like lily of

A chance for Hannah to watch Lake Iliamna wildlife at an island rest en route to Nondalton. *Hannah Breece collection*

the valley; feeling a sharp pang of homesickness, I wished they were white. Another bloom reminded me of arbutus at home in Pennsylvania. Birds on this trail were tame, flying unfrightened back and forth in our paths, but rabbits and squirrels fled from our passage. I always had a comfortable feeling on Alaskan trails, whether going through high grass or crawling over logs and around boulders in forests, because I knew there were positively no snakes. However, spiders could be immense, and poisonous too, and mice were everywhere.

The seven strong Nondalton Kenais who were my guides unloaded the boats and cached the baggage at the lake end. They carried the boats over the trail and then, while one waited with me, the others retraced their steps, got the baggage and reloaded the boats.

We had now reached the Newhalen River, at a spot where it was very wide, swollen and torrential from melting mountain snows and glacial ice. This river, like many other great Alaskan rivers, was dangerous within its great breadth. Many different currents rushed at awful speed. Anyone navigating it must understand those channels. No stranger could simply get in a boat and safely find his own way. The Kenais knew the channels well and, feeling secure, I was free to marvel at the river and appreciate its volume and power.

When we heard the roaring sound of rapids ahead we unloaded again for a portage. We had to scale the steepest bank I think I had ever climbed. It was about two hundred feet high and the ground was soft and crumbly without bushes to cling to. I felt a little nervous whenever I looked down at the river, at the very foot of the bank, but at the top a view repaid that struggle: a vast valley with the mighty river winding through it into the far distance against a background of snowy ranges.

This second portage was only two miles but it included another equally steep bank down, and the men had to make two trips on it, both times heavily loaded. I brought out a lunch for us and made tea; having eaten and rested, all eight of us felt better able to continue with several hours' more rowing.

When scarlet and gold lights flashing across the sky announced that sundown was ending the very long northern summer day, we landed and the Kenais built a large fire to keep mosquitoes away. Then they prepared supper and brought mine to me, nicely cooked and served. They put up my tent, covering its floor with a thick layer of spruce boughs. After I tied the door strings of its mosquito netting, not an insect could enter. I was glad to lie down.

All night the guides took turns guarding my tent, gun in hand, because this spot was known to be a rendezvous for bears. The men had a wholesome fear of Uncle Sam should any calamity befall me, but I think they had even more concern about being held to account by Iliamna village if I were not returned to it safely.

The next morning, the third of this journey, we continued on the Newhalen River and late on that long day reached the lower end of Six Mile Lake and the summer fishing camps of the Nondalton people. It was here that I would live and set up school.

All the women and children came to the shore as we landed to bid me welcome. The men pitched my tent a little apart from the fishing camp and the women took me to it. After consulting with each other, they hurried down to the shore and returned with their aprons full of small round stones. Again and again they refilled their aprons, until the whole floor of my tent was thickly covered with the pebbles. Then away they went after boughs of fragrant spruce to lay on the stones. Most of Alaska is permanently frozen under its topsoil, at a depth varying from two or three inches below the surface to several feet below. Where a tent is pitched, cold water oozes up. The little stones were to prevent my tent floor from becoming soggy mud.

Olga, the young woman who had been so kind to me on my first visit to Iliamna, was here in the Nondalton camp. Her husband, Pete Anderson, had set up a store here; they had with them their two children, who looked utterly Swedish like their father. When everything had been done for my comfort, even to making a fire in the tent's Yukon stove, Olga brought me a nice supper and then I was glad to sleep.

Zackar Evanoff, the Nondalton chief, must have been about sixty years old. I had met him several times before in Iliamna. Although he was only five feet tall, he was an imposing figure because of his strong character and attractive personality. My guides had told me that his father was a Russian Jew. His features could well have been European but his dark complexion and stocky build were typically Kenai. He spoke Kenai, Russian, English and Aleut, and spoke them all well. He was reputed throughout the country to be an excellent businessman, never known to be outwitted in trading, and he not only looked after his own interests well, but those of his people too. A chief did not inherit his office but was elected by his people and then they all stood by him.

During the past winter Zackar had sent word to those at Stony River that a teacher would be coming to the Nondalton camp. The Stony River tribe dispatched an old man to Nondalton to report back what he thought of the school. With him they sent a young boy to see what the school could do for a child, and a large boy and girl to see what it could do for older children. The Stony River people would judge whether the children came back wiser than when they went away.

The hardships of that little delegation's journey were almost inconceivable. They had crossed large, swift rivers, deep canyons, mountain snows and seeping tundras. They had started on their way the first of April, using a dogsled until the thaw. Then they had "mushed" across country, as hiking without the aid of a sled was called, until they were brought to a halt by a river or lake. To cross it they would build a log raft. They had no baggage except for a few axes, guns and ammunition, and carried no food. They lived on the game they shot.

Zackar and
Mary Evanoff.
*James Carter
collection, Alaska
State Historical
Library*

The entire population of Nondalton, assembled at the fishing camp on July 4, 1911. Hannah, wearing a hat, is standing at the extreme left. Seventh and eighth from the left in the same row are Chief Zackar Evanoff (bearded and bare headed) and his wife, Mary. Two future chiefs are also in the picture: Alexie Balluta, third from the left in the same row, who succeeded Zackar in 1930; and Gabriel Trefon, the youth standing second from the left in the back row, who succeeded Alexie in 1947. The present chief, Bill Trefon, is one of his descendants. *Hannah Breece collection*

The last part of their journey was by water for many miles. They made a boat frame, shot moose, covered the frame with the hides, using sinews to sew the skins so that the craft was perfectly watertight.

On the twentieth of June they arrived at the fishing camp, and my heart ached for them. All four were utterly exhausted and ragged and dirty to the last degree. All the women in camp went to work sewing for them, using material I had brought along, and in a couple of days had new outfits for them. They looked like different beings after they were rested and bathed and their matted hair was clipped. Various families took the visitors into their camp homes and treated them royally.

The old man and children attended school every day, and at the end of the summer the man said he was pleased and asked me to come back with him to his people. I explained that I had promised to return to Iliamna. He and the children, I knew, would talk for years to come of all they had seen and heard that summer.

The custom at this camp was for the men and big boys to go to Bristol Bay in June and work in the canneries there. At Nondalton fishing camp the salmon run began later, in early July. This summer the fishing was disastrous. Almost no fish came up the river from the sea. The canneries had sent word from Bristol Bay that there was no work for lack of salmon. Nobody knew why.

Word reached us from Iliamna that the same calamity was occurring there. I was especially sad when I thought of my poor pupils who for the first time had a seine of their own. At Nondalton people caught what few fish they could.

Large boys came to school at night. Women had their hygiene classes and did sewing and basketry in the afternoons. Children came all day. All listened and learned from everything, making the most of their chance at schooling seven days a week, for we had Sunday school too.

One Sunday, however, everyone took a holiday from the fishing camp and school, because it was an important Russian religious day. Nondalton had no church reader, and no priest had ever visited the place. Whenever a priest visited Iliamna, which now had not happened for some six years, the Nondalton people were supposed to travel there for services. Nevertheless, Zackar had seen to it that the village built a church, and on this important day they were all planning to attend it.

They were anxious that I come with them and see the church and their village, which was about three miles away, on the same lake as the fishing camps. It was a beautiful day and the boats on the water made quite a fleet, for visitors had come for this event from outlying places.

We started in the morning to reach the village by noon. All the people promptly went into their houses to put on their best clothes. The men were especially well dressed, even to the point of wearing good dress shoes, and the women put pretty scarves on their heads.

I walked about while they were getting ready and was surprised to see much better houses and furniture than in Iliamna. Whether this was a consequence of earnings from the Bristol Bay canneries or was owing to Zackar's shrewd bargaining with traders, I do not know. Probably it was owing to both.

As was customary, people stood in church, men and boys on one side, women and girls on the other. To me, it was a very strange service. Not one word was spoken by anybody. From time to time, in the silence, people bowed and crossed themselves. For two hours we stood there. I thought it such a pity they could not have, in their language, some of the sermons that were preached throughout the world to so many empty pews.

After the service and lunch we returned to the fishing camp. It was very late at night when we arrived but at this time of year it did not become dark until nearly midnight and then only briefly. Back in camp, people told me the Kenai had never been heathens. Before the Russians came they had worshipped God as the Great Spirit.

They also claimed that they had Bible stories before the Russians came. They told me some of the stories from their tradition, all from the Old Testament. The essential truths came through in their versions but the stories had been clothed in settings that accorded with the Kenais' own environment. Thus, telling me the story of the flood, they said the ark was under the snow and ice of Alaska. They believed their people had seen and described it before it was buried. When one thinks of the incredible animals, such as mammoths, lying deeply buried under snow, their belief does not seem strange.

They believed that three sea otters, rather than only two, lived through the flood. The extra was the only animal outside the ark to survive. He was on the highest rock and when the waters reached him he was able to swim until they subsided.

One day during school I became aware that a deep voice had joined the children's in "My Country 'Tis of Thee." Looking up from the little organ I saw a tall, white-haired man. With his long white beard and handsome sport suit he looked very distinguished. The children and I must have made an odd appearance. Because of mosquitoes we all wore veils hanging from wide-brimmed hats. Each veil had tightly fitted armholes and a drawstring to tie it securely below the arms. In addition I was wearing long leather gauntlets.

The gentleman introduced himself as Warren Smith from Seattle. He was connected with a firm of mining engineers looking over gold prospects in the interior; I believe the project was sponsored by the Guggenheims. The rest of his party was entering the area by way of the Bering Sea, but he was to go by a different route to judge the possibilities of overland transportation.

He asked permission to go into my tent and cook dinner for himself on the stove. As was the custom, I set out food for him to cook, and he talked with the children, who all knew him from a visit the previous year. He told me about his wife and daughters in Seattle, then said he must hurry to reach his next camp before dark. He rowed out of sight in his frail boat with only his Newfoundland dog for company.

In a day or two Zackar came to me much troubled. He feared Mr. Smith would drown. Word had come that a white man, farther along on his route, had directed Mr. Smith up a river from which no one had ever returned. Zackar said the white man knew it was a fatal river and wanted Mr. Smith to die because the previous year Mr. Smith had caused two white criminal outlaws to be apprehended.

I asked Zackar whether he could send some fast rowers to overtake Mr. Smith. He replied that no man would take a boat onto the fatal river, but that messengers could be sent to the river's mouth to head off Mr. Smith in case he should be resting for a few days in a cabin located there. I wrote a letter explaining that all the tribe expected him to lose his life if he attempted the route which had been recommended to him, and that he had better heed their warning. Then I got detailed, minute particulars of the route the natives took instead and included them in my letter.

Zackar gave my letter to his second chief and two other young men and directed them to stay three days in the cabin. If at the end of that time Mr. Smith had not come to the cabin, they were to place the letter on the table and return home.

The messengers returned without having seen Mr. Smith. However, they believed that when he left the cabin he must have expected to return because there was no wood. No traveler left a cabin without replacing the wood he had used. They left the letter on the table. Some weeks later they went back and found the letter was gone. But thereafter nothing was heard of Mr. Smith. Zackar and the other men were convinced he was dead. I doubted that. The letter was addressed to him. It must have been he who took it.

Almost two years later, at the A.C. Point as I waited for a steamer, a gentleman walked up to me and thanked me for saving his life. It was Mr. Smith. I assured him nothing could have been done without Zackar and told him how concerned the Nondalton people had been.

In turn he related what had happened after he left the fishing camp in his bidarka on that summer day. He reached the cabin that night as he had planned, but before starting up that wrong river he wanted to do some surveying and make notes on the topography. While at this work he fell and hurt his back. Fortunately he was close to a different cabin where he had camped the year previously. He crawled to it on his hands and knees. A pail of water was in the cabin, and some wood, but not a bite of food, and he had already eaten the lunch he carried in his pocket. Though he was unable to stand and could only creep about, he did not think he was seriously injured and was sure he could walk in a few days.

His main problem was how to get food. Again he was lucky. Each day his big yellow and white dog brought him a wild duck. He was able to broil the duck sufficiently to make it edible, and then divided it with his dog. He thought the dog brought the ducks in order to get his own share, but whatever was in the dog's mind he saved his master's life. For seven days Mr. Smith was helpless. When he was able to make his way back to the other cabin he found the letter and revised his route.

At the end of my summer with them, I left the Nondalton people reluctantly. In all the ages, it seemed that I had been the only one to come expressly to help and uplift them with no other purpose. It seemed to me dreadful that in all the great world there had been no person to go and tell them that we did care if they were hungry, sick or ignorant. They asked me not to go but all I could tell them was that if I could return the next summer, I would.

The storms of autumn had set in and were so dreadful we had to travel by bidarka on the return journey. A bidarka is built with a very light framework, just enough stiffening to give it shape, which is covered with skin that has been soaked in oil and then tightly fitted and sewn. The top, just high enough to escape the surface of the water, is also framed and covered over except for holes only large enough each for a grown person to get into and kneel. The bidarka to carry me was about fifteen feet long and had three hatches.

In a bidarka one wore a *kamleika,* a waist-length, hooded coat with a drawstring so it could be tied securely around the hatch rim. In effect, it was an extension of the boat to enclose

A bidarka of the kind Zackar Evanoff provided for Hannah. This one, with unidentified paddlers and passenger, was photographed in 1921 on Lake Iliamna. *Courtesy of Robert W. Vreeland*

a paddler or passenger. I bought my *kamleika* from Zackar's wife, Mary. It looked like sheer oiled silk, puffed in four-inch strips. It was made of bear intestines.

I knelt in the middle hatch, and Zackar and his helper paddled. It was necessary to maintain perfect balance. They told me I was the first white woman in that country to take a journey in a bidarka. The two men were so alert and skillful with their paddling, which they rapidly changed from one side of the craft to the other, and I stayed so still that in spite of rough, stormy waves and strong winds we had no mishaps.

14

Fish Famine

My cottage back in Iliamna seemed unbelievably snug and comfortable. Too much so. I had grown used to camping and living outdoors and the cottage smothered me.

Conditions at the Iliamna fishing camps were alarming. Families had been able to catch and prepare only a few bundles of dried fish to feed themselves over the coming winter, and had none to trade for flour, tea and other accustomed necessities. I conferred with Kusma and Epheme and we decided to start the school year at the camps instead of in the village, so the children need not start using dried salmon while it was still possible to catch and eat a few fresh fish.

For the camp schoolroom I chose a fish drying house, a large, lattice-work building with a high roof and a floor of earth as hard and smooth as tiling. The lattice sides were filled in with spruce boughs, and with a smudge in its center there would not be a mosquito to plague us. Normally this fish house was crammed with drying salmon all summer, but this year it had stood empty. Old Matrona volunteered to stay and help care for the children.

The fish house was within sight of the camp located on the opposite bank of the river, but was around a bluff from the camp on its own side, out of sight and hearing. Although the river was about half a mile wide here near its mouth, the fish house was surprisingly within sound of the camp on the opposite shore. The acoustic properties of the water here were astonishing. I set up my tent close to the fish house. The camps had plenty of boats, and travel between them was frequent and easy except in case of storms.

We got school under way in an orderly fashion, with afternoon sewing sessions for women who were not squirrel hunting, but something was wrong. The women, normally so pleasant and eager to make school clothes for their children, were lazy and saucy. They struck me as intoxicated. I suspected hooch but although I peered everywhere in the camps where something could have been hidden, I could find none.

Then one day I noticed a barrel in the corner of one of the best tents. It attracted my attention because it was piled with old clothes. This was not natural because I was always having to remind the women not to stuff dirty or old clothes under the beds, and that barrel looked too carefully loaded. I made a dive for it. It was a whole barrel of hooch in a brown foam, ready for drinking.

I walked into the next tent where Michael Rickteroff, the second chief, lived and told him and Young William, the reader's grown son, to come immediately and empty out the hooch. The second chief demurred, then agreed but proposed waiting until after supper. No waiting! It must be done now!

When I got back to the barrel I saw that about two gallons had been taken out. I could not find it and the woman in the tent laughed while I hunted. I think it must have been in two large tea kettles I did not examine that stood on the stove. I commanded the two young men to carry the barrel to the water. They pled with me not to throw it over but I dumped it down the bank and the entire yeasty, sour mess went trailing into the water.

That night I felt very much alone, miles away from any other white person, and among people who were angry with me and not altogether sober. But the next day the women professed to be sorry for the way they had behaved. They drank no more as far as I could judge.

The following Sunday, Old William invited me to dinner with his family and paid me the honor of a special treat. They were cooking something good and waiting to eat until I could be served first. The odor was appetizing. William removed the lid of the large iron dinner-pot hanging over the fire, and with a sharp, pointed stick speared a big piece of meat and held it up triumphantly.

For an instant I felt faint. It looked exactly like a monstrous, black human foot. They had removed the claws, and the under part of the bear's foot was toward me. I was to be given the prize tidbit. William took out his old pocketknife, and I managed not to flinch while he cut between the big toe and the next, stripped off the big toe and offered it to me. In somewhat of a daze I held out a piece of paper for it. I could not possibly eat it; I could hardly keep from gagging merely by looking at it.

They had been so courteous and kind. Keeping my eyes averted from the toe in my hand, I thanked them and begged leave to take it to my tent so I could have my bread and tea with it. Yes, that was satisfactory. At a safe distance I furtively threw the ghastly thing into an impenetrable thicket. It was wrong to waste food on the brink of such want, but at least I hadn't hurt anyone's feelings, theirs or my own.

With a hard winter facing us, I decided to go to a village a few miles upstream from the Bering Sea where I could arrange emergency allowances and deal with school business. While I was away, people would remain in the camps to take advantage of the few straggling salmon. School lessons this September would have to be postponed for a couple of weeks.

Mr. Nielsen, the Dane who was my guide when Old Dick jumped the ravine, agreed to take me as a passenger on his launch. His Aleut wife, Martha, was planning to go to the coast to visit her mother and I could accompany them. We could bring back on the launch government supplies I planned to pick up at the coast.

I had never been the length of Iliamna Lake, and this trip would take us over its entire distance. I had a canvas-topped compartment about six feet long at one end of the boat and Martha had a similar compartment at the other end. We went aboard at eventide and started very early the next morning, threading our way among the islands.

By late afternoon the following day we reached an open part of the lake. No islands were now in sight and it felt like the high seas. Toward night I became a bit doubtful about our safety because Mr. Nielsen had neglected to bring a trailer lifeboat, and there was neither candle nor lantern aboard. The engine was out of order. Several times that day it had stopped and been difficult to restart. We would probably be all right, I thought, unless a storm should break.

One soon did. The sky became dark and lowering. I suggested to Mr. Nielsen he steer for a rift in the mountainside because the natives had told me that when they saw a sky like this they fled for shelter. He protested that he could not make the shore, it was too rocky, and we might not reach it before dark, so it was safer to stay in deep water.

The waves rose rapidly and we rocked back and forth as darkness increased to inky blackness. Kept dry by my parka, I stood at the prow and gazed intently, lest we threaten to run into a rock. I asked Mr. Nielsen how he knew which way to steer the launch. He said he went by direction of the wind. Now I lost all faith in him. "But the wind is coming from all directions," I said. "It is not in the same direction for two minutes." The waves were now so high that occasionally one would envelop me. He replied that he had no other choice but to push ahead because if we stopped, the boat was likely to capsize.

We were supposedly heading for the short, but wide, Kvichak River, which drains Iliamna Lake into the Bering Sea. We would get through safely, Mr. Nielsen said, if we could reach the river's north bank; if we drifted to its south bank we would be lost upon the rocks. At three in the morning I caught sight of a line on the horizon. What could it be but a hill? Land was near and land might mean rocks. I called out to anchor quickly. Instead of doing so, Mr. Nielsen refused to move and asked why. I was frantic. He had been half asleep. When he did realize we were almost at land he finally did hurry to lower the anchor. In the darkness we could see little, but the water surrounding us was quiet.

As light came we discovered that we were on the dangerous side of the entrance to the river. In a short time we would have been wrecked among the rocks and breakers. By daylight Mr. Nielsen was now able to steer around the reef and reach the safe route.

At the river's entrance stood a high bluff, and on the bluff stood a man as though on lookout for us. Mr. Nielsen said it was the river pilot he had been told to employ, but he was sure there was now no danger so he did not intend to do that. I urged him to obey his instructions, to no avail, so without stopping on we went past Igiugig, a sleepy little village with smoke curling up from underground houses. I had a horror of that village; the previous summer its dogs had eaten a two-year-old child.

We had gone no more than five miles when our launch grounded in this immense, sealike river. Out of its five channels, Mr. Nielsen had chosen a wrong one and we were stuck in the sand. There was nothing to do but hope we would be seen, although we were almost out of sight of the navigable channels. I had a white tablecloth among my things and Mr. Nielsen fastened it to a mast. We had been grounded for thirteen hours when four men appeared in bidarkas. They had spied out the speck of white. They arrived none too soon, because the water was becoming rough.

They tied one of the bidarkas to the side of the launch and fastened the other beside the first, then instructed me to step into a hatch on the first boat and from there to the hatch of the outer boat. This was much worse than the *Dora*'s rope ladder. It took the men about two hours to free the launch and then they steered us into the proper channel; when a good camping place came in sight, they took us to shore. By the time we ate it was daylight again. We reached Koggiung without further incident except to sight a large whale that had come in with the tide and seemed to be lost.

At Koggiung was an underground village, and in between visiting government offices and dispatching my messages I had an opportunity to visit every house in this village. To enter a house one merely had to bend a little, so it was more like going into a cellar with a low doorway than crawling into the ancient, abandoned barabaras whose ruins we had visited on Kodiak Island. The rooms of these houses were large and had surprisingly high ceilings. Although they were not very light, neither could they be called gloomy, because walls and ceilings were neatly covered with flowered wallpaper. They were better furnished than I had imagined. Stoves were good; so were tables and chairs. The most interesting building was the *kashim,* the men's ceremonial community room, also underground. It was large and contained a bath, or kind of swimming pool, with benches arranged like an amphitheater.

The people here were Eskimo, intermarried with Russian. In their appearance, the Eskimo heritage predominated. I was told by them that when Russians came to the north, the better class married Eskimos and the others married Aleuts. They said they were looked up to by Aleuts as superiors, but that Indians looked down on both them and the Aleuts. They had a new government schoolhouse attended by children from this village. The government was now discouraging natives from building underground and they had begun responding to this advice.

On our return trip, after I had accomplished my business, Mr. Nielsen took aboard a river pilot. Upon entering the lake we stopped to examine Igiugig, the underground village where the dogs had eaten the child. The pilot preceded us up the steep trail and had all dogs put out of sight and chained before he sent down for us. These houses were poorly and crudely furnished and less commodious than those at Bristol Bay. They had to be entered on hands and knees, but inside there was ample room to stand upright. The villagers in this humble place did splendid work in fossil ivory brought to them by Bristol Bay traders. I bought a beautiful chain with an attached cross, all cut from a single piece of ivory. I also bought an oblong dish of a kind the villagers made for their own use, carved by hand from birch, with smooth and symmetrical curves.

The first news to greet me back in Iliamna village was that Kusma, the chief, had taken one of the young women, Daluska, as his bride. The way of spreading the news was to say, "Daluska is wearing a net." An unmarried Kenai woman wore her hair in two braids, and a widow wore her hair bobbed. A married woman wore a beautifully beaded hair net that she herself wove.

Only two months into winter, the children looked pale and thin. The summer's catch was already gone, and without their normal fill of oily fish they were hungry almost all the time. So far I had been able to give them two good dinners a week in school, but clearly they were undernourished.

The Kenais accepted the normal hardships and exertions of their life bravely and cheerfully. They were a strong, stoic people. But these were not normal times of normal poverty. In their anxiety and deprivation, they thought that the miserable hooch would help them. I had a suspicion that the children were even less well off than could be expected. So I told them to bring a piece of pilot bread to school the next day and they would get a nice dinner, but anyone not bringing the bread could not eat dinner. Every last one brought the piece of bread.

I had judged rightly. The bread had been made of flour from the fermented mess left in the bottom of hooch barrels. After school that day I stormed to the village and made the biggest racket of which I was capable. They would not, I made sure, use their flour that way again—the flour that should go into good bread for the children and themselves.

As soon as I received authorization for emergency fish vouchers I was able to provide a good, wholesome cooked dinner in school every day for the pupils, the women and the children too young for school. The men were able to feed themselves from what they earned packing for prospectors and traders and chopping wood for the store.

The white men who came through said, "Let them hunt! They are a lazy lot!" But these men did not understand how bad times had become. The villagers had no money to buy ammunition. Their guns were useless, so they pawned them for food. A hunt meant a round-trip journey of about 250 miles, and food for dogs and men on the journey.

I had once thought everyone was poor alike, but the famine made a vast difference out of normally small margins of poverty and prosperity. The dogs of the poorest people died off rapidly and died off first. Some of the men whose dog teams were gone walked more than a hundred miles to Bristol Bay and carried whale meat home with them. They cached what they could not carry for a second trip. But wolves broke into the caches and took all the meat. The men had depended on that meat to supply food for their return journey. They struggled back in the bitter cold, utterly famished.

Hungry dogs crossed the river to where there were two horses in a barn and got one of the animals down. By the time the owner got there with a gun, they had partly eaten the horse alive.

From down the lake word was sent me asking if someone in our village could take two Aleut children. Their mother had fallen on the ice and the dogs had torn her to pieces. I thought it best that they not come to our village because the Kenais did not like the Aleuts.

The Eskimo youths arrived from the reindeer station and were the fastest learners in the school. The difference must have been that the government was rationing them while our children were hungry because, after I was able to provide dinner to Iliamna pupils every day, they took to learning quickly again.

Fish was so expensive we could afford it for the school dinners only twice a week. Other times we had dried beans or dried peas, and at all meals bacon, bread, dried fruit and tea. We alternated sugar for tea with syrup for bread.

Feasts for Thanksgiving and Christmas were out of the question, but for Thanksgiving at least we had vegetables from the school garden. Many families now said they intended to put in gardens the next summer.

Besides being a winter of general disaster, it was marked by particular disasters. The steamer *Farralon* was wrecked in Cook Inlet; it ran aground in a blizzard. Some of the rescued men made their way to our village. They had no snowshoes and had come close to perishing on the trail.

Mondilla Simeon, who still had his dog team, went out alone after wood. He did not return at night and the search party found him lying under a heavy branch with parts of his hands, face and shoulders frozen. Pneumonia set in and I had to make many trips over the trail to his house with food supplies from the school funds for him and his old mother, Seponita. Their wants were simple but I had to dole out the food one day at a time or Mondilla and Seponita would have given fashionable tea parties with a surplus.

A doctor from more than a hundred miles away visited before Christmas, looked over the sick and advised me about treatments. His wife sent me a young chicken that had been given to her, and a quart of milk that was not dried or canned but had been frozen fresh. I sent that to a white woman across the river, because she had not tasted fresh milk for five years, and I had had some two years before. After the doctor was gone, a young man, Sullivan Jackarr, broke his upper arm. Fortunately it was a clean break; with great help from one of the storekeepers, I could manage that. For a man to lose the use of an arm was a tragedy, so getting it set correctly was extremely important.

One sight to make us happy that winter were the new babies. Every day their mothers came to school to eat dinner and drink a good cup of cocoa. The babies knew nothing about a famine; they were chubby.

The snow, this terrible winter, did not develop a crust. The trails were so engulfed in soft drifts that it was impossible to walk them merely wearing boots. Snowshoes were constantly necessary. Mine were about five feet long, latticed and thonged with reindeer sinews very heavily twisted.

At last spring did come, gardens were put in and people left the village to repopulate the fishing camp. Although I was not formally assigned there again, I was told I could go to Nondalton for the summer if I chose and the cost of transportation would be allowed.

A boat owned by two white men with two Kenai helpers was chartered to take me and my baggage on the lake as far as the portage*. This time, instead of tenting, I established myself in an empty food cache raised on stilts. The guides from Nondalton had not yet arrived at this rendezvous but the char-

Hannah and her guide, Joe Kackley, at lunch on a Lake Iliamna island.
Hannah Breece collection

*See frontispiece photograph.—Ed.

tered boat had to return that night. The men were reluctant to leave me alone on the lake shore but I assured them there was nothing to fear. If a wolf should wander near he couldn't get me, for I would draw up the ladder. Furthermore, I would venture that every move I made would be watched because all natives in the vicinity were aware of my journey.

Sure enough, the boat had not long gone when a little Eskimo woman came around a curve in the lake, beamed at me and held out her hand. She was dressed in fur; her black eyes were bright and shining as beads, and a rich red showed through her olive complexion. She was an old acquaintance!

Hannah, seen dimly at left, is preparing to camp overnight on a Lake Iliamna island. *Hannah Breece collection*

This was the very woman who had come with the little Eskimo party all the way to the Point, years before, when I was returning to Wood Island after my first brief trip to Iliamna. I gave her a *Ladies' Home Journal* because all native women, whether Aleut, Kenai or Eskimo, loved that magazine.

During the three nights I spent in the cache and the two days by the shore, I think there was not a single hour in which I was not being watched by someone or other from the Eskimo camp a mile down the lake. At night I could hear the watchers move quietly about, and would go off to sleep knowing I was well guarded.

When the men from Nondalton arrived, they were worried that we might be cut off on the portage by a forest fire. They had not seen a fire but thought they had smelled one a long way off at their camp the night before. So we hurried as fast as we could. Since they were not burdened with boats, they needed to make only this one trip on the trail with the baggage.

On the portage trail we caught glimpses of the fire here and there. Mossy tundras were burning. In the forested portion occasionally a tall tree fell near enough so that we could hear the crash. The air felt hot on our faces. But a forest fire in Alaska does not sweep across the country in the same way it would in the States. If it did, we could never have made it to the river before the fire swept across our path. We walked single-file as fast as we could to reach our boats moored in the river.

On the second, shorter portage around the rapids, the fire had already burned itself out at the riverbank. The ground was still so hot it almost burned our feet. The last part of that trail, through woods, we made on the run. Our reloaded boats carried us across the river to a camping spot on the opposite shore.

The camp site, revealed in the light of a mosquito fire, was

The Eskimos who watched over Hannah while she waited for her Non-dalton guides on Lake Iliamna. The group was probably from a small Yupik (Pacific Eskimo) settlement of the time on the Newhalen River.
Hannah Breece collection

beautiful. As I was gratefully preparing for bed, the guides asked me to walk up the hill and take a look. The whole mountainside on the opposite bank was grasped by blazes. The flames were not a continuous spread, but like fiery serpents zigzagged across the earth. Old spruce trees burned like oil. Blazes would shoot upward, then crash, and a star shower ascend into the heavens. The fire had crossed the last, wooded part of our trail less than an hour after we had outraced it; I shuddered to think of the difference that hour had made.

The wind was coming in our direction. Sparks flew toward us, over the river. It was not safe for us to sleep until the wind changed, which it finally did about midnight. As usual, one or another of the men took turns guarding all night, ready to rouse the rest of us if the fire caught on our side of the river.

The next morning, smoke and heat were oppressive. It was pitiful to see distressed birds whose nests and little ones had been burned. They flew about frantically. Mother ducks were trying to keep their young away from the edge of the hot riverbank, yet not let them get into dangerous currents. Squirrels, rabbits and foxes were destroyed over a great area. Here and there, fires were still raging. This had been Kenai hunting ground for centuries. Its charred wreckage at any time would have been a misfortune. This year it was a calamity, for once again the summer runs of fish had vanished.

At the fishing camp I half expected the children to have forgotten all they had learned the summer before. Not so. Both they and their parents were proud to show me how much more they had learned over the winter. I had left books and writing materials in Zackar's care and he had seen to it they were used. Older children had taught younger ones as far as they could, and went on to read all the books I had left. They had done all the arithmetic problems as far as they had knowledge. So this summer we had a good foundation, and we all made the most of it.

One day the women invited me to go with them to get birch bark for baskets, a round-trip of ten miles. The grove was perhaps the loveliest place I have ever seen, before or since. The white trees stood wide apart, straight and far-reaching, each in its own space, not spindling but a foot or more in diameter. Short, light-green grass, in places almost hidden by the white blossoms of the moss berry, covered the ground. A lazy brook meandered through the gently sloping grove, reflecting the ferns overhanging its banks and the delicate foliage of branches arching above.

The whole day was magical. The women, laughing and happy, wore beaded leather shields at their waists. Drawing sharp knives, they skillfully stripped off as much birch bark as they could carry. They would not permit me to carry an ounce, but when we arrived home they shared with me until I had more bark than anyone. Then they said they would have to use it, for what could I do with it? The next week, among them, they made me seven baskets from my share: handsome, waterproof and durable.

On the important Russian religious holiday we all went to church in the village, as in the year before, even though the rain was pouring torrentially as we made the three-mile trip up the lake in open boats. This time the service was not silent. Zackar stepped out in front of the standing congregation and in Kenai preached a sermon. If his words were as eloquent as his expression and gestures, it was an excellent sermon.

Afterward I asked him about it. He said that ever since the silent service I had seen the year before, he had been speaking this way in church, drawing upon truths from the Bible, sto-

At left is one of the seven birch-bark baskets given to Hannah by the Nondalton women who invited her on the bark-gathering expedition. At right is the carved birch bowl Hannah bought in Igiugig. *Pete Butzner*

ries from the Sunday school lessons and from the discussions and stories told among us in his tent. Like Epheme he was a philosopher, and I am sure his sermons would compare well with those that many a pretentious congregation hears.

At the close of this church service, the men all began to talk together animatedly. I could see that some of the oldest men were angry and the younger ones trying to persuade them of something. Several times I heard the word *teacher,* and realized the argument was about me. Although I knew they were my friends, old superstitions are powerful and I worried that I had unknowingly offended them or seriously transgressed in some way. I felt very much alone, far from my own people.

After what seemed a long time Zackar came over to me and said they wanted to thank me for coming to them through fire and water and had been debating how to express their thanks. They wanted to give me a sacred picture. The oldest folk, he said, had objected that I would ridicule it so it had been decided that he should ask me whether I would promise never to make fun of it. I gave him my promise.

Then he brought out a print of the Madonna framed in white wood. Long ago it had been sent to them from Russia. Everyone in the village gathered around and it was presented with ceremony and solemnity.

They knew this was to be my last summer in Nondalton. They knew they had a hard winter ahead and that there was nothing practical I could do to help them through it, but they were giving me the most unusual and precious object the community possessed.

15

The Second Famine Year

Back at the Iliamna fishing camps after my summer in Nondalton, I again set up the camp school so the children could stay there as long as possible. Since the fish runs had failed again disastrously, the bears were hungry and their accustomed ways were upset too. Perhaps that is why they took to venturing where they did not usually go.

One evening a wind storm set in and the rain poured down cold and steadily. My two nearest neighbors in the camp, Mondilla Simeon and his mother, were away squirrel hunting. I cooked some bear steak, cut from a young, berry-fed cub, and left it over the fire while I went down to the shore for water. The pan caught on fire, the meat was badly charred, and the scent from it seemed strong enough to perfume all Alaska.

Owing to the storm and having no place to visit and no one to talk with, I decided to go to bed early and read by light of the lantern hanging over my bed. As I lay there peacefully, bedlam broke loose. All the dogs in camp, probably thirty, were jumping, howling and snarling outside the tent, sounding as they did the time they were after me that Sunday morning in the village. Only a loosely staked canvas stood between us. Then I heard a lumbering animal moving on the outside of the canvas and knew it was a bear.

I did what I should not have done. I turned out the lantern light and quaked in the dark. The dogs did not cease their snarls and yelps for what seemed an eternity but in reality was only an hour or two. I could do nothing but wait and cower and then, when the dogs finally ceased their clamor, fall asleep.

At two in the morning Old William poked his head in my door flap and said, "You much scared, Teacher?" He said I should hurry and come with them because they were afraid the bear might eat some of us. Every man and boy in the camp on my side of the river was gathered around my tent. They rolled up my blankets, hurried me out and marched me with them to the fishing camp proper. There were not more than two guns out of pawn, so some of the men had axes and some had clubs and I couldn't help smiling at our strange parade through the woods and around the bluff.

Because of the bluff, nobody in camp on our side of the river had heard the dogs over the sound of the storm. But across the water people in the other camp heard them and were frantic to reach me. Try as hard as they could they were unable to launch a boat because the waves were too strong. Finally the storm lulled enough for two young men to put across in bidarkas and rouse the camp on my side of the river. By this time the bear had gotten away with the dogs in pursuit.

The next morning we could see where the big, lumbering animal had lain in the grass beside my tent. Along with its big tracks were tracks of a little bear. We speculated that the old mother bear had been drawn by the scent of my burned steak. That night I transferred my sleeping quarters to an empty fish cache.

The weather this winter of 1911–12 was extremely strange. Although the air was bitterly cold, the earth was warm. The snow was deceptive. From above it looked fluffy and innocent, but below it was melted so that when one walked on it one soon sank into water. Snowshoes were useless in this slush. The lake and the rivers were treacherous. By midwinter snowslides and tremendous avalanches had become dangers.

Elderly people told me their fathers had described the same conditions long ago, followed by fire bursting out of a mountain and smoke and ashes falling about them although the fire was far away. The strange weather added to anxiety about the disappearance of the fish. The Bible was thrown from its stand in the church, which counted as a very bad omen.

The men asked me if they might eat at school with the women and children. I knew that if they sat around in their homes and the school all winter they would die. So I made a proposition to them that they accepted. They were to bring to the schoolyard logs that were twelve inches in diameter at the narrow end and ten feet long. That would leave plenty of firewood for them from each tree. They might work together or alone, as they liked.

For every three logs they could get a fifty-pound sack of flour from the store. For every single log they could get a pound of tea, two pounds of lard and (let us whisper it) tobacco. I rationed stick candy to be eaten with their tea, for in their weakened state it was not advisable to trust them with sugar. I also gave out dried fruit occasionally, and where I was positive a man had no fish, I saw to it that he had it at least three times a week.

I had no way to inform the Alaskan authorities of the work arrangements in return for emergency food, at the time the men and I agreed on them. So I just did what I thought best on my own responsibility. The bills from the store were authorized by the emergency allowance I had arranged with the government. When spring came, I would sign vouchers in favor of the storekeeper and mail them to the proper government auditing committee, which had to scrutinize all bills before they were paid except in cases of great suffering and want, when money could be sent immediately.

We had no deaths over the winter, but only three dog teams were left and those were depleted and the animals weak. The men had to work hard, using only their own strength to draw heavy logs over slushy trails. But it kept them active, which is what I wanted.

Ever since I had come into the Iliamna Lake country I had heard talk about a young Welsh woman, Mrs. Miller, and her aged white husband, who lived in a remote area. They made their living by trapping in the wilderness. Everyone had a kind word for Mrs. Miller but said little about her husband except that he made her do all the work. He was no favorite. Before I had left Nondalton a young, travel-worn woman had appeared at my tent. She was timid to the point of being frightened, and dreadfully bedraggled: barefooted, bareheaded, missing some teeth and others rotted.

I took her by the hand and said, "I am so glad to see you, Mrs. Miller. I have hoped ever since I came that you would come to see me." Tears poured down her face. She told me she had been afraid to come because her clothes were so bad and her teeth so broken. "But your eyes and your hair are so beautiful," I told her. "One doesn't notice the teeth and the dress so much." She eagerly asked if I did really think her eyes and hair were pretty. Long ago, she said, she thought so too but now she did not know.

In the hour or two she stayed she told me of an experience she and her husband had had the previous winter. They were living beside their trapline in a tent from which she could tend the traps on snowshoes while her husband waited in the tent. They were having so little success that they tramped off together from the tent to select a better location and were caught by a blizzard. They crawled into their fur sleeping bags, lay down on the snow and let the soft, fluffy, dry flakes cover them. It was warm, she said, but oppressive. She did not know how long they had lain there when she felt she must get into the air, for she was smothering and would rather die in the blizzard. Although her husband protested, she struggled out of the deep snow. Later they found they had lain there more than two days and that the storm had ceased only an hour or two before she fought her way out.

The next time I saw Mrs. Miller was a month or so later when she and her husband stopped at the Iliamna fishing camp overnight. I invited them to eat with me. In the course of our conversation Mr. Miller referred to a time when he had been wealthy. I had already heard he had been considered so. Yes, he went on expansively, he had known the time when he could command fifty thousand dollars but he had lost it through speculation. In Alaska one learned from acquaintances only what they chose to volunteer about their previous lives; one did not interrogate them or pry. I think he wanted to shock me or instigate an argument, for he volunteered that he was proud of the fact he had earned his wealth by dealing in whisky on the Klondike.

I well realized he was too old to change his ideals, and the heavens were too high for him to hitch his wagon to a star, so I made no comment. Instead I invited Mrs. Miller to sing. She readily did and was true to her Welsh heritage, for her voice was far above the common and she sang on and on. She mentioned that she loved the hymns, for they were what she had sung when she belonged to the Christian Endeavor Society in Wales. Her husband snapped out, "But remember, you do not believe any of that stuff now. You have too much sense!" at which she looked frightened and said nothing. The next morning he stood by and gave directions while she broke camp and then loaded the whole bundle on her own back.

I next saw Mrs. Miller during my trip to the coast. A woman at Koggiung had become interested in her and between us we fixed her clothes and provided what else she needed to look nice for her outdoor life and make her more comfortable. In the presence of her husband, I told her that if anything should happen to him she should feel free to come to me and I would take care of her until she had decided what to do. That devoted husband piped up, "And what will you do with me if she dies first, take me in?"

I answered simply and to the point, "Heaven forbid!"

Not much later, during the winter, her husband died very suddenly while they were five miles away from their cabin and an equal distance from a copper mine where miners were camping. She left her husband's body in the snow and notified the miners of his death. They organized a party to arrange his burial and to help Mrs. Miller arrange her affairs and obtain a guide to accompany her to Iliamna village. Snowshoes were of no use to them because of the strange weather this winter, and they had to take many long detours because usual winter trails were so treacherous.

Mrs. Miller's only friends were in Wales and she had no money to make such a trip. There was no point in her trying to go to the States, for she knew no one there, nor even to another place in Alaska. But before the winter was out, she married a good man in our part of the country. He took care of her, and she of him, and at long last she had a real home.

As spring approached, everyone in Iliamna village grew more hopeful. For one thing, the women cut holes in the ice at the edge of the river, where it was not too slushy, and were able to catch all the grayling trout the village needed. They thought this forecast a good run of fish for the coming season.

And the two years of want were taken as a lesson to be provident by making good gardens.

In the school we made great progress over the winter. The classes were now graded and conducted in much the same manner as in any up-to-date school. Washington was supplying the latest books and materials. The pupils were also well advanced in music, which they loved, and did nice watercolor work. The boys enjoyed any work with hammer and nails, and the girls were good at drawing patterns and making clothing.

Thus everything was in good order for a new teacher to take over. I would have remained longer if it had been really necessary but what I had set out to do had been accomplished. Not that perfection of any sort had been achieved, but the pupils had been awakened. They had a thirst for something better than they had known. That is the longest step in progressing toward a higher civilization. Only the inherent energies of their own minds could carry along their development.

So I steeled my heart in order to go to a new field where I was more needed. The Department in Washington granted my request to leave Iliamna in the middle of April for a vacation, and then a new assignment.

People in Iliamna seemed as sorry to have me go as I felt to leave them. They brought me as parting gifts the prettiest things in the village, treasures remaining from the prosperous sea-otter days: a coral cameo, a Japanese enamelled pin, a gold fleur-de-lis pin and some pieces of fine Russian china. To reject their gifts would have hurt them. I had nothing to give them of comparable value, but I left them everything I could spare.

Waiting for the Steamer

In mid-April summer trails were not yet passable, so my trip to the head of the bay was by a different route than I had previously traveled. Mr. Brown was to be my guide. The night before I was to start I was made comfortable in his cabin for travelers, beyond the village.

Normally we would have set off by dogsled but on account of the strange weather the trail was too soft. So the trip was to begin with a six-mile walk, starting at two in the morning. I was not looking forward to that slog through the slush, but it turned out to be an unexpected joy. A friend of Mr. Brown's from the Lake Clark country was arriving in Iliamna the night I was leaving, and since Mr. Brown knew that both this man and I were from the Susquehanna River in Pennsylvania, he arranged for us to have breakfast together at one in the morning before I started out.

Neither of us had seen anyone from our own homes for years, and upon discovering that we had mutual friends these two wanderers could not stop talking. We realized how we did love the dear old Susquehanna. He insisted on walking with me when we finished breakfast, and the time passed so rapidly that the miles seemed few. At the end of the hike, as I skimmed away on a dogsled, my Pennsylvania friend waved me good-bye.

On this winter trail there were three dangerous stretches. The first was a three-hundred-foot ascent, which was called a precipice, although I would call it merely an extremely steep mountain ledge. A heavy rope had been fastened from top to bottom for travelers to cling to. However, the rope was buried many feet under the snow because the trails were so poor there had been little travel. So the rope was useless to us. Owing to the cold winds in the canyon, the snow was topped by a hard crust and the ledge looked like a wall of marble. When I realized I must climb it I wondered how in the world I could; and after getting to the top I wondered how in the world I did.

A guide took a hatchet in one hand and held one of my hands in the other. He cut step after step and I followed in his footsteps. At the top I was almost exhausted and so was he. We both realized that a misstep would have sent us hurtling far below, and likely buried us in the snow when we landed; this is probably why we felt so tired when the strain was relieved.

He warned me not to move but to stay just where I was while he retraced the trail he had hacked to join the men with the dogs and baggage down below. They needed him to help make a more gradual trail to the top of the ledge for the dogs.

This took about two hours and during that time I experienced some states of mind it is hard for me to describe. Of course, first there was the view: one mountain peak beyond another, some jagged and sharp, others rounded and dome-like. A sky of gray, an earth of marble. Such a space demonstrates the utter smallness of one human being. It is one thing to say this, but actually to feel it is devastating. A desolating loneliness filled my soul. This was followed by fear. I wondered if wolves would appear. With an effort I shook that off and with all my will I determined to enjoy this splendor on the top of the earth so that the wait would become a memory of wonder and pleasure instead of a lonely horror to disturb my dreams.

On the other side of this mountain was a two-mile stretch of extremely dangerous trail. It was a gorgelike pass between two mountains and was subject to avalanches. To one side there had already been monstrous snowslides; to the other, far up on its pinnacle a huge snowbank leaned over, ready to fall. We were conscious that any movement or sound could set off that avalanche. The little feet of the dogs made only the tiniest vibrations. No one spoke a word for those two miles.

Our last bad stretch was over two miles of river where the ice was broken in many places and nowhere was strong enough for perfect safety. While three men stayed with the

Dogsled on the trail from Iliamna village to the head of Iliamna Bay.
Hannah Breece collection

sled, one went ahead and constantly sounded the ice, sometimes turning around and changing course. The dogs were far
enough behind so that their driver did not need to stop at such
times, nor even hesitate while he and the dogs changed
course. Speed carried us over the ice before it could give; hes-
itation could have ended in disaster.

The cabin at the head of the bay looked to me like a mansion. The guides stayed only long enough to fry pancakes and
bacon and make coffee, their first meal all day and mine too.
Tired as they were, at six in the evening, they had to travel
back to the village immediately because by night the trails
would not be as soft as by day. Their departure left me alone
at the head of the bay. That night, every now and again the silence was broken by a muffled, vibrating sound ending in a
roar like sudden thunder, and I prayed that thousands of tons
of snow had not buried my guides on their homeward trail.

A young Kenai from our vicinity who had married an Eskimo girl from the west was buried under a slide earlier that
winter. When his wife heard what had happened she ran to the
slide and would not leave until his body was dug out. The
night after his burial she slipped unnoticed from her home and
lay upon his grave. In the morning she was found dead under
the night's blanket of new snow.

I expected to be in the cabin at the head of the bay only
overnight, until a boat could take me to A.C. Point the next
day. A storm came up and my overnight stay lengthened into
six days. This was tiring because the cabin was furnished with
only a wooden box for a seat and no bed, but at least I was not
worried that the delay would cause me to miss the steamer. I
knew that the same storm which was isolating me would prevent the *Dora* from entering Cook Inlet. I had brought magazines, sewing, paper and pencils, so although this wait of

almost a week was lonely, I was occupied and the days were not unhappy. It was a comfort to think that the old magazines had been new once.

When the storm lifted, Mr. Brown turned up and took me by boat to the Point. It was not lonely there. Martha and Mr. Nielsen were waiting for the steamer's arrival. A number of men were awaiting it in the large abandoned building, which was fast falling into ruin. The *Dora* was due any day.

All of us eagerly scanned the horizon for its curl of smoke. But when we finally saw it, instead of coming toward us it sailed past the mouth of the inlet, eastward toward Seward. The sea was too rough for the ship to hazard the inlet. We had nothing to watch for now and all of us were sad, expecting it

The A.C. Point, nicknamed Camp Patience. *James Carter collection, Alaska State Historical Library*

would be a month, or even more, before the *Dora* returned. My anticipated vacation was disappearing.

Although my cabin was warm I did not stay in it much of the day. Far up on the mountainside, on a ledge protected by an overhanging cliff, I spread a fur rug and fixed a canvas for wind protection. There I sat facing the open sea, marvelous to watch because the storms were almost continuous. Sometimes I heard short, sharp barks but these were only foxes. Sometimes there were sounds of snowslides. But several times I felt, rather than heard, a grinding, grumbling noise from the depths of the earth as if rocks were crushing beneath mighty pressure. At any rate, that is what I imagined because the disturbance was not from the sea nor from snowslides.

After we had been waiting eighteen days, the *Bertha* appeared on the horizon, a ship considerably larger than the *Dora*. It was carrying miners and their wives to the gold fields and taking in freight. A disadvantage of its size was that the old slippery rope ladder over its side was even longer than the *Dora*'s. Mr. Inglis, the same purser who had taken me into Afognak, was now purser on this ship. He said they were glad to see me alive and were providing me the best room and service the boat afforded. I had not slept in a bed for twenty-five nights.

We stopped to unload freight and passengers at settlements all along the west side of Cook Inlet. The tidal bores were at their height, spreading white water far over the land. I was amazed at how cities like Seldovia, Seward—and those farther to the south and east, Valdez, Cordova and Katalla—were booming. They were almost unrecognizable from those same places six or seven years before. Seward was still hustling, although disappointed again at lack of capital to finish the railroad.

The *Bertha* was on its way to Seattle, which was my destination too. The first inkling that this journey might be unusual was the sight of an immense school of whales, hundreds of them, heading from the west and turning southward as fast as they could swim. We were now in the open seas, out of sight of land. The following afternoon the water became much troubled, which was strange because there was no wind or storm. Yet waves became higher and higher, creating great troughs. Then the water took on peculiar shapes. Four great waves would come from each of four directions, forming a high and perfect pyramid for a moment as they crashed together. Look where we might, the massive water pyramids were everywhere.

The *Bertha* rolled into hollows of water. We had to watch from inside, as it was unsafe on deck. Sometimes the boat was so slow in righting herself it seemed we must surely turn turtle. That night we doubted we would survive. The wireless operator was unable either to receive or send messages owing to atmospheric interference. Someone, I did not know who, in the darkness, groped his way to my window and asked if I were frightened. I answered truthfully that I was not frightened but thought we would go down. There was nothing to do but lie still and wait.

By ten the next morning we had sailed out of the area of disturbance. But later that day, as we were at dinner, the *Bertha* gave a sudden whirl halfway around, then as suddenly it whirled back again. The staunchest heart grew sick during that second, for we had been on the rim of the whirlpool at Dixon Entrance between the waters of Alaska and British Columbia. It is like a purgatory with heaven on the other side. Which country is heaven depends on which direction one is going. If our good captain had not veered about on the instant, we would have met the fate of many a ship wrecked in that stretch of dangerous water.

My vacation in Seattle was short but sweet except for the pitiful letters from people who were affected by the eruption of the Katmai volcano. Katmai is connected with the same chain or ridge that I was on when the steamer was so long coming to Cook Inlet. That warm earth, the grinding of the rocks under the mountain ledge, the exodus of the whales from that vicinity and the awful pyramidal waves were all connected with the great eruption.

So soon, I left for my next assignment—to Fort Yukon, far in the north.

17

To the Arctic Circle

Juneau, which was now the American capital of Alaska, could not have been more of a contrast to Sitka, the old Russian and first American capital. Sitka was so charming with its pure white houses roofed in light sea-green moss and cuddled among the dark-spined spruce. It was quaint but dignified, like a dear and proper old lady dozing in her chair. Juneau was like a strapping young fellow striding to his work. It had swiftly become a modern city with department stores, government buildings, an executive mansion and a high school inferior to none in Seattle or elsewhere. Most astonishing to me, its streets were lined with automobiles.

As the seat of government, Juneau was a clean city. All gambling and dance halls in Alaska had long since been forbidden by law, and those laws were enforced in Juneau, as they ought to have been in all other cities of the Territory.

Skagway, north of Juneau and close to the British Columbia border, was the jumping-off point for the Yukon. Everyone who knew his way around Skagway stayed at Mrs. Pullen's. Mrs. Pullen had been left a widow with two small boys. She ran so fine a boardinghouse that nobody missed the absence of a modern hotel. Her best advertisement was her breakfasts. Guests sat at small round tables, two or three to a table. On each table's snowy linen, the centerpiece was a flat pan filled with the previous night's Jersey milk. The cream, rich and heavy, had not been disturbed. Guests skimmed it off to suit themselves. She had the faculty of combining great elegance, polished silver and good china with the ability to make everyone feel comfortably at home. No wonder everyone came back.

At Skagway we boarded the railway cars to their terminus at Whitehorse in the headwaters of the Yukon. From here on river steamers were the key to travel between coast and Yukon settlements. All freight and most passenger travel, therefore, was practical only between the thaw in late spring and the freeze in early fall. Between Whitehorse and Dawson the steamers were small, much like the indomitable *Dora*.

Because navigable channels were forever shifting, it was a commonplace for these steamers to become grounded on underwater sand banks and to be released by a "dead man." Sailors from a marooned ship rowed to the nearest shore, letting out a line of heavy rope from a coil. On shore they dug a deep grave and sawed a heavy log about the length of a man, tied the rope around it, placed it in the grave and filled in the earth. At a signal, sailors on the ship wound the rope on their windlass, or jinny, as they called it. Since the "dead man" could not stir, the steamer had to move.

I was surprised to see what an innocent and unremarkable stream the Klondike looked to be. It does not take much to stir up the world if a stream like that and what it contained could create so much excitement.

In Dawson, a very British city, we had to pass through customs. I had a new telescope organ on which duty was expensive. But I knew there was no duty on tools, so when the customs officer examined it, looking stern and commenting that it was new, I said "Yes, but it is to use in school and it is my tool."

"How do you make that out?" he asked severely. What I like to think of as my Irish heritage came to the rescue. "I manufacture squeals with it, sir," I replied. He burst into laughter and let it pass.

From Dawson the riverboats were large and more comfortable than many of the steamers plying the coast. Eagle turned out to be as characteristically an American city as Dawson was British, and I rejoiced to be where the Stars and Stripes were flying over me once more. The next place of importance was Circle City, so named because in an erroneous survey it was supposed to be crossed by the Arctic Circle, which, in reality, is much farther north. After several days' more travel we did reach the Arctic Circle and Fort Yukon, eight miles above the circle.

This settlement, to be my new home, consisted primarily of an Indian village, strung out along the riverbank for about a mile, containing the public school and teacher's house, which were combined in one large log building. The Episcopal mission home was downstream from the village. It was a big square two-story building with sleeping porches and verandas. At the end of Fort Yukon was also an Episcopal log church, four stores and accommodations that included one well-patronized restaurant for white men who trapped in the vicinity. The stores catered mainly to natives. They were fur trading posts that took furs and handicrafted articles in barter.

The permanent white residents were the Episcopal archdeacon of the Yukon, Hudson Stuck, who was often absent, looking after the many other settlements that were his far-flung responsibilities; Dr. Grafton Burke and his wife, both in their twenties, and their small child; the storekeepers; and I. Dr. Burke was a missionary doctor. I had heard that his wife was a lovely young woman and I did hope she would like

me, for I would certainly appreciate her friendship if I succeeded in gaining it.

The essential point about my work in Fort Yukon was to
carry on in harmony with the missionaries. It was not my
duty, as government teacher, to work in subjection to them,
but it was clear that the representatives of two great institutions for good, government and the church, should cooperate
when conditions of native life required it. This was especially
necessary when serious questions arose concerning the laws
for protecting native interests and well-being.

The natives in Fort Yukon were Athabaskan Indians with
Scottish blood. The settlement had been an old British garrison and Hudson's Bay Company fur trading post in the days

The Fort Yukon Episcopal mission church and cemetery. *Hannah Breece collection*

before a re-survey allocated the region to the United States as part of Alaska.

The year's economic cycle began in September, when natives departed for the haunts of the great white rabbits, bringing them back by the hundreds. They sold for twenty-five cents apiece. Then throughout the long winter other and more valuable fur-bearing animals were trapped in huge quantities.

A minor but important form of trade blossomed in summer when hundreds of excursionists visited Fort Yukon by boat, living on the excursion steamers during their short stays. They bought fur coats and hats and leather goods decorated with beads and porcupine quills. Thus native women, particularly the older ones, were continually busy making fur garments and tanning moose and caribou leather, not only for their own families' use but to sell as decorated cushions, gloves, belts, leggings and mocassins. The women and children ordinarily wore handsomely decorated clothing. Mothers carried their babies on their backs, suspended on beautifully beaded straps.

Food was abundant. It included dressed rabbits, ducks, grouse, king salmon and white fish, all of which were prepared by September in time for the hard winter freeze and were thawed for use as needed by soaking them in cold water. To try to cut meat or a head of cabbage or loaf of bread while it was frozen at thirty below zero was like trying to chop iron with an axe. Fort Yukon had the answer to my winter hunger for bread. It could be frozen too, I learned. Put frozen into the oven and heated thoroughly, the bread tasted fresh-baked.

It was every native woman's ambition to make three new dresses for herself each year, to wear at three dances held during the holiday season. These were fashionable outfits copied from up-to-date fashion papers that the stores carried, and were made of silk or velvet, which the stores had on hand at exorbitant prices. The women were natural-born dressmakers, with a fine sense of style. The men sent to Fairbanks, or went there themselves, to get the best dress suits the city carried. Both men and women possessed fine and fashionable dress shoes although these were totally unsuitable for getting around in Fort Yukon. They never wore hats, however, because the wind was too strong to keep them on. Besides, the women did not look well in hats.

The houses were not all alike, but a typical Indian home was solidly made of logs with the usual single room, about twenty-five by thirty feet, and a corner entrance protected by a corridorlike vestibule. In the entrance corner was a good cooking range, cupboards, dining table and enough chairs for the family. In the corner beyond was a suite of bedroom furniture with a Brussels rug on the floor. At the other end of the room was a sewing machine, a phonograph and some easy chairs, and along the back wall between this area and the bedroom suite were narrow built-in beds, usually homemade. In the middle of the room was a Jumbo heater. Hanging on the walls were guns, fur coats and beaded clothing. One nook in the cooking and eating area would have pails, old shoes and what-not. Here and there were trunks for holding best clothes and other treasures. A house was snug with double-framed and double-glazed windows, and in the ceiling was an opening that could be closed at will, an excellent ventilator.

All water had to be brought up from the river, although the best water was melted from ice cast up over the high riverbank and into the town during the ice break-up in spring. At the school and teacher's house we had a large iron tank kept filled by Old Fred, who climbed up the bank with two five-gallon cans on a shoulder yoke. In summer the water was so muddy it had to settle for a day or two. An engineer from the Bureau of Mines who stopped by briefly in summer told me he thought the water could be pumped up from the river, but I doubt that he realized how intensely cold the winters were.

Every person spoke English except at home, where they used their Athabaskan tongue. The children had biblical names: Esau, Jacob, Isaiah, Isaac and John were favorites for boys; Mary, Ruth, Sarah and Rachel for girls. Bibles and hymnbooks were translated into the Athabaskan language. A native minister, supported by the Episcopal mission, held Sunday morning services in the church; white people had their church service in the evening.

In the past Scottish trappers and storekeepers had married Indian women, and those marriages were regularized and taken seriously. But marriage of Indians and whites no longer occurred here. Nor did whites intermarry with the Eskimos who came down with their furs on the Koyukuk and Porcupine rivers. These two river systems, along with the Chandalar, were routes for water travel in summer and dog team trails in winter, and the vast territories to which they gave access enabled trappers and traders to carry on the vast fur business.

The scanty trees were stunted by the climate. I counted rings on trees not more than five or six inches in diameter and found them to be a hundred years old. Logs for building were all rafted by water from southern forests. The flat plains extending from the village as far as the eye could see were covered by beautiful wild grasses varying from a tinge of wine color to bright red, and summer flowers, beginning with a delicate white bloom peeping out before the snow disappeared, which the natives called the snow-flower. Later, forget-me-nots and wild roses were everywhere.

Snow was seldom seen falling in Fort Yukon. Beginning in August a kind of frost would seem to fill the air and in no time the ground would be white. Since these accumulations did not thaw all winter, a heavy layer of snow would build up, packing so smooth and hard that a trail was almost like a marble pavement. In spring the snow would evaporate, so there was no slushy season. All at once it would dawn on us that the snow was gone. Then the dust would begin to blow.

The great flats had fertile soil but it was not productive without irrigation because no rain fell in Fort Yukon all summer. And since the growing season ended in early August, it might seem that gardens were impractical even with irrigation. But my pupils cultivated a successful school garden by carrying water to it from the river. All ordinary northern vegetables matured in the very long, sunny summer days; peas were especially productive.

The great events of summer were arrivals of the steamers, often carrying men of letters and other people of note. The steamer arrivals were announced by the dogs. One particular dog would leave the village and stand at a little distance up or down the river. He would appear to be listening. Then, still before any sign of a steamer was apparent to a human being, the listening dog would lift his head and howl. At this signal, all the dogs would hurry to that end of town and be rejoined by the listening dog. They all would stand quietly together until, well before the steamer itself came into sight, they saw its smoke. At this point a few dogs would howl, then all quiet down until the steamer blew its whistle. Every dog then would take to howling and keep it up until the boat was at anchor, and the gangplank had been thrown from the upper deck to the street. The docking point was across the street from the school because the riverbank was so sheer there that the gangplank could bridge it. The first people off the steamer would be the kitchen boys with pails of scraps to feed the dogs, which may explain why the animals were so attentive. But I could never learn how they sensed the arrivals so far in advance.

Fort Yukon's government school and pupils. Hannah is the tallest figure, center rear. At the right is the steeple of the Episcopal mission
church. This is probably the school photograph that Archdeacon Stuck
showed in fund-raising slide lectures. *Hannah Breece collection*

As far as ordinary school responsibilities were concerned,
life had become much easier for me. Dr. and Mrs. Burke
made a round of each house in the village at least two or three
times a week. All I had to do in case of sickness was to report
to the doctor any child who looked undernourished or otherwise did not appear well. Once in a while a motherless child
looked dirty or neglected and I had only to tell Mrs. Burke.
She either gave me clothes from her mission boxes or else appointed people in the village to take proper care of the child.

Archdeacon Stuck had organized a town council, where the
business of the community was conducted as in any organized

town. I was always invited and because I was the government teacher, people were encouraged to regard me as a representative of their country.

The archdeacon took a close interest in the pupils and their lessons. Many a time he stepped quietly inside the door, and while I went on with my work he would walk up and down the aisles, helping wherever a child seemed to need encouragement, patiently tracing letters or figures. Sometimes he stood outside when school was dismissed. Then what a shout went up from the little boys! One would be carried on his back and the others crowd around him until he reached the mission gate. He would always have something in his pockets, and when they received their treat the little fur-clad, rolypoly figures would head for home.

So primarily the job of a teacher here was class work in the ordinary subjects and in manual training for boys. But I had observed that the girls and younger women were less engaged in leather and bead work than their mothers or other older women. So I organized a club with prizes for those doing the best handicrafts. This did a little something to help revive younger women's interest in this profitable employment. I often visited the homes, primarily for the pleasure of talking, admiring the work the women did and teaching those who were interested how to bake bread.

There were no suitable places of recreation for native people, so one of my activities was to provide frequent entertainments in the school. Both children and adults were natural and gifted actors. Both as performers and spectators they all seemed to enjoy the entertainments. And this kept me busy.

18

Long Journeys to Court

I planned to remain in Fort Yukon until serious questions involving the interests of the native people were settled by law. In connection with these problems I was subpoenaed to attend federal court in Ruby. Dr. Burke and his wife went too. It was a five-hundred-mile trip down the Yukon, a thousand-mile round-trip.

Travel by river steamer was no hardship; it was much like living in a beautiful, moving hotel. The cost was correspondingly high. The water was so quiet that all the ladies sat in the observation parlor and sewed, read or wrote. Once we left the flats, the scenery was wildly beautiful.

Our business in Ruby occupied several weeks. Ruby was a gold mining town in an early stage of settlement. The streets were not graded or drained and there were no planks at crossings, so mud was apt to ooze over one's shoetops. In the school there were two teachers but only fifteen pupils.

Both going and returning we stopped in Tanana, a center from which vegetables for winter use were sent in all directions. On our way to Ruby in July we saw the flourishing gardens and flowers. In August, on our return trip, the flowers were frozen and everything covered with snow. Tanana is also a center of gold mining and lumbering and the site of the Fort Gibbons military post. Whites lived in elegant and refined homes as well as humble ones, and Tanana boasted a church resembling an old English cathedral. The native settlement was about a mile distant and included a government school and an Episcopal mission that had almost completed a hospital building.

Days at Fort Yukon shortened very rapidly after September set in, with the sweep of the sun falling lower toward the horizon and east and west merging closer together until only a faint flush of light appeared between them, and then not even that, for the long, cold night was upon us. Lights burned all day long and no one could go outside without a lantern whether it was noon or midnight. But the darkness was not thick and black. The moon, the stars, the snow and often the

The Canadian vessel *Dawson,* one of the Yukon River steamers that brought summer tourists, excitement and glimpses of luxurious travel to Fort Yukon. *The Albertype Co.*

aurora borealis modified the Arctic night into a soft, velvetlike blanket. For weeks we did not see the sun, and a melancholy seemed to settle upon my soul. I could not dispel it. But life continued just as when day and night were divided.

On our return from Ruby, the winter cold had come so early and was so intense that the Yukon froze early and rapidly from source to mouth. If it had stayed that way, all would have been well for travel by dogsled. But heavy fall rains at the headwaters filled tributaries to bursting. The floods worked under the iron ice sheet on the Yukon with such force that the ice broke into myriads of cakes that climbed and tumbled, crushing their way down the channel, rushing toward the Bering Sea, much as happens in the great ice break-up at the time of the spring thaw.

But this was not spring. The ice did not float out to sea. All up and down the river, the chaotic ice blocks were arrested. This was the only highway for dog teams and the only mail route. We hoped in vain for the trail to improve; the best to be expected was that the most passable route would be marked.

I was to travel this route to Fairbanks. Another subpoena had been sent and must be obeyed. In any case, it was in the interest of the native people. School was moving along nicely and I arranged as best I could for work there to continue while I was absent. I did not dread the cold, but I dreaded that rough trail we would have to endure for about a hundred miles before the route turned and followed the mountains.

We had three sleds and dog teams. Mrs. Burke and her child were in one sled, Dr. Burke in another, and mine was the third. My driver was Ginnis, whose wife, Rachael, was a good friend of mine. The sled was actually a sort of toboggan without runners. Its framework was made almost in the shape of a canoe and covered with untanned white caribou skin.

Flaps of the skin were left hanging over the sides of the sled, and the edges of the flaps were perforated. Ginnis and Rachael spread a bearskin rug in the sled, allowing the sides to fall outside. They spread a large fur blanket over that. Then I got in, and they tucked the blanket and rug in snugly and spread another blanket of fur. Now the leather flaps were folded over and laced up like a shoe.

On my head I wore a knitted hood, much like an aviator's, under my parka hood. Around my neck I loosely threw a large woolen scarf, for when it is forty degrees below zero, the saliva flows from the mouth in streams. When one spot froze on the scarf, I moved it, to keep a dry place over my mouth. No clothing could be tight. My shoes were large enough so I could move my toes at will; otherwise they would have frozen. Three pairs of gloves were necessary: the first of soft wool fiber threads; the second, knit mittens; the third, large fur mittens with long gauntlets.

We set off at two in the morning. I will never be sorry I saw the Yukon in its mighty ice chaos, but that first day we bobbed, jerked and bounced over ice cakes until I thought I could not endure it. Dogsled drivers never ride unless to stand on the runners of a Yukon sled. On the type we were using there is no place for them to stand. Ginnis kept up his rhythmic, even lope all day long. Before an hour had elapsed, his fur coat and hood were on top of the sled. In a short while more, his woolen sweater was lying on the coat, and he was perspiring in his shirtsleeves. But at the shortest stop he got into his discarded garments as quickly as possible.

Even when the trail is in a normal state the Yukon is treacherous. It has many holes above its subterranean hot springs, with little bursts of steam rising from some. One dog in a Yukon team, called the mascot, does not help pull the sled but instead, on a long lead, ranges well ahead of the pulling team.

His work is to seek out airholes and thin ice if they lie ahead, and veer to a safe path. The mascot warns; the team obeys.

However, all morning on our second day the dogs were hard to manage. The leader of our pulling team was not obeying the mascot. He seemed possessed to run close to airholes. Ginnis had to swear and yell to get the team to follow the mascot. His swearing was so outrageous that finally I remonstrated with him. "Ginnis, what would Rachael say if she heard you?"

He asked me if I did not want him to swear anymore and I replied that I certainly did not. He said, "All right, Teacher."

For a short time everything went well, until the dogs made a dive toward a hole in the ice. Ginnis called in vain, using very proper language, and we were getting ever nearer to an awful gap. I called, "Swear, Ginnis! Oh, swear!" With that permission he soon had the dogs back on the trail. I suppose I was accountable for the blasphemous manner in which it was done, but was glad not to be lying cold and stark in the Yukon.

At night we stayed in roadhouses built of logs where there were facilities for taking care of dog teams, as well as feeding travelers and making them comfortable. As we traveled south the trail became smoother and we came to splendid spruce forests. Nevertheless, we were all glad to see one little spot of lighted window far ahead of us. There were no habitations on these lonely trails apart from the roadhouses. They were all much the same: warmth to enjoy from piping hot stoves after we had held our hands in snow, then cold water, until the pain in them eased; the same bountiful meals; and the same comfortable beds built on the walls.

After three days' travel we reached Circle. Since it was Saturday we were to rest there in the hotel until Monday. On Sunday evening another party from Fort Yukon arrived, four gentlemen who had been in Kamchatka in Siberia during the summer. On their return their ship, the *Wolf,* had frozen fast in the Artic Ocean on the coast of northeastern Alaska. The group, composed of the ship's captain, a Seattle *Times* reporter and two young men from Boston, had traveled on snowshoes and by dogsled to Circle, and they too were on their way to Fairbanks.

From Circle we took to the trail in early morning hours, as before, and traveled for very long days but had midday respites at "halfway houses," necessary on this part of the journey because the mountains were so dangerous, the drifts on the trails so hampering and the air so bitterly cold. A warm dinner and a rest made the days shorter and enabled the drivers to keep on the run later at night. Thus day after day passed until we reached a small town near Fairbanks, where again we rested over Sunday. From there the drivers and teams returned to Fort Yukon and we took passage into Fairbanks on a small local railroad.

The import of our trip to Fairbanks occupied six weeks and was a source of great anxiety. Apart from that I had a pleasant time because friends whom I had previously known in Seward did everything they could to make it so.

Fairbanks had two distinct classes of people. The majority were pleasure-mad. But a different group was composed of quiet, educated people who derived their amusements from intellectual sources and loved to play tennis and go sled riding. However, that might be said of any city in the world, and there was really no difference between this city and any other of similar size in the States.

Only one or two of the gold mines in the vicinity were in operation; I gathered that additional capital was needed. The Episcopal mission operated a large hospital. The schools were among the best in Alaska. It was the hope of Fairbanks businessmen that the government would complete the railroad from Seward. I had no doubt that Fairbanks would become a metropolis when the Seward railroad connected it with the Pacific, and a Tanana line connected it with the Yukon. If Alaska is destined to be thickly populated, Fairbanks must surely become a great city.

Our journey back to Fort Yukon was much like the journey out, but not as cold. At no time was the temperature lower than forty below zero, and in midday it was higher. On one occasion, when the dogsled was plowing through fresh snow, the dogs crossed tracks where caribou had lately been tramping. They went wild. The driver could hardly hold them. He would not have been able to except that fortunately we were among trees and he jerked the team around a tree trunk. Of course the toboggan upset, and while I was on my face I thought the snow would smother me.

I was so glad to get back to my school pupils and find that the children had not been idle. But the darkness much oppressed me. When the light returned, I knew every woman would clean house. No matter how clean houses seemed to be in the dark winter, when the sun returned they presented quite a different aspect.

The day when the faint glow between east and west became a rim of gold on the horizon, all the children ran out to see the top of the sun and sang out to it, "Beautiful sun." The melancholy rolled off my soul and I knew I had been homesick, oh, so homesick, to see the sun.

As night disappeared and the long day came upon us, we reversed the hours of day and night. Now everyone slept through the hot hours of the day. Doors were locked and curtains drawn, for the still air made the sun seem hotter. Cool winds from Arctic snows blew over the parched land during the sunlit night hours, so it was then that people cooked and ate their food, men built houses, I taught school, mothers walked the riverbank with babies on their backs, there was buying and selling and the streets were full of life.

All winter the river ice had grown thicker until in the coldest spots it was frozen almost to the earth floor of the channel. How the ice resisted the force of waters rising below it! Finally, with an awesome crash, the sheet of ice, which spread out for miles, broke into a million pieces, cutting thousands of tons of earth from the village street and hurling tons of ice into the village.

During the thaw no one could venture to the river for water. After the ice from our part of the Yukon and the Tanana River on the south had passed, the Chandalar, Porcupine and Koyukuk to the north must empty their ice. These masses would cause backwaters and the banks would again be torn asunder, making the river water thick and muddy until far into the summer. In anticipation of all this, every tub, boiler, pail and what-not was filled with ice cast above the banks. Tumbled into barrels and tanks, this would be the only clear, pure water until summer was almost half over.

When the ice was gone from the river, and men were rafting logs from forests to the south, and the gardens were in, and many people had moved into tents, and plans were afoot for an Episcopal hospital, it was time for me to move too. There was no more special work I could do in Fort Yukon, as far as I could see. I hoped to work where I could live farther south and see and consider some of the results and problems that educational work and other policies had brought to native people.

Last Assignments

Once more I made the trip up the Yukon and over the White Pass Road to Skagway and the coast. Our coastal steamer stopped in Sitka and I remembered to ask the priest there, "Where is Bishop Innocent?" His reply was crisp and short, "He is in Tibet." That was all I was able to learn of his fate.

For the next two years I was assigned to Wrangell in the southern panhandle. Wrangell's mild weather was a contrast to Fort Yukon's: in summer not too warm, yet in winter too warm for much snow. It rained and rained, a gentle, steady downpour that no one seemed to mind.

Although Wrangell was on the coast it was secluded. Through the mountainous islands that ringed its ocean side were only two passes, each barely wide enough to allow a ship to enter. On the mountain nearest the ocean the native people a few years before had been frightened by seeing John Muir, the great student of nature, walking in the dead of night through a terrific storm, waving a lantern. In spring, avalanches thundered down the mountains, and the snow dust rose for hundreds of feet from abysses where millions of tons of snow were being hurled.

On the tundra stretching to the east many gold claims had been filed but only a few were being operated. However, one that was, an undersea mine called the Treadwell at Juneau, was said to be the largest gold mine in the world. Nearby were a garnet mine and a ranch where ginseng was successfully cultivated. The streets of Wrangell were well planked and lighted. The dark green of the spruce and the scarlet of mountain ash and elderberry made it, I thought, the most attractive coast city in Alaska. Both cherry and apple trees grew successfully but only a few people had ventured to plant them.

This section of Alaska was poetically known as the Land of the Totem Pole. The chief of the native people in Wrangell, an aged man named Shaaks, told me a totem pole story concerning his father. This must have occurred during the early part of the nineteenth century or possibly at the close of the eighteenth century, since Shaaks was probably born in the 1830s.

His father, said Shaaks, accidentally broke his strong cane into two pieces one day when he was walking. He concluded that an evil spirit was after him, and to appease it he had fifteen slaves killed and buried under Wrangell totem poles. The pieces of the old cane were still kept in a crude museum near Shaaks's home.

Shaaks, who was a short man with gray beard and hair, looked more like a Scot than an Indian. He was the last chief of Wrangell, and with his death, which occurred while I was there, a centuries-old dynasty ended. Although he was much venerated, the Indians wanted to discontinue the tribal system because under U.S. law Indians ruled by chiefs were not considered citizens.

At Shaaks's funeral, his wife gave the death wail, very similar to the Jewish funeral wail, one of the customs that led some of the Indians to speculate that they and the Jews had a common prehistoric ancestry. A few days after the funeral, Shaaks's son, who had ambitions to succeed his father, was assassinated. Tom Tameree, whose father was Hawaiian but who was of Shaaks's family on his mother's side, was next in line. However, he was a peaceful lieutenant in the Salvation Army with no aspirations to power, and was not harmed.

In the past the Wrangell Indians had been warlike. They and the Haidas of British Columbia continually raided one another for slaves and to exact vengeance. The slaves killed and buried under the totem poles by Shaaks's father were captured Haidas. One of the leading families in Wrangell was descended, it was said, partly from Haida slaves and partly from the royal family of Austria. One of the possessions in which Shaaks took pride was a marble pyramid presented to him by the government because he restrained his people from sending a punitive expedition when one of his sons was killed by raiders.

Southeastern Alaska had long interested me because it was the home of hundreds of native people who had been sent to the United States for their education, in hopes that they would be able to solve problems for their race at home when they returned. The older native people had looked forward to bright days when these educated young people returned. But often, instead, the educated sons and daughters turned into one more problem.

I had happened to tutor one such exceptionally promising pupil in Fort Yukon, a bright and gentlemanly youth named Walter Harper who accompanied Archdeacon Stuck on his long dogsled trips. The archdeacon carefully supervised Walter's education and had me correct his written compositions and give him a start in algebra and geometry to help him prepare for college studies in the States. Poor Walter! We could never know whether his brilliant promise would have been fulfilled. He perished, along with many others of my acquaintance, in a steamer grounded and wrecked in a gale near Wrangell.

The possibilities of splendid pupils like Walter, and the creditable achievements of a few of those sent out of Alaska, seemed hopeful and made the question of sending pupils away from their homes and people well worth studying. But on the other hand, happy outcomes seldom occurred.

Were the disappointments and tragedies of these young people a transition stage that must be passed through in a race's development? This question had long bothered me.

My last Alaska assignment, after two years in Wrangell, was in nearby Douglas, an island across from Juneau, where the same puzzle presented itself. Observing cases instance by instance, it seemed to me that the returned students were usually so uprooted and dissatisfied that their unhappiness annulled what knowledge they may have gained in distant places of how to improve conditions for their people. I finally reached the conclusion that native children and young people should be taught in their own settlements, in schools adapted to their own ways of life.

From the disappointments I observed, I could also see that liquor was a major stumbling block for once promising but dissatisfied youths. Alcohol was the curse of the north. Fighting it became an important part of my work in Wrangell and Douglas. In this cause I made numerous trips to the capital, Juneau. It was small use to teach a school if standards could not be elevated among the people as a whole.

Many others, especially missionaries, had enlisted in the cause of betterment of native life in southeastern Alaska. Among those with whom I was associated, or knew by results of their work, were Dr. Hall S. Young, Mrs. William Thomas, Mrs. George Barnes, the Reverend and Mrs. S.

Bollinger, the Reverend and Mrs. David Wagoner, the Reverend and Mrs. J. S. Clarke, Dr. and Mrs. J. P. Mooney, the Reverend Corser, and Dean and Mrs. Christian, a noble band of men and women. It is hard for those at a distance to realize what they had to combat, and I count it one of the great privileges of my life to have come in contact with them or their work.

Although Douglas was close to Wrangell, its climate was entirely different. In winter, snow sometimes lay sixteen feet, and bitter gales blew fiercely through the channel among the islands and over them from Taku Glacier.

While I was at Douglas the sea broke into the great Treadwell undersea mine and flooded it. Everyone was saved except one miner. His children were my pupils. The mining company gave their mother ten thousand dollars so the children could be raised without want.

Usually in Douglas trails were dug down through the deep snow. But while men were away from the town for weeks because of the Treadwell accident, snow was allowed to lie and pile up on almost deserted streets. People just tramped on its surface. Since it reached a fifteen-foot depth, one's head was higher than the electric wires on their poles. People reached their doorways down below by steps cut into the hard-packed snow.

One stormy night, picking my way down the steps to my door, I slipped and broke my leg. I was afraid to move for fear my foot would come off; that is how it felt. I could make only one person hear me through the storm, a woman who with her little boy had moved into one of the miners' temporarily vacated houses. I called to her, shouting what had happened, but although she wanted to help she did not dare approach me for fear the devil would get her. It was a tenacious superstition that a cry for help is a ruse of the devil's.

City street in Douglas. The snow was usually shovelled from walks, as here, but Hannah's fall occurred when deep snow was left lying and makeshift steps cut down to doorways. *Hannah Breece collection*

Finally a tall, strange man passed along the trail. When he saw me he picked me up, opened my door and got me into a comfortable chair with blankets about me. He ordered me not to faint which is what I probably would have done, but he had so much authority in his voice I thought I had to obey him. After he had made me comfortable, he pulled a tremendous gold watch out of his pocket and said he must go, although he hated to leave me alone. I assured him that someone would come soon and he left.

While I was recovering I made inquiries about him. It seemed that not another soul in town had seen this man, nor had any ship come in that day. My surmise was that he was investigating one of the gold mines and wanted to be as inconspicuous as possible.

The men from the mines near Douglas were of every nationality. When we entered the World War many Americans were doubtful that these men would permit the American flag to remain aloft on the school flagpole. But the flag was raised daily without interference, and many of these men, whose loyalty had been doubted, served the United States bravely. Alaska was almost depleted of men. Many of my former pupils enlisted, some as aviators, and many did not return.

After our country entered the war, I was made president of the Red Cross for the native people of Douglas. I noticed that the schoolchildren were becoming thin, and looked wan and hungry. In response to my questions, their mothers told me they were eating only fish, no bread, "because the people of the United States are at war and the poor little children there need bread." Agents of the government were amazed at how heavily the Douglas natives subscribed to liberty bonds. The amount they contributed was not huge, of course, but it was very large in proportion to their numbers and means.

The public school buildings at Douglas were all built on piles within the tideline. At night when I was alone in the large empty building with the waves dashing and lashing under it and the snow piling high on the roof, I often felt that literally there was no safety in the heavens above nor in the waters beneath. Sometimes a good-sized iceberg was serenely hovering near, and it was not uncommon to see roofs within sight crash under the weight of snow.

But from my windows I could also see the buildings where the gold stamping mills and crushers were banging and pounding, day and night. The lights shone out from rows and rows of windows on the mountain and clustered along its sheltering side. In any direction I might look, toward mines named Thane, Juneau, Treadwell or Little Mexico, a dazzling electrical display met my eye.

Figuratively, too, the light was beginning to shine out brightly. The men and women of Alaska had made the liquor business illegal. The Seward railroad was going to be completed by the government and the outside world connected with the Arctic. There were hope and possibilities for primitive races and their grateful, affectionate people. The patter of the little feet of the malamutes would be succeeded by the whir of airplanes as they carried the mail over great rivers and icy plains. The dance halls and gambling houses were to become faraway memories, replaced by magnificent schools, churches and hospitals. And I was glad that I had had a small part in blazing the way for better things in this most beautiful, most wonderful land.

COMMENTARY

Puzzles, Tangles, Clarifications

1. Educational Policy and Sheldon Jackson

Now and again Hannah alludes to the aims of the government's educational policy or mentions that what she was doing was in accord with it. What was this policy? Was what she did in accord? The answer to that last question is a resounding yes—infused with a subtle no.

The policy, as set forth officially by Sheldon Jackson in an 1892–93 report to Congress, addressed

> [A] work of great magnitude, in a new and untried field, and with unknown difficulties. It was a work so unlike any other that experience of the past . . . could not be the sole guide . . .
>
> It was to establish English schools among a people the larger portion of whom do not speak or understand the English language . . .
>
> It was to instruct a people, the greater portion of whom are uncivilized, who need to be taught sanitary regulations, the laws of health, improvement of dwellings, better method of housekeeping, cooking and dressing, more remunerative forms of labor, honesty, chastity, the sacredness of the marriage relation, and everything that elevates man. So that, side by side

with the usual school drill in reading, writing and arithmetic, there is need of instruction for the girls in housekeeping, cooking and gardening, in cutting, sewing and
mending; and for the boys in carpentering and other
forms of wood working, boot and shoe making, and the
various trades of civilization.

It was to furnish educational advantages to a people,
large classes of whom are too ignorant to appreciate
them, and who require some form of pressure to oblige
them to keep their children in school regularly. It was
a system of schools among a people who, while in the
main only partially civilized, yet have a future before
them as American citizens.

This policy, to which Hannah hewed in subjects prescribed, was the creation of one man, Sheldon Jackson, and
was long administered by the same man. "Government policy" was Sheldon Jackson policy.

Jackson was a Presbyterian clergyman born in May 1834 to
a religious family in Minaville, New York, and educated at
Union College in Schenectady and Princeton Theological
Seminary. He was a small man, five feet four inches in height,
rejected by the Presbyterian Board of Foreign Missions as too
frail to withstand the hardships of foreign mission work, but
the church did commission him to work on the American
frontier, where he ministered to white pioneer settlers and
transients in the Rocky Mountain territories and Indians in
many parts of the west. He founded church after church in
these fields and distinguished himself for endurance, energy,
bravery and sometimes foolhardy obstinacy. He had married
happily at the age of twenty-five but incessant traveling allowed him little time at home. His wife was the perfect model
of a missionary's wife: loyal, supportive, uncomplaining as

she raised a family under conditions of hardship and frequent household moves.

In 1877, at the age of forty-four, Jackson went to Alaska on his own initiative and with the help of a benefactor and teacher from Seattle started a mission school in Fort Wrangell, in the southern panhandle.

At the time nothing was known by Americans about the possession they had acquired ten years before, apart from scrabbles of information brought back by crews of New England whaling vessels, a few other wealth-seeking adventurers and soldiers and sailors from small garrisons and coast guard stations. As Jackson's biographer points out, the area had been without civil government after the Russians departed. There were no civil servants, courts, judges, American records, including census figures, and no schools other than a few attached to the Russian Orthodox Church, supported from Russia. The one American public school, which had been founded by white citizens in Sitka, had died away four years before Jackson reached Alaska.

Between 1877 and 1884 Jackson made two more trips into this great unknown, gave some nine hundred speeches about Alaska to American church groups and politicians and started five mission schools. He also wrote a book, *Alaska,* published in 1880. Together with his speeches, this book established him as America's foremost authority on the area. Its frontispiece was an alarmingly fanatic-looking portrait of himself.

The text and illustrations were even more alarming. He portrayed the natives as almost subhuman demons from hell: frenzied men who ate dogs alive; cannibals who tore into raw corpses with their teeth; killers of babies; sexual abusers of little girls; polygamists; evil sorcerers; sinister witch doctors; women universally prostituted; nude men parading themselves like proud horses; torturers; mutilators; enslavers;

murderers; etc. Their very funeral rites of yells, whoops, chants and rattles were an offense against "the civilized ear."

This lurid volume has long been out of print and copies are rare. (The one that edified me is in the Baranov Museum's rare book section in Kodiak.) When admirers of Jackson acknowledge it at all, they do not describe it. One explained it away to me as a "work of persuasion," specifically intended to rouse church people to the need for good works and politicians to the need for action and control. Indian fighting was still an American preoccupation at the time; Custer's Last Stand, the American military's defeat at the battle of Little Bighorn, had taken place in 1876, only the year before Jackson first visited Alaska; the long, bitter U.S. military campaign against the Nez Percé ended in Montana only in 1877.

Perhaps Jackson's *Alaska* was indeed merely a cynical anthology of horrid nuggets to serve his propaganda purposes. But after sampling his later and more sober-sounding reports, I think this embarrassing polemic was truthful in the sense that it genuinely portrayed its author's emotional position. At any rate, apart from abstract pieties about solicitude, he conveys

Etching of Sheldon Jackson, frontispiece from his 1880 book, *Alaska*. *Published by Dodd Meade and Co.*

no respect for the lives that unchristianized native people created for themselves, and much that continued to be damning.

It was not only his writing that revealed his policy of totally expunging native ways, root and branch, and exerting total control. In his own boarding school for boys and girls in Sitka (which has now evolved into a college named for him), pupils were signed in through five-year contracts with their parents, and so completely institutionalized that no contacts with families or influences from their communities could touch and taint them further than they were already contaminated. Education itself would imperil these individuals without continual control over them, Jackson explained to Congress:

> [T]he brighter the girl the greater her danger; for, as she improved in the school, she began to dress more neatly, comb her hair, and keep her person more cleanly; the dull, stolid cast of countenance gave way to the light of intelligence, and she began to be more attractive and consequently in greater demand. To save these girls necessitated the establishment of a "home" into which they could be gathered and taken out from under control of their mothers . . .

In 1880, the same year his *Alaska* was published, Jackson arranged to parcel out Alaska among Protestant churches willing to establish missions with schools or orphanages. The cartelization mutually agreed upon allocated to the Presbyterians the southern panhandle, where Jackson had already been establishing schools, and Point Barrow far to the north, where another mission was planned. The Baptists got Kodiak and Cook Inlet; the Episcopalians, who already had opened a mission in Fort Yukon, got the Alaskan Yukon; the Methodists got the Aleutian and Shumagin islands; the Moravians got the valleys of the Kuskokwim and Nushagak rivers; and the Congregationalists got the Cape Prince of Wales area. The Russian Orthodox Church was neither brought into the discussions nor alloted a field. In the eyes of the Protestant missionaries it was little better than heathen itself.

Even with this efficient rationing of their efforts, the churches' funds were too thin, and the authority their missions could exert too weak, to control and civilize Alaska. Nor could they support enough schools for supplying this vast territory with its hundreds of settlements, all very small. Jackson and his supporters exhorted and lobbied Congress to take action. Because of their efforts, Congress proclaimed a District of Alaska (it did not become a territory until 1912) and in 1884 adopted a civil code for the district to replace military administration.

Ironically, among the very first fruits of civil government was a custody case that Jackson's Sitka school lost. An Indian woman from the state of Washington asked the school to release a niece who had been orphaned since being signed into the school by her parents. The school refused. The aunt then applied to the new civil court for a writ of habeas corpus, which the court granted. Next, another student's parent applied for a writ, and not only was the parent granted custody, but the judge then ruled that he would fine or imprison anyone who interfered with a child leaving the school. Promptly, half the school's 104 students ran away.

One can understand why, considering the school's regimen. They were denied use of their mother tongues not only during hours of school instruction, but for twenty-four hours a day. "Without any legal power to hold the children," said a report by the school on its program, "it has been very difficult to exercise the authority necessary to secure the best results in speaking English." When pupils in the Sitka school

were not engaged in formal classwork, their days were con-
sumed in endless duties and drudgeries. One becomes exhausted merely reading the list. In the long, grim description
of laborious school activities—the scouring, mending, lamp-
cleaning, pickling, care of slops, stump extractions, wood-
cutting, grading, yeast-making and on and on—not one word
is given to sports, games, entertainments, arts or free time.
Not to put too fine a point on it, the children were little
slaveys. One can only wonder at the half of the student body
that didn't clear out when it got the chance.

The same year that it installed civil government, Congress
created, at Jackson's urging, an agency for Alaskan education
in the Department of the Interior, and the next year Jackson
was put in charge of it. But Congress was so miserly with its
educational appropriations, then and later, that Jackson continued eking out with church schools. The result was a system
that combined government-supported schools (the part of the
network employing Hannah) with mission schools, called
contract schools, that got a pittance from the government. In
1904, when Hannah entered the system, hundreds of little
settlements were still without schools, including those that
were clamoring for them such as Iliamna, Nondalton, Stony
River and the Eskimos Hannah encountered in the Iliamna
region.

Jackson persisted in believing that only compulsion could
guarantee school attendance. Throughout his administration
of twenty-two years he beseeched Congress to legislate com-
pulsory attendance, but Congress always balked. The military
government in Sitka, before the civil code was established,
had the right idea! A commander of a U.S. ship stationed
there, one Captain Henry Glass, "caused a label to be made of
tin for each child, which was tied on it so that if a child was
found on the street during school hours the Indian policeman

was under orders to take the numbers on the labels and report them, or the teacher each day would report that such numbers from such houses were absent that day. The following morning the head Indian of the house to which the absentee belonged was summoned to appear and answer for the absence of the child. If the child was wilfully absent the head man was fined or imprisoned. A few cases of fine were sufficient . . ."

Differences between Hannah's and Jackson's educational styles are obvious. She relied on getting children into school by contriving ways for them to enjoy education. Far from alienating families, her tactics depended on family enthusiasm. Her conception of educational enrichment went well beyond official guidelines. For instance, she was eager to open her pupils' eyes to the great world beyond their hermetic ken through study of geography, stories and pictures of other people and how they lived; nature study that went beyond the economic and practical; introduction of new games and toys, evidence that people far away knew and cared about them. She not only told her pupils about elections and the abstract idea that people could direct their government democratically, but held elections on classroom issues and abided by the results. True, she may have been reasonably sure of election outcomes in advance, but not necessarily always sure. Sometimes she asked for a show of hands to get soundings, like a public opinion pollster, before taking a step. On one occasion at least, she broke the taboo against use of languages other than English when she had Kenai translations read of the president's and governor's Thanksgiving proclamations. She discouraged children from speaking in their mother tongues in school and did not help them out by resorting to native phrases she must have picked up, but she did not punish children for lapsing into their own languages in school or at play, as was done in many Alaskan schools.

At the root of differences between Jackson's and Hannah's approaches to schooling was a profound difference in their conceptions of the purpose of education. Jackson thought of it in terms of control, Hannah in terms of nurturing. In the government archives is a letter to a cantankerous supervisor in which Hannah defends a decision she had made on a fuel wood purchase; she granted that she had not acted like "a sensible businessman" in the way she had put the contract out to bid (she had encouraged a bidder who would employ natives against a rival who would not), and then she added parenthetically, "but I'm a woman and cannot think and speak like a man."

What did she mean by this? Hannah recognized that some men acted fairly and nurtured people for whom they were responsible. She liked men in whom she saw those qualities, such as Zackar, the Nondalton chief, for example, the two Baptist mission superintendents with whom she worked, and the Russian Bishop Innocent. But many little observations, as well as many little silences in her memoir, add up to the impression that she thought men, by and large, behaved like controllers of other people when they were in a position to do so, and all too often were ready to take advantage of those in their power. She did not regard this as usual behavior for women. There are many ways of controlling, and many of nurturing, and one may doubt the validity of her assessment. But it is clear that what she saw as a gender difference was something she did not care to change in herself.

Sheldon Jackson was not only a controlling sort of man, but implacable when he was crossed. For instance, he disposed of the judge, the U.S. attorney, a U.S. marshal and the governor, all of whom had run afoul of him in the custody cases and various other suits concerning his Sitka school; he had them investigated and removed by Washington. How could Hannah admire this bossy and intolerant man?

But Jackson was no one-dimensional martinet. He was a complicated man. For all his anger and loathing, he was certainly no sadist. Early in his career he left a school for Choctaws in Oklahoma because he disliked whipping boys to maintain discipline. No doubt he thought his rigorous policies and methods directed to natives were less coercive than concerned.

Toward his American colleagues he extended appreciation, trust and a spirit of partnership—not the castigation, suspicion and attempts at domination he reserved for native peoples and his white enemies (of whom he had many).

Hannah kept few letters. Among the dozen or so she treasured was one from Jackson, written soon after she began work in her first post at Afognak:

> Madam:
>
> Your letter of October 1st, is received and it comes with good news, like the election news that we have been hearing the past two or three days.*
>
> I can not tell you how glad I am that you are getting hold of those children. You are in a very important field and one where you can accomplish a great deal of good. I have often noticed that the out of the way and the inaccessible places of the earth, that on that account are avoided by some workers, prove to be the most fruitful.
>
> On October 11th, we ordered for you, 10 yds. of black-board cloth, 3 doz. slates, 3 boxes slate pencils, 3 Gospel Hymn books with notes, and 9 Gospel Hymn

---

*This was the November 1904 election of Theodore Roosevelt as President; Hannah much admired Roosevelt as a conservationist.

books without notes, and one half doz. small scissors. They have just been received at the Office and will at once be mailed to you. In addition we will now send you 4 doz. First Readers; 6 doz. tablets and half a ream of foolscap paper.

I also received from the school Commissioners a very complimentary letter, with regard to your success.

On November 2nd, we shipped your school some new school desks, but you have so increased the school, that there may not be desks enough. If your school gets so large that you can not handle it, you had better divide the school, teaching certain grades in the forenoon and certain other grades in the afternoon. Let me know if you need more desks and if there is room in the school house to place them.

Very truly yours
(signed) Sheldon Jackson
U.S. General Agent of Education in Alaska.

After we get over our amazement that the top administrator of Alaskan education was concerning himself with three dozen slate pencils and half a dozen small scissors, we get the message that Hannah cherished: he personally cared about her needs; he stood behind her as helper and well-wisher.

Jackson had one personality for colleagues and an entirely different personality for those whom he saw as unbridgeably alien. Hannah shared Jackson's aim of spreading civilization. But Hannah had only one personality, whoever she was with and wherever she was. That is why in her classrooms the gentler, nurturing schooling of Bloomsburg, Pennsylvania, wormed its way into the Sheldon Jackson Alaskan policy and riddled its harsh core of rejection and control.

2. The Reindeer Project

The reindeer superintendent who behaved so callously toward Hannah was a Norwegian Lapp named Hedley E. Redmyer, who had immigrated to the U.S. in 1883. Redmyer's letters in government archives show that he wrote English fluently in an educated, copybook hand. Jackson must have had confidence in him to have placed him in charge of an isolated government reindeer herd rather than at a mission reindeer station, where he would have been under closer scrutiny.

Neither the investigation of Redmyer nor his subsequent discharge were owing to Hannah's report on him. After the apologies and expressions of sympathy she received from officials, no further attention seems to have been given her account.

The Redmyer investigation was triggered more than a year and a half later by a letter to Washington from one Albert W. Young, mechanical engineer. Here is what he had to say:

> I must respectfully beg to call your attention to the irregularities connected with the management of the Reindeer Station at Iliamna, Alaska; but that is not the word (fraud and injustice) fraud to the U.S. Gov't and injustice to the people residing in this section of Alaska. To begin I have lived in Alaska eight years prospecting etc., etc. On the 29th of Oct. 1907, while at Iliamna Bay awaiting steamer from Seattle, I heard Mr. Redmyer of the Reindeer Station remark that he always lost a large part of the Gov't supplies before he could get them to the Reindeer Station, they would either be stolen from A.C. Point or else stolen while in transit between Iliamna Bay and Iliamna village, a distance of about twelve miles. On the 25th of Dec., as no steamer had arrived, I returned to Iliamna Village and ascer-

tained the following from the residents there who are mostly prospectors, and men of good repute. A Mr. Peter Anderson has for the past four years conducted a trading post at Iliamna Village and on several occasions has done freighting for Mr. Redmyer and whenever he is short of supplies for his store he simply helps himself to the Gov's rations belonging to the Reindeer Station and sells them over the counter, done so last winter and *is doing so at the present time.*

Mr. Wm. von Hardenberg of Lake Clark informed me that he came to Iliamna Village last winter wishing to purchase bacon. Mr. Anderson told him there were none, but that the Reindeer Station supplies were being sledded across the portage to Iliamna Lake and part were cached on the trail he would send and get a box of bacon, as he (Anderson) had Mr. Redmyer's permission to use whatever he wished. He instructed the natives they would find two boxes of bacon on the trail, to go and bring the largest box. When the bacon arrived Mr. von Hardenberg bought half the box at exorbitant prices and Mr. Anderson remarked he would keep the rest for his own use, as there was no bacon in the country. Mr. B. S. Foss told me that at another time Mr. Redmyer complained about bacon (another box) being stolen from cache close to the village. Mr. Foss was indignant at the insinuation as he resides there with his family. He said to Mr. Redmyer, Redmyer you know very well Anderson took that bacon and you have got to stop insinuating people living here are thieves. Mr. Redmyer somewhat alarmed begged him to say no more about it, saying it was not Gov't rations but his (Redmyers) private stock and he would let it go as he did not wish to make any trouble about it. Last winter

Mr. Anderson sent to New Dalton Village on Clark Lake, for trading purposes a tierce of lard labeled (so I am informed) "Iliamna, Alaska, Industrial School." They have also sold stoves, tents etc., etc., it is also asserted Mr. Redmyer and Mr. Anderson have made out "Labor vouchers" promiscuously. Mr. Joseph Oakley, Peter Rather, Mr. Chambers, Mr. Walker, Charles Jensen, Dr. Dutton, B. S. Foss & Son, admit they know more or less about the fraudulent management and would welcome an investigation.

I have the honor to be most obediently yours,

Albert W. Young, M.E.

Iliamna, Cooks Inlet, Alaska

January 2nd, 1908.

This letter did produce action, culminating in suspension of Redmyer's salary and then his removal for financial irregularities. This also probably explains why Hannah's kind friend Olga was not in Iliamna when Hannah returned there in 1909. Olga's husband, Pete Anderson, was a self-employed storekeeper so he couldn't be fired by the government; however the scandal may have made it advisable to take himself, family and store out of Iliamna and off to Nondalton.

This reindeer station was only one of many, part of a grand Sheldon Jackson project. Jackson was hipped on the subject of domesticated reindeer. It loomed as large in his plans for remaking Alaska as Christianization and education. He counted on a combination of these three elements to transform native life.

The most picturesque part of his vision was a proposed reindeer-sled express to transport freight over snow and ice to whaling fleets and wilderness mines, and carry mail to missions and trading posts everywhere from Point Barrow at farthest north, to Afognak and Kodiak in the south. He mapped out main lines and branch lines, as if he were designing a railway system complete with depots, expeditors and supervisors. Deadly serious, he set about raising appropriations from Congress and contributions from mission societies.

Jackson argued that domesticated reindeer would save Eskimos from extinction by supplying them with meat, hides, bones, employment and cash. He expected wild caribou to vanish, just as wild buffalo herds had been vanishing from the American prairies; former Indian caribou hunters could herd domesticated reindeer as a substitute. The people of the Aleutian Islands, who had been engulfed in poverty since the collapse of the sea otter trade, would also be saved by reindeer. And most important to Jackson, heathen barbaric hunters would rise into civilization as tamed Christian herders.

First he had to get reindeer and people who could handle them. In 1892 he sailed to Siberia to buy reindeer and recruit Samoyed herders, the start of hundreds of thousands of miles he was ultimately to travel in search of deer, herders, and money to pay for them. It was slow going. On his first trip he was able to bring back only 170 deer; in 1893, only 127; and in 1894, only forty-eight. Each purchasing voyage entailed dickering for a few deer here, a few there, hither and yon along hazardous, unfamiliar coasts during the brief summer. Jackson formed a plan to set up a permanent purchasing and recruiting station in Siberia so herds and herders would be assembled and ready to sail when ships called. But he had to drop this plan, in part because the Samoyed herdsmen he had recruited were such a disappointment. They fecklessly allowed the domesticated deer to mix with caribou and revert to the wild. They were careless with fawns, which had unacceptably high death rates. They were shockingly cruel to the animals. On the sly, whenever they wanted they killed government deer and ate them. Altogether, they set bad examples to the Alaskan natives they were supposed to be teaching and civilizing.

Jackson counted on a systematic apprenticeship scheme to multiply herds and herders. Each youth employed under supervision of a station received his pay in reindeer. At the end of four or five years of apprenticeship he would have the start of a herd, since of course he could keep the fawns too. Graduate apprentices were expected to employ, pay and train apprentices in their turn, multiplying both herds and herders geometrically.

In 1897 Jackson gave up on Siberian herds and Samoyeds. But he had gotten promising reports about Scandinavian Lapps. So he sent an agent to northern Scandinavia who managed to buy five hundred Lapland reindeer and to make employment contracts with forty-three Lapps, fifteen Norwegians and ten Finns. Dependents coming along too included nineteen wives and twenty-six children, most very young.

Jackson at this time was sixty-four and in frequent severe pain, but he set off for northern Norway to shepherd these people to Alaska along with a cargo of three hundred of the deer, two hundred sleds, and baled moss to feed the deer.

It must have been an unforgettable voyage. It has been described by Arthur J. Lazell, Jackson's biographer. Trouble began at the dock. At the last minute the Lapps balked at boarding. They were awaiting delayed delivery of four kegs of whisky. When the kegs arrived Jackson had the police confiscate them and tell the Lapps they had the choice of boarding or going to jail.

At long last—there had been many previous delays because of storms, fogs and blizzards, finding a ship to charter and overcoming quarantine difficulties—the trip began with a bang-up party in steerage, where the Scandinavians were assigned quarters. They had managed to smuggle some bottles in with their belongings, and drunken pandemonium lasted all night. The next day came the first of a series of North Atlantic mid-winter storms that hardly let up during the three-week crossing. The Scandinavians were violently seasick, and their quarters wet and filthy. Jackson's own cabin was ankle-deep in water.

The animals were on deck in a good stout pen, but the storms were so severe the pen threatened to give. A new pen had to be constructed and the animals relocated while the ship was plunging and shuddering. Measles broke out among the children.

In New York the animals, sleds, feed and people were loaded on a train for Seattle, where a steamer was to meet them. The ship was nine days late and the feed gave out. A substitute diet killed a dozen deer and made many others sick. When the herd disembarked in southeast Alaska the animals were unable to walk. Moss for feed was supposed to be waiting for them but it was not because of a week's delay in sending the cabled order a distance of five miles. Nor did tents and other equipment that had been ordered for the reindeer men and their families arrive on time. The deer were too sick and weak to reach nearby moss beds. Moss was hastily gathered and brought to them but by the time the herd could travel, half the animals were already dead and more died in the weeks following. Jackson was much criticized and ridiculed for presiding over this fiasco.

In light of all this, one can understand why Hannah's complaints of Redmyer were given short shrift. A competent—or supposedly competent—herdsman was valued no matter how unchivalrous. And measured against the hardships and anxieties of everyone connected with the reindeer vision, Hannah's miserable day-trip and painful feet were trivial.

An average of fewer than a hundred reindeer a year had been successfully imported to Alaska between 1892 and 1906, but by 1906 the 1,260 imported had multiplied to 12,826. Fifteen stations were opened between 1899 and 1906, one of them the Iliamna station. They employed a total of seventy-eight apprentices, among them the six Eskimo youths Hannah taught. Half the herds by then belonged to natives. Almost five hundred deer had been broken to harness for commercial transportation. Jackson regarded these accomplishments as a rebuke to skeptics. He never wavered in his faith in reindeer power. When he was close to death in 1909 he was cheered to learn that Sir Wilfred Grenfell, the founder of a mission for fishermen in Newfoundland, was satisfied the project had succeeded and was thinking of repeating it in Newfoundland.

Alaska's reindeer population peaked in 1930 at what was said to be 600,000 animals, but that may be an inflated figure because by 1950 there were only 25,000. This precipitous decline was variously laid to depredations by wolves and eagles (which were a major menace to fawns), overgrazing, excessive butchering, and mixing of herds with wild caribou.

The underlying reason, a historian who has looked into the subject told me, was that the scheme made no sense from the viewpoint of native people. Moose and caribou did not disappear as Jackson expected them to, and thanks to hunting regulations still remain plentiful; indeed, at the present time they are increasing. It is more sensible for a native to get deer meat and skins from wild caribou that look after themselves and their fawns than it is to pen deer, protect them from other wildlife, rear their fawns and haul feed.

Today domesticated reindeer are scant in Alaska, their economic importance negligible and their social significance nil. The same is true of other Alaskan stock-raising. Over the years many experienced ranchers from the American West have thought that places like Wood Island, Kodiak and the Matanuska Valley near Anchorage were ideal for raising beef cattle or sheep, but these enterprises have failed. When the wolves and bears didn't do in the animals, the high comparative costs of rearing and marketing did.

As for the two anachronistic forms of winter land travel— dogsled and reindeer sledge—only dogsled racing is a competitive sport today. Nobody seems to find excitement or fun in reindeer, Santa Claus notwithstanding. Many people who Jackson consigned to herding to achieve a slow and logical climb into civilization have responsible jobs within the businesses of air freighting and air-taxi services.

Jackson, for all his personal idiosyncracies, was a common type: the know-it-all (who also possessed a supposed knowledge of the future) who wades into a piece of the world and its population with visions of how to transform the whole she-bang and proceeds to try doing it. The people who founded and shaped the Soviet Union were such types. So were many imperialists who lorded it over colonies in Africa and Asia. So were American slum-clearers, public-housers and city planners. The World Bank today is full of such types. The visions differ; the hubris and impulse do not. Some take their authority from science or pseudo-sciences like sociology and economics. Jackson thought he took his authority straight from God; he sometimes said just that.

As for Hannah and the reindeer, after she settled into Iliamna they were still to be one of her vexations, as we shall see.

3. The Bureaucracy

When Hannah first saw the school and teacher's cottage in Il-iamna she noticed they were sited idiotically and the paths looked dangerous. That wasn't the half of it.

She swiftly made a request to her top Alaskan supervisor for gray building paper or siding to conceal the black tarpaper, blotched and stained with nonadhering whitewash, on the classroom's inside walls, and to provide a better barrier against cold than the flimsy muslin ceiling. She was at pains to add that these were minor problems and no reflection on her predecessors, who "had done wonders in the short time they were here." As between the cottage and the school, "I would prefer if I had my choice to have the schoolroom beautiful; for these children have such dingy homes." Since the requested covering did not get to her that winter, Hannah tacked up some paper she found. In the meantime she heard that siding had been sitting unprotected on a distant dock and probably was now worthless.

In April, having experienced winter in these buildings, she wrote a further list of requirements. The good news was that it was fortunate that the building paper had not been sent— because the bad news was that the paper she tacked up had soon become dirty and disreputable from rain beating in. She suggested "after much pondering" that there was nothing like heavy canvas to keep out the cold and winds, and its shipment was both less uncertain and less expensive than siding; true, canvas would require two good coats of paint but so would lumber. The roof and floor should be painted too to prevent deterioration. Furthermore, the log walls were not tight. The chinking had been so poor it had flown out with the wind. These shortcomings required exorbitant amounts of fire-wood. And that was another thing: no woodshed. Soaked wood brought in from an outdoor woodpile took up classroom space while it dried out for days and made the place unpleasantly damp. There was no place for chopping kindling except the classroom. She outlined specifications for a woodshed, emphasizing that it would need a floor raised off the ground. The schoolroom also needed a cupboard with a lock on it to protect groceries.

As for the cottage, it was even more open to wind and weather, so even colder. The window casings had not been packed and must be removed to repair that omission, but they had been bolted to the logs in such a way that they couldn't be removed without destroying them. She doubted that the upstairs rooms could ever be made habitable in winter. The open stairway leading to them, "a snare and a delusion in this climate," also made the first floor impossible to heat, so the stair would have to be closed with a door and partition. A railing along the steep path to the river trail was essential because the level trail to the village was like a glacier in winter and nobody used it.

She had been told by a "shrewd" white man that the property had never been surveyed and was subject to encroachment, so she urged that boundaries be settled, allowing sufficient space for a school garden on a sunny flat near the cottage.

She attached a condensed, formal requisition list, down to hinges, doorknob and work to be contracted, not failing to add parenthetically, "Information regarding U.S. Gov's Land."

All this went to Mr. William T. Lopp in Nome, who was now the chief of the education department within Alaska. Although Hannah was probably not aware of it, these requests put Mr. Lopp in an awkward position. Information to which Hannah was not privy is today accessible to anyone interested in microfilmed archives of the Department of the Interior, dispersed among various libraries in Alaska, Seattle and Washington. The archive I sampled, which deals with the Iliamna school and the reindeer station during Hannah's years, is in Anchorage.

The designer and the construction supervisor of the school was Dr. Henry O. Schaleben, of whom we shall hear more. After he finished his work on the school, leaving the results to Hannah, he applied for a cost overrun of two hundred dollars above the four thousand dollars that had been authorized for the job. The overrun was such a serious matter that it had to travel through numerous layers of the bureaucracy all the way up to the Secretary of the Department of the Interior. He approved it at the behest of his department's educational agency, which in turn had relied on what its Seattle office chief had written, and this man had depended upon assurances from none other than Mr. Lopp. The salient portion of Seattle's approval read:

> Dr. Schaleben was industrious and careful in every way to protect the interests of the government. Mr. Lopp who has seen the school house and residence since its erection, is of the opinion that the money has been economically expended. In our combined judgment this excess of cost is due entirely to Dr. Schaleben's filling plans made by him which could not be carried out within the limit of cost and for this, in our judgment, he should not be, under the circumstances, held responsible.

That marvelous last sentence is worth wistful memorizing by any architect.

Mr. Lopp would have to send Hannah's requisitions and the reasons for them along the same bureaucratic route—although in this case not all the way to the Secretary of the Interior—as his earlier reassurances about the satisfactory job. How embarrassing for Mr. Lopp!

It is unclear how much of Hannah's wish list he gradually granted. Apparently, she never did get the woodshed, but she did get the school cupboard. And when summer came she employed a workman to bank earth around the two buildings and chink the logs. She had the workman take the earth from alongside the paths so that simultaneously they could be widened and made safer, and had him build a railing. Mr. Lopp complained of the cost of the labor and she replied that for lack of equipment, even so much as a wheelbarrow, the work had been time-consuming.

In her memoir Hannah conveys a sunny picture of her relationships with those who supplied and supervised her—so much so that one is tempted to believe she worked within a bureaucracy that wondrously combined efficiency with flexibility, and prudence with sympathetic imagination. But she omits glitches, meanness, obtuseness and neglect that cost her heavily in frustration and anxiety.

When the system tied itself into knots, as bureaucracies are wont to do, she was stuck in the catch-22s. For instance, she was supposed to use various expense forms, but the forms did not arrive in Iliamna when she arrived (perhaps were never sent). In their absence, she used school notebook paper to list her travel costs from Wood Island to Iliamna, and enclosed receipts. The total came to $107.37. At the time her salary was ninety dollars a month payable from September through May; she got no vacation pay. After much delay she heard from Washington that it was impossible to honor her bill because it was not presented on the required form. But in recognition of the fact that she had no forms, a solution had been found: her pay, instead, would be extended through June. She replied she was glad they had found a solution, even though it left her with a shortfall of $17.37, and added that she looked forward to earning the salary extension by working through June.

Hannah was routinely harassed by Mr. Lopp about the school expenses she turned in, and when he was not sufficiently sharp-eyed the Seattle office was. For example, among the modest expenses for her summer school at the Nondalton fishing camp were arrangements for a patriotic party to celebrate the Fourth of July. She provided tea, part of a sack of flour, some raisins, and candy for the children. She also gave a prize of a harmonica to the boy who could play it best. The bottom of her requisition bears this notation by the Seattle office, "Candy and harmonica disallowed, $1.60."

Mr. Lopp was part of a bureaucratic layer that had been interposed, for reasons I shall come to later, between Washington and workers like Hannah. He was a Congregational minister from Indiana who had been one of the first four teachers to Eskimos chosen by Jackson from among twenty-four applicants who had responded to advertisements in church publications. He was also one of Jackson's earliest and staunchest lieutenants in the great reindeer project, and in that capacity had given exceptionally heroic service occasioned by a shipwreck in the far north.

Dr. Schaleben, designer and builder of the outrageously bad Iliamna school and residence, was a young physician who had been recruited, along with his wife, Gertrude Ramslund Schaleben, in Minnesota. Upon being hired he had been assigned immediately to design and build the Iliamna school. Then the couple were to be stationed there. His wife was to be the teacher, and he was to serve as public health officer and physician to numerous native villages. That was the plan. However, after one winter in their new schoolhouse and residence they got a new assignment (at whose initiative the archives do not reveal) to Koggiung on the Bering Sea, where Dr. Schaleben was commissioned to design and build another school. Presumably the doctor had learned from experience, because the couple remained at that school and were joined by Mrs. Schaleben's brother, another teacher. The Schalebens' move to Koggiung was the reason why the Iliamna post, which Hannah had so much coveted, finally fell to her.

Hannah mentions in her memoir that when she had been sent on her wild-goose chase to start a school at the reindeer station, she was authorized to put up one or two buildings there, but had no authorization to put up buildings or spend any money at Iliamna, where the school should have been, so was laying the whole matter before Washington. The logical next move would have been for Washington to assign her to Iliamna and transfer her building authorizations there. That is plainly what Hannah hoped and expected, and we may be sure her buildings would have been well chinked, properly banked, furnished with a woodshed and more intelligently placed on surveyed land.

Washington flubbed this because of a bureaucratic reform set in motion in 1906, the same year as Hannah's abortive trip to the reindeer station. Jackson (in his letter to Hannah, see p. 206) had rejoiced too soon over the election of President Theodore Roosevelt. Because of anger in Alaska at the influence there of Presbyterian mission policies and Presbyterians in high places, and complaints about lack of home rule, Roosevelt ordered a report on the situation. The report's author, Frank C. Churchill, a civil servant in the Department of the Interior, was extremely negative about Jackson's administration of the schools and the reindeer project and the intimate mixing of government and church mission responsibilities. Jackson's biographer, Lazell, says Churchill backed up his criticisms and made his recommendations with scant or no evidence. Be that at it may, Churchill did note that "I know of no adverse criticism that should be made as to the quality of service rendered by the teachers employed."

As a swift response to animus against Presbyterian influence, Roosevelt asked for the resignation of Governor Brady, who was a businessman but who also had the misfortune, under the circumstances, of having previously been a Presbyterian minister and having come to Alaska as a Jackson protégé. As governor, Brady was actually not a notable supporter of mission policies (for instance, he was not a prohibitionist), and he was also not subservient to commercial pressures; arguably he was the most evenhanded and competent governor Alaska had received thus far. Jackson was not asked for his resignation as head of the education agency, but the following year, 1907, he voluntarily resigned—with small thanks from the government—because of age and ill health, and he died in 1909.

Among his other recommendations, Churchill urged that as far as practicable, persons skilled in medicine should be employed as teachers in the Arctic and Subarctic, and he also urged closer bureaucratic control over schools and reindeer stations both from Nome and from Washington.

Mr. Lopp's and Seattle's pettifoggery over such items as harmonicas and much else, the travel expense forms that couldn't be gotten around even when they had not been supplied and the employment of a medical doctor with no relevant experience to design and build a school, were obviously among attempts being made—to put it in bureaucratese—at implementing the new guidelines. As far as Hannah was concerned, reform was no improvement; on the contrary.

At the same time he was transferred to Koggiung from Iliamna, or soon afterward, Dr. Schaleben was made district superintendent over four schools, one of which was Iliamna.

Hannah had much looked forward to meeting the Schalebens and eagerly anticipated a promised visit from the doctor to discuss what she was doing, get his counsel and give him her reports for relay through Mr. Lopp and on to Washington. However, the doctor's visit did not materialize and he was so unresponsive to her communications that she evidently concluded he was uninterested in the school and her work. In her frustration, as the school year was drawing to a close in April, she took the rather drastic step of bypassing the unresponsive doctor by sending her reports on school attendance and other school matters to still another physician, Dr. Romig, the district superintendent in Seward. She used the disingenuous excuse that since Dr. Schaleben signed himself "Assistant Superintendent" rather than "District Superintendent," she hoped she was not doing wrong. She ventured that Seward was the more logical seat for superintending Iliamna. She received a kind reply complimenting her reports and work, with an assurance that the reports were being sent on to Washington but making it clear that Seward could not superintend Iliamna.

So Hannah was thrown back on the unresponsive Dr. Schaleben. Before starting the second school year she made, on her own initiative, her hazardous trip to Koggiung, to deal with the doctor, finally, face-to-face, get him to make decisions and recommendations regarding emergency relief, send on word of the recommendations (probably to Mr. Lopp) and await replies. Her unspecified school business to be accomplished concerned Nondalton. When she had returned from the summer session at the fishing camp, she had written a long report on the educational situation there, as well as a report on her summer's work, and put forward a proposal for a six-month Nondalton school session beginning the next summer as soon as school finished in Iliamna. She gave this to the doctor and received assurance that he would add his recommendation.

Evidently this meeting with the doctor was small pleasure. The Schalebens did not so much as invite her to their home for a meal, an unusual breach of hospitality—or snub—under the circumstances. They were young and perhaps she came across to them as a tiresome old fussbudget, or perhaps it was an embarrassment to them that she knew how bad the Iliamna buildings were.

But far worse than this was the fate of her Nondalton proposal. It was never even considered in Washington because her reports and other material were never received there, nor did these seem to have gotten even as far as Mr. Lopp. Hannah learned this by chance just before winter closed in, and it was too late for further communication with Washington. Giving Dr. Schaleben the benefit of the doubt, she preferred to think he had indeed sent on his promised recommendation, but that without the supporting material it had merely mystified recipients; as far as the archives show, there is no indication he sent anything on. This was a very bitter disappointment to Hannah.

A couple of months after she realized her proposal had fallen into a black hole, she finally did receive a visit from Dr. Schaleben in his role as physician. He was the doctor she refers to who examined the sick, gave her advice on their treatment and whose wife sent along a chicken and a quart of frozen milk.

It must have been on her visit to Koggiung that the doctor saddled her with the unsought title of "assistant superintendent" of the reindeer station. Among his many other duties and titles the doctor was now also the reindeer superintendent. The replacement for the disgraced Mr. Redmyer had not worked out and the doctor had been given that responsibility too. The chore he handed to Hannah seemed simple enough: she was authorized to see that one reindeer from a native's herd was transferred to Samuel Foss, a white Iliamna businessman, in payment of a debt owed him. What a mess that turned out to be!

The ins and outs of the affair are too tedious to relate, but the upshot was that Mr. Foss and his wife, who laid claim to being intimate friends of the Schalebens—a claim Hannah credited—tried to bully Hannah into giving them two and a half reindeer from the native's herd, then upped it to three, and when Hannah stuck to her written authorization for one, made their grievance a cause célèbre among the whites. Hannah needed Dr. Schaleben either to revise his instructions to her or else to support her, but although she wrote him at length and in obvious agitation, the ugly situation was simply left to fester.

Hannah's isolation during this second Iliamna winter was desperately hard for her to bear. She had incurred further unpopularity among a faction of whites by opposing importation of a large consignment of whisky. Part of a previous consignment had been illegally traded to natives and she knew this would be repeated. Furthermore, a few of the native men, who she had reason to believe had been prodded by these white enemies she had made, were claiming that famine relief food was a gift from the white people in Washington and she should have nothing to do with it.

She had no one to talk with about any of these problems other than the U.S. recorder, a clerk, without whose counsel, as she wrote Washington later, she would have been utterly alone. She was also becoming frightened. In March, as the winter was drawing to a close, she wrote a personal letter to Elmer E. Brown, who now held the position that Sheldon Jackson had filled. She said it had come to her ears that opponents "intend putting me out of here this summer," and enclosed her application to be appointed for a third year in Iliamna. She said:

> I am not worried about my position (if you only understand the true state of affairs). I have more faith in the Department than to think you would recall me without knowing the truth. You remember I gave up a $100 a month salary to come to these people and I would not ask to remain if I did not think it for the best interests of the work here. I can get along with the Indians and when it is known that *you stand by me*—the other trouble will right itself.
>
> But if it is to be known in any way that I have written this letter (Doctor Schaleben *not* excepted) I want to be given time to get out of the country *first*. I am *too* alone . . .
>
> I will feel quite uneasy about my appointment . . . It would be dreadful to be left here all winter and another teacher sent in. October is an uncertain month and the last two years, I think, has brought no boat [to A.C. Point] in September. There is not a vacant cabin here and what I should do I do not know.

She pointed out that the office of U.S. commissioner had been vacant since the previous October and recommended the recorder, Thomas Hanmore, as a man of integrity with few enemies who could give an unbiased report of conditions. She concluded her letter with an incongruous chatty paragraph about a dear Alaskan friend who had met President Taft in Seattle and received from him a cabinet photo in an ebony frame with a personal inscription. The unstated implication was that if her nightmare came true—if she were to be marooned and abandoned in Iliamna—the president himself would hear of it. Her grasp at this pathetic straw of political pressure—so unlike her—reveals how alarmed she must have been.

Her letter is stamped as received in Washington on May 20, 1911. On this same date the department received a letter from Hannah's niece, Martha Robison, reporting that no word, directly or indirectly, had come from Miss Breece since the previous October; her family and friends were becoming much alarmed. It probably did not hurt that Miss Robison wrote on the letterhead of the Presbyterian Board of Home Missions, her employer. Five days later she was sent a reply that the department had just received letters from Miss Breece, the first to get to them since October, and that she was "in good health and spirits, happy in her work and she had requested reappointment commencing next September."

In short order Hannah was informed of her reappointment. She even received a salary raise to ninety-five dollars a month. Her nightmare was over.

Hannah was not the only one to suffer from her superintendent's insouciance. Her successors as teachers at Iliamna were a man named J. L. Brown and his wife. In their first winter on the job, Mr. Brown wrote Mr. Lopp that Dr. Schaleben had delegated him responsibilities concerning the reindeer station. Brown had found the chief herder was making "bad use of his authority" and slaughtering deer merely to make a big showing. Another herder was doing no work, merely slipping into the station to pick up supplies. When Brown told the herder he must attend to his herd, the man refused, whereupon Brown suspended him and recommended his dismissal. Dr. Schaleben, instead of supporting the suspension, told Brown to send the man to work again. "Does he intend I send him back by force?" wrote Brown, adding that the recalcitrant herder now had the idea that Brown could suspend no one and was making mischief among the other herders. He concluded his letter to Mr. Lopp thus: ". . . I do not wish to make complaints of any one else. So will merely ask that you count this place vacant at the end of this year and either send me some where else or allow me to quit the service."

It is hard to know what to make of Dr. Schaleben. He and his wife were much admired as heroic, vigorous, charming people and devoted, gifted teachers; they are still remembered as outstanding Alaskan educational pioneers.

We can be sure the doctor was overworked. He was the only physician serving native people in some thousand square miles or more. Considering his many additional duties, it is little wonder that he brushed off requests for attention and decisions, leaving others to bear the consequences as best they could. His own letters to superiors radiate optimism and confidence.

I surmise that along with his other gifts and abilities, he possessed one of the important attributes of a successful courtier or valued bureaucrat. That is, instead of saying no to superiors or plaguing them with complexities and difficulties, he gladdened their hearts with assurances of Can Do, No Problem, and Everything in Hand—a man they could gratefully rely on to deal with the system.

4. Fort Yukon Troubles

With their plentiful food, Brussels carpets and satin party dresses, Fort Yukon natives were far richer than those in Afognak, Iliamna and Nondalton. Why did a teacher who aimed at giving children a first leg up out of poverty choose such a prosperous settlement? And why would a teacher who preferred strenuous assignments choose an already well established school where by her own account both living and

Dr. Henry O. Schaleben, second from right, with native guides.
By permission of Mrs. Ray F. Schaleben

teaching conditions were easy and routine? Hannah merely says that she had the interests of the native people at heart.

To put her choice in modern terms, it was as if she had elected to take up work in a community that was rolling in money but that was also gripped in epidemics of crack cocaine and AIDS. Floods of alcohol—some imported under license and then illegally traded to natives, some smuggled in by mail carriers and others—were demoralizing and killing Fort Yukon's native people, and diseases new to them were also killing them off at an alarming rate. Hudson Stuck, archdeacon of the Yukon, had been tracking the rising mortality and falling birth statistics in this and other far northern trading settlements. He concluded that Athabaskan Indians were headed into extinction unless the laws could be enforced against unscrupulous whites exploiting them or else unless they withdrew into remote settlements isolated from whites.

Law enforcement was at an impasse because a succession of corrupt U.S. marshals were in league with the lawbreakers. This was a wide-open, raunchy settlement, abundantly furnished with saloons, gambling dens and brothels. With alcohol as the lure, young Indian women were recruited into prostitution, and fathers and husbands were inveigled into selling daughters and wives in return for alcohol, silk umbrellas and other "glittering trash."

Archdeacon Stuck had gotten Hannah to come to Fort Yukon not only to teach but to enlist in the battle for law enforcement. Her memoir mentions a native town council in which she participated as a representative of government. The council was an attempt by the archdeacon to promote partial native self-rule and self-discipline. Its primary function was to admonish Indians who succumbed to alcohol, and if necessary punish them. These defensive measures proved to be ineffective, so during Hannah's second year in Fort Yukon the archdeacon and his few allies went on the offensive.

To this end the archdeacon tried to persuade Dr. Grafton Burke, a young Episcopal medical missionary, to accept the post of U.S. commissioner and justice of the peace. The doctor refused until a young Indian trapper of his acquaintance, Stephen Crow, froze to death because of being "drunk to stupefaction," leaving behind his wife and two small children, whom the Burkes took under their care. The trader who had sold Crow the whisky went unpunished because no official would prosecute him. This so outraged Dr. Burke that he agreed to take the job, and the archdeacon arranged for Judge F. E. Fuller of Fairbanks to make the appointment. The job was vacant and unsought-after because it carried no salary. However, as the title "commissioner" stated, it entitled the holder of the office to charge fees or commissions for attending to official work such as registering land claims, issuing licenses, and the like.

As commissioner and justice of the peace, Dr. Burke represented the force of the law, and he had powers to subpoena, to adjudicate local cases and if necessary send them to a federal grand jury. Wasting no time whatever, Dr. Burke proceeded to charge three whites and subpoenaed them to appear before the grand jury in Ruby. Two were accused of selling alcohol to natives, and one was accused of cohabitation with a native woman. Evidence against all three seemed ironclad.

The cohabitation charge can probably best be understood in our terms as a charge of living off the avails of prostitution. At any rate, in a New York newspaper article the archdeacon wrote about the case, he said it was unnecessary to describe such men because Robert Service had already done so in depicting the low-down white, and had not overdrawn "this despicable type." Here are the first two and the last verse of "The Low-Down White" in Service's *Ballads of the Yukon:*

> This is the pay-day up at the mines, when the
>   bearded brutes come down;
> There's money to burn in the streets tonight,
>   so I've sent my klooch to town,
> With a haggard face and a ribband of red en-
>   twined in her hair of brown.
>
> And I know at the dawn she'll come reeling
>   home with the bottles, one, two, three—
> One for herself to drown her shame, and two
>   big bottles for me,
> To make me forget the thing I am and the man
>   I used to be . . .

She will come with the dawn, and the dawn is .
    near; I can see its evil glow
Like a corpse-light seen through a frosty pane
    in a night of want and woe;
And yonder she comes by the bleak bull-pines,
    swift staggering through the snow.

The low-down white charged by Dr. Burke was a young fellow whose gangrenous arm the doctor had saved a few years previously. Now he purposely paraded his "unlawful cohabitation" to challenge the doctor's authority. The two whisky sellers may have been much like someone we have already met in Hannah's memoir: Mrs. Miller's husband. However, the two from Fort Yukon were apparently better connected than Mr. Miller.

Hannah's luxurious trip on the Yukon steamer was for the purpose of testifying at the three men's arraignments before the grand jury in the small river town of Ruby. The trip was a success. All three were indicted.

Then in January of 1914 came their trials in Fairbanks at which Hannah also testified—the reason for the long dogsled trip and unspecified anxiety she described. The prosecuting district attorney, Mr. James J. Crossley, was a courageous man who for years had been opposing the granting of liquor licenses in instances when the trade was obviously directed to Indians. The defense lawyer seems not to have troubled about the evidence Mr. Crossley drew forth, other than to claim that Mrs. Burke and Hannah attempted to coach native witnesses by nodding their heads yes or no.

The white male Fairbanks citizens who comprised the jury deliberated ten minutes on each case and returned verdicts of not guilty on each. One of many accusations leveled against Mr. Crossley by his enemies was that he was "a carpet-bagger

ignorant of western ways." In this instance he was flouting the
unwritten rules that no white man was supposed to testify
against another in a trial involving natives, and that no native's
word would be taken against a white man's.

When the Burkes and Hannah returned to Fort Yukon after
their failure in Fairbanks, they became targets for the fury of
storekeepers, saloon keepers and traders who exploited Indians. This was to be expected. It was more devastating that almost all other whites in the settlement either turned away
their faces or lay low. Archdeacon Stuck was not present at
the trial, nor during the aftermath at Fort Yukon. He was in
New York and Washington on church and government business. But in a long newspaper article published in the *New York
Evening Post* he spoke of their tribulations:

> [A]t Fort Yukon, the Government school teacher, Miss
> Hannah Breece, has given Dr. Burke most loyal sup-
> port, and has not shrunk from her share of the
> dislike and unpopularity . . . [T]his young physician,
> his devoted wife, and the government school
> teacher, maintaining a little garrison for defence of the
> Indians . . .

Dr. Burke was the chief target. His enemies attempted to
have him removed as commissioner on charges of malfeasance. When this was unsuccessful he received anonymous
threats, and shots were fired outside the mission building
where the Burkes lived. Then a dynamite blast destroyed the
veranda and blew out the windows. At one point a drunk former U.S. marshal came after the doctor with a pistol and a
bear claw. The doctor beat him senseless with his fists. Previously the doctor's "infectious smile, youthful good humor and
willingness at no cost to stitch up wounds and repair broken

bones of whites as well as Indians" had made him the most popular man in town, according to Archdeacon Stuck's biographer. Now he was the most hated, although held in grudging
respect for beating up the man with the gun and the bear claw.

A campaign of unspecified vilifications was directed against
Hannah. Whatever the calumnies and complaints were—attacks on her character? her competence?—they were serious
and persistent enough for the archdeacon to vouch for her in
Seattle and Washington and for Mr. Crossley to defend her in
a letter to Mr. Lopp:

> July 17, 1914
> On Board Steamer *Delta*
> near Tanana, Alaska

Sir: I am reliably informed that some persons at Ft.
Yukon have made complaint against Miss Hannah
Breece, the Government teacher at that place, and I
hereby beg leave to advise you that such persons are
very undesirable citizens and some of them are not
even citizens. The law-abiding element and the best
white people at Ft. Yukon are with Miss Breece, who
was drawn into the fight by being subpoenaed as a wit-
ness by me as U.S. Attorney in our efforts to clean up
the awful conditions of immorality and vice that existed
at Ft. Yukon and to prevent the vicious whites from
driving off of their land which the said Indians had occupied for such a long time.

Not only has Miss Breece been on the right side of
law and order but when put upon the witness-stand she
has told the truth and this aroused the bitter enmity of
the lawless element who have annoyed and insulted her
in every conceivable way they could possibly think of
doing. Furthermore, the first deputy marshal sent

there, A. F. Stowe, was an habitual drunkard and the marshal knew it and he was abusive to Miss Breece for he joined right in with the lawless element. After his removal on account of drunkenness the new deputy marshal Thomas E. Wonecoff, who had been a member of the grand jury that had attempted to indict the Commissioner, Dr. Grafton Burke, for malfeasance in office and other trumped up charges merely because Dr. Burke tried to enforce the law, was sent to Ft. Yukon as a reward for his services in trying to have Dr. Burke removed as Commissioner and the U.S. Attorney removed because they were trying to enforce the laws and maintain decent order at Ft. Yukon, and he too, no doubt, is trying to make it hard for Miss Breece. This man Winecoff [sic] has been ousted from the position he held as minister in both the Episcopal and Methodist Churches and is absolutely unreliable in every way.

Miss Breece has done her utmost to protect the Indians at Ft. Yukon from the vicious whites and she has been a noble mother to the Indian children at Ft. Yukon where she has raised their standard of living.

Dr. Burke and Miss Breece have both had very difficult positions to fill at Ft. Yukon and in my opinion every officer of the Government who wishes to help the Indians of Alaska and who wants order and decency maintained and the laws enforced should stand by them and give them every assistance as both Judge F. E. Fuller and I have tried to do as best we could.

I should be pleased to answer any inquiries you may care to make of me concerning conditions at Ft. Yukon.

Later that year Mr. Crossley successfully prosecuted a case against white encroachment on Indian land *(United States* v.

Cadzow) in a trial presided over by Judge Fuller. This caused an uproar throughout Alaska, and such intense political pressure was exerted against both men in Washington that Woodrow Wilson's administration had them both removed from office.

Dr. Burke, who had intended to return to the States for post-graduate medical training but delayed his departure because of the trial and melee, left Fort Yukon later in 1914 to study at Bellevue Hospital-Cornell Medical School in New York City. When the Burkes returned to Fort Yukon in 1916, after a period in which the settlement was afflicted with a replacement who was less competent and whose wife was thought "shrewish," many of their former critics were only too glad to welcome them back. They remained in Fort Yukon until the doctor's death from cancer at the age of fifty-five in 1937. He is still fondly remembered by older people in the community who had known him when they were children.

Hannah finished out the school year and then took up her new assignment in Wrangell. Why did she omit this gritty material? I do not think it was because it was too painful for her to dwell on, because otherwise she would hardly have kept, among the few letters she treasured, the signed copy of the letter from Mr. Crossley to Mr. Lopp. I have a reason for thinking she enjoyed reliving these wild events, which I will tell in the next section.

As for other reasons: As I explained in the foreword, Hannah put her memoir together from letters to family and friends. Perhaps she had not wanted to alarm or distress her correspondents—just as she omitted all references to her fears, approaching despair, in her second winter at Iliamna. But I suspect that her main reason was that she could hardly describe these events without reference to the demoralized and pitiable condition, at the time, of so much of the native population in Fort Yukon, and she was determined that she, for one, was not going to provide handles that would be eagerly seized by the very kinds of racists and bigots she was now engaged in battling.

On two occasions Hannah considered leaving the Alaska teaching service and inquired of the Office of Indian Affairs (also in the Department of the Interior) about returning to work she had previously done among Indians in the western United States. On both occasions the Alaska service indicated it would not oppose her transfer. The first time was after her wild-goose chase to the reindeer station, when she seemed to be stuck in her easy position at Wood Island.

The second time was in January 1915 after the Fort Yukon troubles, when she applied to Indian Affairs as either a teacher, or preferably a field matron visiting homes and teaching women and girls the arts of housekeeping and gardening, she also expressed a preference for working with Navajos. Here in full is the reply she received, dated January 30, 1915:

Madam:

Answering your letter of January 19, you are informed that even if you were eligible for reinstatement as teacher in the Service you could not be appointed field matron until you had passed the required field matron examination. Further, there are no vacancies in the Navajo country at the present time, nor is the Office aware of any contemplated vacancies for which you could be considered.

Very truly yours,
(stamped) E. B. Meritt
Assistant Commissioner

It may possibly be that she was thought too old. A jotted memo attached to her application notes that in 1902 she was "43 yrs of age now about 56 yrs" (actually she was fifty-five; in any case not a great age for teachers in these services).

But it is also possible that she had gained a reputation for partisan defense of native interests. Surely officials in the Indian Affairs office had read Archdeacon Stuck's prominent New York newspaper article of less than a year before in which he extolled the government schoolteacher Miss Hannah Breece as one of a little garrison maintaining defense of the Indians, and they must have been aware of his many talks on conditions and events in the Yukon—some given in Washington—in which he repeated his praise of her by name. The Indian Affairs office, to understate matters, was not notable for defending native interests and rights. At any rate, the cold and brusque reply she received conveyed an unmistakable message: "We wouldn't touch you with a ten-foot pole."

5. Fellow Teachers

On an occasion when Hannah visited my family in Scranton, Pennsylvania, I accompanied her to an orphanage and nursing home called The Home for the Friendless—later more sensitively renamed Friendly House. I was eleven years old at the time. We were calling upon an old lady who had taught with Hannah in Fort Yukon.

She was bedridden in a tiny room with a cramped window view of a service yard and no furnishings other than an iron cot, a dim lamp that illuminated the old woman's small white face and wispy white hair, and a scarred bureau. Two kitchen chairs were brought in for Hannah and me.

Then to my surprise, because the surroundings had prepared me for a mournful and boring ordeal, a flood of laughter and chatter filled the room. It was about people I did not know and occurrences I did not understand, and to my regret now I retain only one sentence: "He was rotten with syphilis."

The moment the old lady said this Hannah put her finger to her lips and they both paused and looked sidewise at me. I realized I was not supposed to have heard what had just been said and so remembered it. Since the old lady had said it with a giggle, it was probably gossip about someone they disliked. On our walk home Hannah told me the old lady was a brave and wonderful person and that she was soon going to die.

Some years later, during another of her rare visits, my brother Jim and his wife, Kay—who was then his girlfriend, they were high school students at the time—drove Hannah to a poverty-stricken anthracite coal-mining town outside of Scranton to visit another old Alaska teacher. Jim and Kay waited in the car outside the small, dilapidated house, so they have not even as much as my one scrap of conversation to remember. But they both recall how joyfully the two old women greeted each other and how much the visit meant to Hannah.

One wonders how many aged, impoverished Alaskan teachers were scattered across America: people with memories as vivid and strange as Hannah's.

Hannah liked other teachers, and she liked the company of people she had known in Alaska. She happened upon McMinnville, Oregon, during a visit there in 1915 with Dr. and Mrs. Coe. Dr. Coe had been the Baptist mission superintendent who hired her at Wood Island, and his wife had persuaded Hannah to stay on for a second year. In a letter to Hannah Archdeacon Stuck told her to have a good rest in McMinnville, but prescribed activity as the best form of recreation. She must have busied herself sufficiently in the life of McMinnville to make up her mind that this was where she wanted to teach when she left Alaska and where she wanted to spend her retirement afterward.

She was living in McMinnville at the time she and I visited the old Fort Yukon teacher, and on our homeward walk she told me it had the best climate in the world as far as she knew. It was cool and mild. It was also full of good friends, she said. McMinnville, I have learned since, was a great Baptist stronghold with a notably strong and active church and was renowned in Oregon as a highly progressive town with good government and attention to the well-being of children and other citizens. This, of course, would have attracted Hannah, but one of its chief attractions must have been the presence of its teachers' college and the company it afforded. It was at the urging of people in McMinnville, who had heard her talk about teaching in Alaska, that she began retrieving her letters to put together her manuscript.

It is curious that Hannah omitted fellow teachers from her memoir. She worked with other teachers at Wood Island, Fort Yukon and later in Wrangell and Douglas. But she does not name them, let alone characterize them or relate any of their experiences. She hoped and expected that her memoir would be published during her lifetime, which of course meant also the lifetimes of teachers she had worked with. It may be that she did not wish to single out some and thus appear to be ignoring or snubbing others. Or maybe she thought she should speak only for herself, leaving others to speak for themselves. Whatever the reason, I regret that I know not a thing about the old lady who lay in a bleak room for the friendless, waiting to die, except that she was "brave and wonderful" in Fort Yukon.

6. Miraculous Rescues

Mr. Inglis, the purser, welcomed Hannah aboard ship after her long wait at A.C. Point in 1912 by remarking he was glad to see her alive. He was not being facetious. Fatal accidents

Hannah at about seventy years of age in her Oregon garden. She jotted on the back of the snapshot that it was "the last I intend to have taken," and apparently it was. *Hannah Breece collection*

were commonplace in Hannah's Alaska. So were survivors' tales of narrow—seemingly even miraculous—escapes. Hannah gives us two of these from her own experience.

Many people believe we each have a personal guardian angel; it is an appealing idea but, like Hannah, I am more comfortable with mundane explanations. Hannah tried to account for the mysterious stranger who saved her when she broke her leg in Douglas—a stranger nobody else saw—by supposing he must have been in town on business so secret that he succeeded in keeping out of sight. But this is pretty lame and implausible, considering that no ship had arrived that day. In any case on this island, which could be reached only by ship, the arrival, presence or departure of a stranger—and a tall and distinguished-looking stranger at that—could hardly have gone unnoticed.

The business about him pulling out a tremendous gold watch and consulting it does not add a touch of plausibility; on the contrary. The clothing the man would have worn in the dead of winter, bundled up against the cold, would hardly have been an outfit from which one casually extracts a pocket watch and tucks it back. Nor in that time and place did anyone traveling arrange a rendezvous in advance by the persnickety dictates of hours and minutes; he was lucky if he could hold to arrangements setting the day.

Here is my guess. I think Hannah must have rescued herself that night: got through her door, grabbed some blankets and, ordering herself not to faint, fallen into a chair. In her extremity ("Hear what happened to Miss Breece? Froze to death! Right on her own doorstep!") she managed her almost superhuman feat of overcoming pain and panic, I think, by dint of a halucination: a halucination of a good old Pennsylvania authority-figure of the early 1860s, who had a waistcoat pocket holding an imperious gold watch—a watch "tremendous" to the eyes of a small child.

Hannah did not even try to explain the irrational fear that saved her, only just, from being swept under the lake ice at Wood Island. But she gives us the clues. Somebody from the school drew water from the lake for the day's clean-up, and always placed a pole in the hole. Like the dog that did not bark in the night in the Sherlock Holmes story, the significant fact was that a new pole which should have been there was not there.

The pole's absence would have set off alarms in Hannah, even though she failed to realize why in her hurry to make up for her lateness. Hannah was a virtuoso in the use of intuition: observations subtly and swiftly incorporated into judgments without conscious analysis. She was accustomed to trusting her intuitions too. This was one of her ordinary, everyday faculties that made her so splendid a teacher and in this instance must have saved her life.

7. *Who Was Gregory?*

Spruce Island, lying between Kodiak and Afognak, was shaken and inundated with ash during the great volcanic eruption of Katmai in 1912. This would have been an appropriate moment for the promised, portentous opening of the grave of the monk Gregory, whose ascetic way of life and mystifying burial were recounted to Hannah in Afognak and again in Kodiak.

No grave split open, then or since. But what is really surprising is that the Gregory in Hannah's story has now been so thoroughly forgotten as to cast doubt on whether such a person ever existed. The folklore Hannah heard may have elided the story of two different monks—or it may have been a garbled version of the life of a celebrated Spruce Island monk named Herman.

If "Gregory" and Herman were one and the same, then the monk described by Hannah did indeed become a saint. In 1970 Herman was canonized by the Russian Orthodox Church, the first Alaskan saint. Today his bones, brought from Spruce Island, rest in a golden coffin beside the altar in the domed wooden Church of the Holy Resurrection in Kodiak.

Pilgrims, both clergy and others, nowadays come from afar to worship and pray at his crypt, and also at a chapel above his original burial place beside Monks Lagoon set within a thick forest on Spruce Island. The pilgrims take away with them bits of holy earth from beneath the raised floor of the chapel, the earth in which Saint Herman was initially buried. They believe it can work healing miracles.

Saint Herman arrived in Kodiak in 1794 along with nine other monks sent from a monastery in Russian Finland. They were the first Christian missionaries, of any denomination or sect, to go to the American Northwest. They built a church in Kodiak but within five years death had reduced their numbers to four. These came into conflict with the Russian-American Trading Company and its powerful manager, Alexander Baranov, because they protested the brutal treatment of natives by the trading company and decried the licentious lives of Baranov and his associates.

An archbishop from Russia who was to have led the new mission died in a shipwreck off Kodiak, and leadership of the church fell to Herman. With no archbishop to protect the monks or intercede for them, Baranov persecuted them so successfully that, as far as history records, only Herman remained steadfast in support of the natives against Baranov.

Some time between 1808 and 1818, Herman fled to Spruce Island. He called it New Valaam after the monastery that had sent him and his companions to Alaska. On the island he lived in a hole in the ground, probably a barabara, with a deerskin-covered stone bench for a bed and two bricks for his pillow. He wore a smock of deerskin and like "Gregory" encumbered himself with a heavy weight, an iron cross and chain now displayed beside his crypt. He ate almost nothing, and what he ate he grew in a garden or was given by followers who fished. He preserved wild mushrooms for winter, using salt that he made from seawater. He was small but very strong.

So far, Herman and "Gregory" do sound alike. But now the stories diverge. Herman opened an orphanage on Spruce Island for native children. He is said to have been an inspired teacher, and to have made cakes and cookies for the children, a skill he had learned in the Valaam monastery where he had been a baker and had quarried stone. None of this detail, including the important fact of the orphanage, attaches to the "Gregory" story.

Nor does any story of fantastic burial and prophecy attach to Saint Herman. However, a number of stories of sea miracles do. The most important in the eyes of the modern church was his rescue of an archbishop and others in the early nineteenth century by miraculously calming the waters that were about to wreck their ship. He is also said to have halted a tidal wave by planting an icon in the sand at a spot on Spruce Island thereafter known as Icon Bay. He was reputed to heal people.

How Herman's bones were exhumed and protected and the present-day chapel to his memory built on the island brings a much later monk into the history.

In 1916 a twenty-eight-year-old priest, Father Gerasim Schmaltz, came to Alaska from Russia and was assigned as parish priest at Afognak, the successor to Hannah's friend Father Petellin. He intended to return to Russia in a few years but the Russian communist revolution marooned him in Alaska. He remained as priest in Afognak for eighteen years. Cut off from the Russian funds that had generously sustained Father Petellin, he was in effect a pauper-priest. He helped Afognak women and children with their gardening and received food in return. He was very pious but also an exceptionally sweet and merry man, given to singing happy folk melodies and engaging in gentle clowning as he swept up with a broom. His manner was open and childlike and he was loved in Afognak.

While he was serving there, he became attracted to the memory of Herman and decided to devote himself to protecting Herman's bones and memory. In 1935, with no support or approval from Church authorities, he moved to

246 / A Schoolteacher in Old Alaska

Spruce Island as a lone monk. He set about restoring a chapel to Herman that had been built years before over his grave and was falling to ruin. Close by the chapel he built a small cabin for himself, simple but cozy and pretty. His restoration and elaboration of the cruder, earlier chapel is the lovely little shrine that today's pilgrims visit. A few natives from Spruce Island helped Father Gerasim build his cabin and the chapel; to earn money for the building materials, he made embroideries, a skill he had learned as a boy from his mother.

Father Gerasim exhumed Herman's bones from beneath the chapel, washed them, and placed them as relics in the chapel, where they remained until Saint Herman was canonized and they were moved to the golden coffin in Kodiak.

An archivist of Russian-American manuscripts in the Library of Congress, Michael E. Vinokouroff, was another who revered Herman's memory. In Washington he heard rumors that "a fanatic hermit" on Spruce Island was doing "unlawful" things with Herman's bones. He was furious. He joined a delegation commissioned to collect archival material from old Alaskan Russian churches and chapels, with the primary object of getting to Spruce Island and putting a stop to whatever was going on there. But upon meeting Father Gerasim his anger immediately dissipated. He was awed by the monk's devotion and his way of life. The two became fast friends and kept up a correspondence in their joint efforts to promote Herman's memory and see to it that his relics and burial site were protected.

Father Gerasim could have done with some friends. Church authorities repeatedly tried to drive him off the island. When this did not succeed they attempted to squeeze him out by settling rival monks there. During World War II rumors circulated that he was really Rasputin, the Russian monk who attached himself to the Czar's court and was murdered in

1916; the rumors were picked up and widely published in America. According to one account he had to prove to the U.S. military that he was not Rasputin. The rumors were given plausibility by the circumstance that Father Gerasim had arrived in Alaska the same year Rasputin was murdered, and by the fact that photographs of the two men superficially resembled each other, thanks to their beards and black gowns, and the fact that Father Gerasim's photograph had been taken later, so the discrepancy in their ages (Rasputin was older) was not evident. The rumor was traced to an erstwhile friend of Father Gerasim's in Kodiak, a bon vivant who had mischievously concocted the tale from thin air to create a sensation.

In his last few years Father Gerasim became a parish priest once again, this time in the village of Ouzinkie on the opposite side of Spruce Island. One of his chief endeavors there was adamantly to oppose drunkenness and importation of alcohol. He died in the Kodiak hospital in 1965 at the age of seventy-seven and was taken back to Monks Lagoon for burial in a funeral procession led by a bishop. He missed witnessing Saint Herman's canonization rites in Kodiak by only five years.

Now to get back to "Gregory." A chief discrepancy between the story of Saint Herman and the story Hannah heard was the dates of their deaths. Saint Herman died in December 1836. That was only seventy years before Hannah heard the story of Gregory from the old woman in Kodiak, said to be the last person alive who had heard the monk's story from his followers. But the old lady would have been a grown woman at the time of Herman's death, and many other people, in 1906, could have heard of Herman's life from his followers. Furthermore, those who had been told the Gregory story thought his hundred-year-old grave was due to open soon. Gregory, if he existed at all, must have died twenty-five years or so before Herman, perhaps a little more.

Puzzling with me about this, the Reverend Fr. Peter Kreta of the Church of the Holy Resurrection in Kodiak mentioned that Father Gerasim discovered the grave of another early monk whose name and history were undocumented and whose bones still remain on Spruce Island. We can speculate that perhaps another monk fled to the island before Herman, or accompanied Herman or else joined him there later and soon died.

Father Peter added that perhaps still other monks may be buried on the island because comings and goings went unrecorded in the dim early days of a religious presence there. Indeed, from the evidence of an old icon, there is some reason to suppose the island for a time had some ongoing connection with the Monastery of Mount Athos in Greece.

If a Spruce Island monk named Gregory did exist, his memory was preserved only in the folklore accounts that Hannah heard. And these accounts themselves now are forgotten, except in Hannah's retelling of them.

Bishop Innocent, who to Hannah's disappointment did not pooh-pooh the story of "Gregory" and his putative saintliness, is himself all but forgotten now. To establish that he really existed, the clergy in Kodiak had to look him up in ecclesiastical records; they assumed at first that I must have confused a bishop Hannah met with an earlier and much celebrated Bishop Innocent who left Sitka in 1850 to become Archbishop of Siberia and later the Metropolitan of Moscow, the highest dignitary of the Church, and was canonized in Russia as Saint Innocent, Apostle to Alaska.

The Bishop's House in Sitka, where both Bishops Innocent dwelled in their time, has been made into a museum and memorial to the canonized Innocent and is under the care of the U.S. National Park Service. Nothing is known at the museum of the fate of the Bishop Innocent Hannah knew, nor do church records in Alaska say a word about him after 1909, when he was recalled to Russia.

As Hannah described him—a man with an open, childlike enjoyment of Christmas gift dolls, lighthearted under the gaze of his glowering entourage—he sounds a little bit like Father Gerasim. The curt word-of-mouth report that Hannah picked up in Sitka in 1914, "He is in Tibet," seems to be the last that was known of him, at least in Alaska. Hannah's report of that comment may thus be the only record regarding his later history, unless it is preserved in archives in Russia.

———◦———

Epilogue

Future-gazing—a comparison of how things will be with how they are—is no more to be relied upon than Sheldon Jackson's plans for the reindeer express. A memoir is a different sort of time machine. By transporting us into the past, it makes possible comparisons with the present. Using Hannah's memoir in this way, we can get some idea of how the settlements where she taught have changed, starting with Fort Yukon above the Arctic Circle and working back to her first post, Afognak, far to the south.

1

In Hannah's time, Fort Yukon had hardly any government presence. Now it has been taken to the opposite extreme. Although it has a population of only 220 people, including sixty schoolchildren, and a very scantily populated hinterland, it boasts a city hall, a native village office, a state building, a federal post office, a branch of the University of Alaska, a clinic and health center, a fire station, a public works maintenance yard, a youth and community center, a library and radio station, a center for the elderly, a district school administration building, an elementary school and gymnasium, a high school, a reconstruction of the old Hudson's Bay Company Fort, and an airfield for passengers and freight.

The old native village that Hannah knew has moved itself a mile downstream to mingle among this loosely assembled plenitude of institutions. Indeed, apart from the institutions, the transplanted Indian village is about all that remains of Fort Yukon. The Episcopal mission is long gone, its only trace a foundation hole littered with the twisted and rusted debris of a fire in an otherwise empty field. The once powerful fur trading establishments have vanished except for the Alaska Commercial Company, which has turned into a supermarket with nothing to buy and sell but the same detergents, cereals, crackers, cucumbers, hamburger, chicken pieces, olives, margarine, candy bars and so on, in the same shelving and display cases to be found in any American supermarket. What appears to be the only visible remnant of the wild old days is a battered and somnolent café with a few rooms above.

The only tangible reminders of Archdeacon Stuck and Dr. Burke are their graves, side by side, marked with a large stone cross and two plaques in a small, well-kept cemetery in a pretty little grove near the old mission foundation hole. The Episcopal church, embellished with splendid beaded altar cloths, does not figure prominently any longer in the life of the town and has often had periods when it lacked a clergyman. A newer, modest evangelical church is more successful.

Although Fort Yukon is the only intermediate stop on daily passenger flights between Fairbanks and Nome, it is no magnet. "Why do you want to go to Fort Yukon? There's nothing there."

Nothing is there at Hannah's old school site in the former location of the Indian village, where the river steamers used to stop and the dogs clamor for galley scraps. The Yukon River steamers themselves have vanished; so have the sled dogs from the center of town except for a single menacing malamute chained to his heavy doghouse.

In Hannah's time, during summer people turned the clock around, making day from the hours of the night and vice-versa. We were told in Anchorage that this was no longer the custom because government workers have to keep conventional hours and so other people have conformed too. Nevertheless, the old custom does partially prevail and for good reason: evening and night breezes suppress the mosquitoes, and feel too fresh and pleasant to miss by going to bed early for no reason. Except for a few holed-up government workers, Fort Yukon slumbers all morning in summer, the windows of its snug log houses curtained and the doors closed.

The first inhabitants to emerge, about noon, are little boys on bicycles. Gradually, as the afternoon wears on, customers appear in the supermarket, somebody gets out an all-terrain vehicle, and children and teenagers pile on. The town taxi driver, who comes from Montreal—his wife is a native of Fort Yukon—is finally ready for business. When the morning plane came in, it was the middle of the night for him.

There isn't much to do in Fort Yukon. If one isn't a government worker, almost the only jobs are fighting forest fires during the short summers. Men recruited in Fort Yukon are flown throughout the state as needed.

But people in Fort Yukon are not poverty-stricken. Like each Alaskan citizen—man, woman or child—each gets a dividend as a personal, no-strings-attached share of the state's oil royalties. The amount varies, depending on oil prices and volume sold, but averages about a thousand dollars annually per person, bringing some $220,000 into the community for discretionary spending. Many households share in profits from investments by the native regional corporation set up when native land claims were settled in 1971. And of course there are funds for special purposes and needs, such as higher-education scholarships, old-age pensions, subsidized home mortgages, disability payments, welfare disbursements, and so on. People are well dressed and still display the panache and the sense of style and becomingness that Hannah admired. Houses look comfortable, and the tradition of having a nice rug on the floor lives on.

Still, there isn't much to do. One of the last of the old-time trappers, now retired at seventy-four years of age, is Fred Thomas, the community's oldest resident. The young men, he says, envy what they suppose was a thrilling life out on the traplines and like him to talk about it but can have no understanding of how hard that life was. "They think life is dreary now, but they couldn't survive in the bush."

Mention old schools, and everyone is eager to tell that the old Indian schoolhouse (a successor to Hannah's building) burned down. The teacher did it, say some. No, pupils did it, say others. In any event, the interesting arson occurred before anyone now alive can remember.

The brick-colored elementary school building would delight Hannah: solid, ample and well windowed, a suburban-looking school. But it would dismay her too. It reveals no outward evidence of student life, is surrounded by a high chain-link fence and is locked in summer.

If and when overnight tourists come, they are apt to stay in a simple but adequate lodge with a rudimentary restaurant and dance floor, run by a local family at the edge of town. If they are lucky in the day they hit town, and well heeled, they may get a tour led by the director of the radio station, a serious local historian. His wife, who arranges the tours and sometimes substitutes for him, is a daughter of the family that runs the lodge. She speaks in a knowledgeable-sounding way about grants in the offing . . . famous names . . . symposia . . . international conferences . . .

Fort Yukon is like a big backstage where one impresario

after another has lugged in scenery and props; but the program doesn't begin. In the meantime, Fort Yukon gets along, sort of.

The administrative district of which Fort Yukon is the center is called Yukon Flats, and flat it is. The river is surprisingly ill-defined, appearing in summer to be spread water rather than running water. As is not surprising, the two physical glories of the place are the same as in Hannah's day: the many-colored and voluptuously textured wild grasses underfoot, and the infinitely huge sky overhead.

2

The people of Nondalton and Iliamna who Hannah knew as Kenai now prefer to be called Dena'ina.* The village of Nondalton that Hannah visited on the important religious day each summer moved about three miles from that site in the mid-1940s, taking up a new location on the shore of the small lake between large Lake Clark and the Newhalen River. All that remains of the village Hannah saw are cemetery crosses and the log walls of one house. Elsewhere in the United States— or indeed in most places of the world—when a settlement becomes a ghost town usually some ruins advertise its former presence for a considerable time, and often a last few residents hang on indefinitely. But in Alaska, when a native village site is abandoned, everybody leaves and takes along everything of value which usually includes the logs and beams of their buildings.

Villages evanesce in this way for a variety of reasons, among them epidemics, and a desire of the villagers simply to improve their quality of life. The Nondalton Hannah knew in 1910–11 was a new village, although she did not realize that,

*Pronounced De-NAH-ee-NAH, said rapidly.

probably because the building materials were not new. It had moved from Kijik, some twenty miles to the north at the mid-point on the length of Lake Clark, the ancestral home of the Nondalton people and the place where Zackar was born.

The village at Kijik had been the largest Dena'ina settle-ment of the mid-nineteenth century, but in 1902 and 1903 it was devastated by measles and influenza epidemics, which was the reason it moved. The reason for the mid-1940s move was that more than thirty years of occupation had taken the shine off the place, and silt deposits were making access to boats dif-ficult. People wanted a clean slate.

After about fifty years' occupation this time, Nondalton seems to be satisfied with its village, which incorporates mod-ern improvements and is on native village corporation lands, protected from outside encroachment. The village church now has its own resident Russian Orthodox priest who is him-self a Nondalton native, vindicating Zackar's determination to maintain the institution against all odds.

Instead of going to the transplanted village, we followed Hannah's footsteps by going to the fishing camp. Offhand, this would seem to be the most fragile of the native settlements she knew, but it has been the most enduring. Not only has it stayed put, its summer meadows are still dotted with wooden racks festooned with vivid pink-orange fillets of drying salmon.

Only nine families use the camp now, and only to fish for their own use, not to produce great bundles for trade. But Zackar's great-great-great-great-grandchildren play about in boats and watch their mothers deftly gutting and filleting big silver fish moments after they are pulled from the water by Zackar's handsome great-great-great-grandsons; Zackar was their mother, Martha's, grandmother's grandfather.

The camp is an almost magical place. One understands after only a few hours at this lovely, breeze-swept waterside why Hannah felt smothered by her house when she returned from the camp. Part of the magic is the general air of exuberance and purpose that pervades the doings and the people here, from the oldest to the youngest in the three generations present. Simple summer houses, interspersed with canvas shelters, have radios, electric lights and propane stoves but no plumbing, and one catches a glimpse of how the old life was arranged, with a stove and table at one end of a main room, sleeping and sitting benches at the other, and shelves and clothing hung on the walls.

Zackar's great-great-granddaughter, Martha Trefon, is married to the present Nondalton chief, Bill Trefon. He was away from the camp at a meeting. His wife says the job of chief has changed since Zackar's day. "Then the chief was always talking with the people and doing everything along with them. Now a chief is so busy with papers, and he doesn't have so much time for people. Lots and lots of paperwork and politics, and he goes to so many meetings." The paperwork, she said, is about "hunting rights, fishing rights, health, native courts, all that kind of thing."

The only dogs in the fishing camp are terrier-like pet mongrels frisking with the children. Martha Trefon calls them "No good for anything; noisemakers." But in the village, people still breed Nondalton's strain of fierce malamutes and these Martha respects. "If your snowmobile breaks down or runs out of gas you're in big trouble. With a dogsled you could always get home." Even though the malamutes are now little used for work in comparison with machines, one gets an impression that the continued attachment to them represents a cherished link to the past and, like the ancestral land itself, contributes to the people of Nondalton's obviously proud sense of their identity.

The fishing camp lies just within the Lake Clark preserve, which adjoins Lake Clark National Park, established in December 1, 1978, by President Carter. The two together—park and preserve—encompass four million majestic acres containing black bears and grizzlies, wild mountain sheep, wolves, coyotes, red foxes, lynx, wolverines, martens, mink, ermine, weasels, marmots, beavers, river otters, moose, almost two hundred species of waterfowl and other birds, five species of salmon and five other kinds of edible fish. It is also part of the range of one of Alaska's fastest growing caribou herds, which increased from 2,600 animals in the early 1960s to more than 180,000 by the fall of 1994.

Hannah is remembered in Nondalton, but only as a disembodied name, Miss Breece—remembered because she was the first teacher to come.

3

Iliamna village has vanished, leaving only a grassy clearing with traces of old cabin foundations and cellar holes: another instance of relocation, this time because the portage from the head of Iliamna Bay was partially realigned and extended to a new terminus at Pile Bay on Lake Iliamna. The portage is a few miles longer than before but easier, and the lake terminus accommodates larger vessels than the old village, which was upstream from the lake.

The extended portage has been furnished with a narrow gravel road over which, in season, it is possible to haul fishing boats, tanks of propane, construction materials and other heavy freight on flatbed trailer trucks. With its warehouses, storage yards and docks, Pile Bay is a depot for the Iliamna-Lake Clark region and even, to some extent, for Bristol Bay.

About twenty-five miles to its west a gravel runway capable of serving jet planes has been constructed. This is the major commercial air hub of the region. The small settlement at this facility now bears the name of Iliamna.

However, in spite of its name, this is not the successor village to old Iliamna, nor is Pile Bay its successor. At the time the old village was abandoned in the 1930s, most families chose to move to Pedro Bay, a lake shore of many inlets protected by islands, some seven miles west of Pile Bay. The village houses are loosely scattered among the inlets, all but out of sight of one another, and the winter population of sixty people is only about half as large as old Iliamna village's population in Hannah's time. The population is still gradually declining as people filter out to live and work elsewhere. Those who remain in Pedro Bay earn their livings doing depot work, guiding wilderness visitors, hunting and fishing for their own needs and fishing commercially.

Some who have left come back in summer, like Annie and Walter Johnson, who we visited. Home base for the Johnsons is the town of Homer on the Kenai peninsula, where Mr. Johnson is a clergyman. Their Pedro Bay great-grandchildren join them in their summer home.

Annie Johnson is one of two Iliamna women who have fragmentary, secondhand memories of Hannah, passed down to them by their mothers. Annie's mother's report was not a happy one. When she was a young married woman Miss Breece invited her to school, she told her daughter, but she was so dismayed to find that only English was spoken that she refused to return. The other reported memory is more cheerful: Rose Hedland, who we did not meet—she now lives in the air-runway settlement farther down the lake—was told by her mother that Miss Breece gave her a porcelain doll.

Iliamna was the village where women looked so aged compared with an outsider like Hannah. But neither in Pedro Bay nor in other settlements I saw did this seem any longer to be true. For instance, Annie Johnson and I were the same age, seventy-eight, at the time of my visit. But she was the one who looked younger, as well as being more agile.

Like most places in Alaska, Pedro Bay get most supplies by air. Any bit of water—a harbor, a pond, a gentle bit of lake, a quiet reach in a river—is a ready-made airport for little planes fitted with floats. Any level stretch of snow is a landing spot for planes fitted with skies. Next to the big airport in Anchorage for national and international flights are other fields, stretching mile after mile, containing thousands of the small planes that penetrate everywhere.

From Port Alsworth on Lake Clark we had taken a float plane to Pedro Bay, landing at the Johnsons' doorstep, and then flew over the portage that Hannah traveled by foot and horseback. The tiny plane maneuvered along a crooked air-path between awesome mountain peaks and glaciers to both sides of us. The ground down below was so rugged and jumbled it looked impossible to negotiate. Innumerable rivulets tumbled in little cascades and gorges from the melting glaciers. Somewhere down there was the narrow present-day gravel road, but its presence was hard to discern on the chaotic ground except in one or two spots. Shortly before we reached the ocean-bay end of the portage we had to abandon our sight of the ground trail: too turbulent now to be safe, down between the mountains, the pilot said. One of the great windpaths from the Pacific to Lake Iliamna was defeating us.

The old A.C. Point on Iliamna Bay in Cook Inlet is an empty shore with nothing to mark its significance when it was the rendezvous point with steamers for travelers like Hannah from Iliamna and a wide hinterland beyond.

4

Woody Island (which Hannah knew as Wood Island) is a mere twenty-minute run by motorboat from the town of Kodiak. It is still "beautiful beyond compare," with its sweeping wildflower meadows and moss-upholstered, parklike ancient spruce forests, as awesome, magical and rain-dripping as Hannah said. But the lakes she described were altered by shifts in ground levels caused by the terrible 1964 earthquake.

Some of the old green-and-cream Baptist mission buildings remain, still prettily reflected in water, but the mission itself moved into Kodiak after the earthquake, dropped its school and orphanage, and converted into a facility for juveniles in trouble with their families or the law; increasingly it has concentrated on working with troubled families. The village and its gardens that Hannah knew have vanished too, along with the mission.

During World War II the army established a signal corps station in a clearing at the highest point. Surrounded by forest, the now-abandoned station is visible only from the air. A few of the men attached to the station fell in love with this rain-drenched isle, and they and their families built houses and set about raising cattle, enterprises that failed. Nobody now lives here in winter. Among the few summer residents is Yule Chaffin, the eighty-year-old widow of one of the former signal corps men; they raised their family here. She is a passionate lover of the island, a gifted photographer, and the author of a book on the Kodiak archipelago and its people. The very few visitors to the island nowadays tend to be admirers seeking her out.

Woody Island comes alive with children again only during twenty-one days in the summer when the Kodiak Baptist Church borrows the remaining mission buildings for a boys' and girls' camp. Then the pastimes in which Hannah's pupils delighted—beachcombing, nature study, exploring the tide pools, fishing—also come alive, for these are the same activities the camp emphasizes.

In Hannah's time, Alaska was a great place for building air castles and even Woody Island was not immune to this form of future-gazing fantasy. After the island was connected to the outside world by wireless in 1911, apparently anything seemed possible and mission people seriously expected that Woody Island was destined to be the commercial center of all central Alaska. In anticipation, a 1912 publication of the Women's American Baptist Home Mission Society, after declaring the island was the logical focus for "regions rich in mines and agricultural prospects," said that therefore the question facing the society was "Shall the commercial center of Alaska be a Christian center?"

Woody Island is today emptier of inhabitants than at any time, probably, since ancient wanderers from Asia first discovered it and fished its waters. In spite of its enduring beauty, the island might sadden Hannah now. She would find it so lonely.

5

Afognak was demolished by the tidal wave that accompanied the earthquake of 1964, but people in both its Russian and native sections had sufficient warning to race to the hills ahead of the water. One person only, a man out in a boat, was killed. In the quake, the bluff on which the schoolhouse and Mrs. Pajoman's cottage had stood shrank to an unremarkable knoll.

The full brunt of the wave hit Afognak because its approaches were unprotected by other islands. Furthermore, since it lacked even a decent bay or harbor, it was a precarious anchorage at any time. The villagers decided to abandon this impractical site in favor of a more protected place on an uninhabited part of larger Kodiak Island. They named the new village Port Lions in gratitude to the Lions Club for disaster aid and help in financing the move.

Superficially Port Lions resembles old Afognak because most of the buildings are scattered about on slopes. However, even the humblest of the houses has basic modern utilities and conveniences and the usual amenities, and all give the appearance of being cherished. Sergai Sheratine, the elderly great-nephew of Tichon Sheratine, Afognak's church reader in Hannah's time, compares his store-bought wall finish with can labels and newspapering and jokes, "It used to be like living in a library. You could read the walls."

The buff-colored one-story school building, set as before at a little distance from the village, would please Hannah not only with its spaciousness and light, but because the tradition of the school garden lives on in a homemade looking green-house on the open, unfenced grounds. The north wall of the greenhouse is covered with an ecology mural showing land and sea creatures and plants, painted by the children.

As before, many houses have their holy corners with lamps and religious pictures. As before, the cemetery is a fenced lit-tle thicket of wooden Russian crosses, but it is a bit harder to keep in order because bears, bumbling about, knock the crosses awry. Kodiak Island has about three thousand of the huge brown grizzlies—the largest land predators on earth perhaps more than in Hannah's time because they are better protected. Bears and human beings coexist warily and re-spectfully but, by all accounts, safely. Instructions, if one meets a bear, are absolutely not to run, look off at the distance instead of at the bear, slowly back up or move away sidewise, and the bear will go away; so they say.

The community still welcomes outside residents who

marry into it, but nowadays these include wives from outside as well as husbands. The few general stores have failed, but a former mayor of the village and his wife, who is from Idaho, now plan to open a supermarket.

The biggest single change is the neat little anchorage with breakwaters, walks and lighting, home port to a dozen or so modern fishing vessels. The fishermen talk exactly like Canadian grain farmers who have made large outlays on farm machinery. They worry about getting enough yield to cover their high capital costs.

No road links Port Lions with the town of Kodiak. People depend on boats, or if need be upon air-taxis based in the town of Kodiak. But the strongest links between the two places are those of blood.

For a generation before the quake and tidal wave, starting at the time of World War II and the boom it brought to Kodiak's economy, people had been leaking out of Afognak and into Kodiak. When Port Lions was built, many entire families chose to relocate to Kodiak instead, so today descendants of the old Afognak population are about evenly divided between the two places.

Kodiak (the town) has been a major asset for Afognak people. It affords a feasible avenue for them into a larger economy and also a feasible avenue back. The pilot of the air-taxi we used, Willie Hall, is a grandchild of Afognak. When he finished high school he became a truck driver. One day on the road in Oregon, homesick for his Alaskan archipelago, he decided he could as well drive a plane as a truck. He tethers his float-plane sometimes in the Kodiak harbor, sometimes among water lilies in a small landing-lake at the edge of his pleasant Kodiak garden. His wife, working from their home, is his dispatcher, a common arrangement for pilots of small planes.

In Hannah's time, although Kodiak had only about four hundred residents, all of whom knew each other, she thought of it as something of a metropolis, a center of things. Today, with a population of 7,600, everybody somehow still seems to know everybody and it still carries the air of being a cosmopolitan little metropolis, a center of things.

One thing of which it is the center is the Alutiiq movement, named for the old Aleut language. The movement fosters Aleut rituals, history, music, crafts and knowledge of the language. Descendants of old Afognak are prominent in the movement. Among the costumed children we watched performing dances inside a modified reproduction of an ancient, sod-covered underground community room were descendants of Afognak. The next day they were off to perform in St. Petersburg, Russia.

Their teacher of Alutiiq has made the same discovery as Hannah: Children learn a new vocabulary most rapidly from songs. Language classes are part of the program at the unpretentious new Alutiiq cultural center and museum in the center of town. One of its workers is Mary Patterson, who comes from Georgia and married into Kodiak. She explained that the museum had been financed by a fragment of the compensation paid by Exxon for the Valdez oil spill, which jeopardized marine resources on which Port Lions and Kodiak fishermen depend.

However, the main impetus behind the center and museum derives indirectly from the state's 1971 native claims settlement, which allocated forty million acres (approximately 11 percent of Alaska's area) to native ownership and paid $962,500,000 as compensation for other lands. Two sorts of organizations—twelve regional corporations and two hundred native village corporations—were chartered by the state to invest the money and make decisions concerning uses of communal lands as well as to direct various other communal affairs.

The organization governing uses of Afognak Island, which belongs to descendants of its former inhabitants, was riven for seven years with paralyzing policy disputes and legal suits that nobody wants to talk about now that bitter feelings have been mended. At bottom, the conflicts centered on the rival merits of conservation versus exploitation. Both sides of the controversy are now having their innings on Afognak Island. Forests are rapidly being clearcut for quick timber profits, to the quiet outrage of conservationists. But the faction that wanted to protect the island has managed to establish appreciable reserves furnished with all-year-round cabins and a few small lodges for visiting wilderness lovers, photographers, elk hunters, fishermen, hikers, snowshoers and archaeology buffs. The Alutiiq center's archaeological scholar supervises digs at pre-Russian settlements and camps, of which it is believed there may be hundreds extending back at least six thousand years. Paying visitors, put up in tents at whatever dig is underway, participate in the excavations and laboratory work and attend lectures. Whatever is found goes to the Alutiiq museum.

The oldest building in Kodiak, indeed the oldest existing Russian building on North America's west coast, was built by Alexander Baranov in 1808. Under its white clapboard siding, its walls are of massive logs. Hannah stayed there as a house guest when it was the home of the manager of the Alaska Commercial Company. By the 1950s it had fallen on hard times as a boarding house. It had survived three days of heavy ash fall from the 1912 Katmai volcanic eruption and then the earthquake and tidal wave of 1964, which destroyed much else in downtown Kodiak, but it almost fell to urban renewers in the 1960s, who decreed it an eyesore. Protests by townspeople saved it by a hair.

Now it is the Kodiak Historical Society's charming Baranov Museum, owned by the town and leased to the society. Hannah must often have sat in a parlor beside the front door in what is now the museum's library, glancing out at the same view across the veranda and lawn to the harbor. The iron bust of Czar Alexander I, which Hannah's host mistook for Peter the Great when it crowned the steep front gable of the house, is displayed indoors a few steps from the library.

A daughter of Afognak, the late Eunice von Scheele Neseth, whose mother was an Aleut from Afognak's native village and whose father was a Swedish immigrant who kept a store in Afognak, was the practical visionary who established the historical society, the first curator of its collections and the moving spirit in saving the grand old house and converting it to a museum. Mrs. Neseth also revived the almost lost art of Aleut grass-woven basketry.

Hannah appreciated the ingenuity with which Alaskans used what they had. An ingenuity that has surfaced since her time is "raw Alaskan fireweed honey," in answer to Alaska's lack of honeybees. People steep fireweed blossoms, heavy with nectar and pollen, in a syrup of sugar, water and alum. Some add clover blossoms. The decoction carries a honey bouquet and the slightly waxy texture of strained honey.

The old A.C. Point, so totally empty of human life now, has in a sense been transplanted to many places, one of which is in Kodiak. Men who once waited for the *Dora* or *Bertha* recur as types Hannah would recognize. There they are, at six-thirty of a summer morning in the hotel restaurant overlooking the harbor—geologists, zoologists, engineers, explorers, adventurers, in no-nonsense outdoor clothing—waiting for their float-plane or boat transportation while they plan their day or week over huge breakfasts of ham and pancakes. There is even a faint reminder of the Reindeer Man on the menu: reindeer sausages, something for tourists to try.

Descendants of the Afognak people Hannah taught have strong opinions about the educational policy of her time and later. They are outraged, and in retrospect incredulous, that English was the only school language allowed. After a glorious Saturday evening service at the Kodiak Russian church, a group of middle-aged and elderly women chatting in the vestibule bring up the subject of segregated schools for whites and natives maintained from Washington between 1912, when Alaska became a territory, and 1958, when it became a state. These women had themselves been segregated as children, some in white and some in native schools; which children were which depended on the provenance of their fathers, who themselves were sometimes mixed. "Wasn't it crazy!" "Why did they do such a thing?" "We had no say at all!"

6

Whether in cities, towns or villages, when people are asked about social problems, they still identify alcohol, Hannah's "curse of the north," as the worst. It seems too that every city, town and village is combating it—with temperance societies, counseling, education, religious sanctions, chapters of Alcoholics Anonymous. Posters and signs exhorting avoidance of alcohol and illegal drugs abound in youth centers and schools. Anchorage, where half the state's population of 570,000 lives, and much more than half the state's population of cars is to be found, is fierce in the battle against drunk driving. Not only does punishment entail long suspensions or permanent revoking of drivers' licenses, but under a municipal ordinance the cars of repeat offenders are confiscated without compensation and sold by the municipality.

All this is rather surprising to a visitor because one sees virtually no evidence of overt drunkenness anywhere. Apparently most excessive drinking takes place at home or in private gatherings rather than in streets, parks or taverns. When Hannah was combating the secretive consumption of alcohol in Iliamna, she associated addiction with poverty and the anxiety and stress of famine. But it seems that economic conditions have little or nothing to do with it. As a man in Fort Yukon remarked, "They used to think people took to drink because they were poor. Now they say it's because they're rich." In Fort Yukon one is tempted to assume that lack of work abets the "curse of the north" but that is equally facile.

Other things do change, and radically. Archdeacon Stuck had good reason to fear that Indians were imperiled by extinction, and Sheldon Jackson to suppose that Eskimos were. But today the state's numbers of native residents (classified as Aleut, Eskimo and Indian) are increasing. In the decade between 1980 and 1990, the increase was from 64,103 to 85,698.

As elsewhere in America opportunities for women in Alaska have increased, how much depending of course on where they happen to live. Poor Mrs. Pajoman! She had been the very first Aleut to become an American government schoolteacher, although Hannah did not know that; the fact was pinned down recently by a scholar at the University of Alaska in Fairbanks. In 1911, after Hannah was no longer in Afognak but still in correspondence with Mrs. Pajoman, she was appointed postmistress there. Four years later, at the age of forty-seven, she suddenly died of a massive heart attack while she was working at her desk on postal business. She left an eight-year-old son. His father, the pleasant-spoken "ogre," journeyed to his native Estonia, remarried there, returned to Afognak and became rich as a fox farmer and cannery owner on nearby islands. He and his wife retired to Estonia in 1936, and according to his son he died in 1944 from heart failure while he was picking a pear in his garden. After his father's retirement, the son took over his father's holdings and lives in Kodiak.

Mrs. Pajoman had scant enthusiasm for schoolteaching, and probably little for postal work. But how she would have reveled in a musical career! In modern Kodiak she would almost surely be appreciated for talents she had such pitifully little opportunity to use and develop in the time, place and choices given her.

There is no way to assess whether people were happier in communities Hannah knew than their descendants are today. Even those descendants cannot make the judgment since they themselves did not experience the old life. However, the elderly people with whom I talked, those who were closest to it in experience and handed-down memories, were unanimous in thinking that life had become not only easier but richer in the intangibles it offers as well as in material things. Hannah had it right, it seems, when she said, "It was foolish not to take advantage of opportunities that could be useful in life," and that after pupils had been awakened "the inherent energies of their own minds could carry along their development." The bit part she hoped she contributed would seem to have been justified. What more could a pioneering teacher ask?

NOTES AND CITATIONS
◄◦►

(sequence follows texts)

FOREWORD NOTES

Hannah's birthdate was July 22, 1859; she died April 22, 1940, and is buried in Old Rosemont Cemetery, Bloomsburg, Pennsylvania.

The name Breece is Scottish, a variant of "Bruce."

"Kenai" as an ethnic designation is now obsolete, replaced by "Dena'ina" for Indians of south-central Alaska. "Athabaskan" and "Indian" remain in use. So does "Eskimo"; the designation "Inuit," which has become standard in Canada, is known in Alaska but has not caught on either among Eskimos themselves or others. The Eskimos Hannah knew are a Pacific coastal branch, "Yupik." To avoid anachronism, I have retained the vocabulary of Hannah's time not only in her memoir but in some other contexts.

Hannah's salary figures are spotty because the Civil Reference Branch of the National Archives was unable to find her in the personnel records of the U.S. Official Register except for the years 1903 and 1911. I have used the 1903 figure for her 1904 salary (when she switched to Alaska from the Indian service, which were both in the Department of the Interior), in the absence of any evidence that it changed. The figure for 1909 is from a telegram in Anchorage archives offering her the Iliamna post. Alaskan teachers' average salaries for 1993–94 are from the Department of Education, State of Alaska, Juneau. The 1993–94 data also note that the average number of pupils per classroom teacher is now 15.4.

"America the Beautiful" is by Katherine Lee Bates, a professor of English at Wellesley College, who wrote the song in 1895 and revised it in 1904. She thus shared Hannah's period of American history as well as her sensibility. Hannah combined the first four lines of the last (fourth) verse with the last four lines of the second verse, and this version (the one I heard Hannah sing) is reproduced here.

One of many who urged Hannah to write her memoir, and publishers to publish it, was Ray M. Cole, superintendent of Columbia County Public Schools in Pennsylvania, who said her lectures, which he had heard, held the interest of both teachers and children and that a book could give readers "an opportunity to sit with a great teacher." Letter in custody of editor.

MEMOIR NOTES

Chapter 1: Prelude to My Assignment
Jackson had a new concrete octagonal museum built from funds he raised privately, and according to Jackson's biographer this had been accomplished by the time of Hannah's first visit to Sitka. But Hannah was precise and accurate about buildings she visited; perhaps the collections she saw had not yet been removed from the "old Russian building."

Chapter 2: Welcome to Afognak
The *Dora* had thirteen staterooms on its lower deck, and thirty-one steerage bunks in the hold. Much of its cargo was carried on its upper deck.

John G. Brady was Alaska's governor from 1897 to 1906.

Chapter 3: Organizing the School
Aleuts and Eskimos are biologically and linguistically related; their divergence into two groups from a common ancestry is now thought to have occurred between four thousand and eight thousand years ago. Archaeological evidence of Eskimo cultures on Kodiak Island much predates evidence of Eskimos in Siberia, the Bering Sea area, Canada and Greenland, leading to speculation that Kodiak was

the Eskimo cradle. *Who Are the Native People of Kodiak Island?;* Kodiak, Alutiiq Studies, Kodiak Area Native Association, 1992.

Chapter 4: The Sunday School Crisis
Bishop Innocent had less authority than his title would seem to imply. In 1903 he had been appointed a suffragan bishop (deputy of a superior in Russia). At the time of his Afognak visit he was a vicar bishop whose see was not administratively independent. For example, he could participate in the ordination of priests but could not appoint priests to parishes; he probably had little, if any, say in the selection of the entourage that Hannah observed. Prior to becoming a bishop he had taught in the Russian seminary in Sitka. His duties seem to have been in part diplomatic. He met with President Theodore Roosevelt, Sheldon Jackson and other Alaskan and U.S. educators, and with officials of Russia's embassy in Washington.

Chapter 7: Kodiak, Wood Island and Seward
The bust on the old mansion roof ridge was not of Peter the Great but of Alexander I, czar from 1801 to 1825. When Hannah was a guest at the mansion it was owned by the Alaska Commercial Company. Subsequently the Kodiak holdings of that company were bought by a merchant named Erskine and the building became known as Erskine House. It is now the Baranov Museum. It was built about 1808 and used for fur storage before the much larger storage building Hannah saw was erected. The large building, close to the water edge, was removed early this century to make more wharf room. It was taken apart log by log, like a toy "Lincoln Log" house at huge scale, and the long logs then sawed into shorter lengths. Where they went I have been unable to learn.

Six of the elegant Seward houses of "Swell Head Row" still exist, still privately owned and occupied, but now are referred to more politely as "Millionaires' Row."

Chapter 8: Wild-goose Chase into the Interior
The rendezvous spot in Cook Inlet was called A.C. Point because the Alaska Commercial Company formerly had an establishment

there. It also bore a nickname, Camp Patience, for obvious reasons. The "surprisingly large building" on the Point was built by either the Trans-Alaska Company, established in San Francisco about 1900 to build a horse-drawn winter sled route from Iliamna Bay to Norton Sound on the Bering Sea, or by the Alaska Short Line Railway & Navigation Company, which in 1903 planned to build a four-hundred-mile railroad from the bay to Anvik on the Yukon River. Both companies were short-lived.

Chapter 9: Life on Wood Island
Hannah's leave-taking of Wood Island in the summer of 1909 was noted by Mrs. James McWhinnie, a visitor from Cambridge, Massachusetts, in *Tidings,* the mission's newsletter: "We were glad to meet Miss Hannah Breece, the government teacher, who has in so many ways shown her interest and love for the Mission. The old school-room had been made attractive by her skill and taste. The white table covers (used only on special occasions) and the everyday red ones and the fresh paint on Orphanage and church were all gifts from Miss Breece. In vain we urged her to remain, but duty called her to a hard Mission field in Iliamna and sorrowfully we bade her good-bye and God speed."

"Bull" was unseemly, verging upon the obscene (particularly if spoken or written by a woman) in America in Hannah's time. Hence her circumlocutions in identifying the fearsome imported animal.

At the time of the editors' and publishers' rail excursion in 1909, about fifty miles of track had been completed. The population of Seward, according to the 1910 census, was 534. In 1914 Congress authorized construction of the Alaska Railway, extending from Seward to Fairbanks (still a spectacular trip), which both towns expected would make them major metropolises. Surprise: Instead, an initially temporary tent city of construction workers in the wilderness at the head of Turnagain Arm evolved into Anchorage, now by far the state's major city and its largest with a population of about 270,000. Seward's population has never reached 3,000, although it is approaching that figure now.

Chapter 10: Back to Iliamna
The Dena'ina Indians Hannah knew as Kenai were not separate and distinct from all others. They are a branch of the great Alaskan group, Athabaskans or Athapascan.

In about 1800 the Kenais destroyed a small trading post the Russians had established at Iliamna village. The massacre of Kenai men and large boys must have occurred before 1821, when the Russians reestablished a post there. John Branson suggests that the foundation logs which Hannah found in the area of the school garden (next chapter) may have been the remnant of the fort destroyed in 1800.

The Rickteroff brothers' birthdates were: Old William, 1844; Kusma, 1849; Epheme, 1859. Old William must have looked ten or fifteen years younger than his age. Old Madrona (Matrona Pedro) was born in 1859, the same year as Hannah. Both were fifty at this time.

Sentiment concerning native-white intermarriage has changed again since Hannah's time, when it was being discouraged. The wife of Jay Hammond, Alaska's governor from 1974 to 1982, is the daughter of a Scottish father and a Yupik (Southern Eskimo) mother; she is as popular and much admired as her husband who was born in New York State, the son of a Methodist minister. To have native blood or a native spouse is not looked down upon; indeed, it is often a point of pride, although I got the impression intermarriage is now treated matter-of-factly, no big deal.

Almost immediately after she arrived in Iliamna, Hannah joined with the village heads and businessmen in petitioning Washington for a post office. Nothing came of that initiative. In the winter of 1910–11 Iliamna was utterly cut off from incoming and outgoing steamer mail for more than seven months.

Chapter 11: School in Iliamna
The prospectors for the Seattle mining company may have been Mr. and Mrs. Oliver B. Millett. However, Mrs. Millett was listed in the 1910 census as fifty years of age which does not correspond with

Hannah's characterization, a "young woman." Her husband was forty-five.

Chapter 13: Nondalton Fishing Camp

Olga (Agafia Sava) Anderson was a native of Iliamna; her husband was a Swedish immigrant. In 1911 the couple turned to prospecting and in 1917 moved to Bristol Bay, where Mr. Anderson became employed in a cannery. Olga died there in 1925 from tuberculosis. Mr. Anderson and several of their children moved to the San Francisco Bay area. (See "Commentary: The Reindeer Project," p. 189, for the possible reason the Andersons moved from Iliamna to Nondalton.)

Zackar Evanoff was born in 1852 and remained chief of Nondalton until the early 1930s. He died in 1935 at the age of eighty-three.

Nondalton's population numbered forty-four when Hannah reached there. The smaller Stony River group may have split off at the time both groups abandoned their ancestral Kijik settlement. Stony River is about seventy-five miles from Nondalton, not a difficult journey by dogteam nor by snowmobile today.

Hannah thought the fish famine was caused by traps canneries were using that in effect "corked" river mouths so that virtually no fish could get through to spawn. These were illegal and she wrote Washington in late summer of 1910 reporting locations of some. While traps undoubtedly were partly responsible for the dearth of fish, the 1910 and 1911 famines were so widespread that it is now thought a natural freakishness of some sort was also responsible—such as change in water temperatures or presence of ocean gasses connected with underwater emissions. In the late 1920s another widespread famine occurred, so extreme that Nondalton people had to travel fifty miles to catch any salmon, and then few. Nondalton elders say that canneries "corked" the river at that time too.

The first Russian to visit the Nondalton area is believed to have been Vasilii Gregorevich Medvednikov. He put up a cross near the con-

fluence of the Newhalen River and Lake Clark in 1792, which is in
the immediate vicinity of the Nondalton fishing camp.

"Warren" Smith from Seattle, John Branson suggests, may have
been Warriner E. Smith of Seattle, chief engineer for the Alaska
Short Line Railway Navigation Company. He was definitely in the
Lake Clark area in 1904–05. By 1910 that company was bankrupt,
so if he was again back in the area it must indeed have been on different business for a different employer, as Hannah reports. The
dangerous river was possibly the Kijik, which drains into Lake
Clark; it was never reported to have been successfully run by kayak
until the summer of 1994.

Bidarkas have two or three hatches, distinguishing them from
kayaks, which have only one. Since Mr. Smith had a bidarka, his dog
evidently occupied one hatch as if he were a person.

If Hannah's *kamleika* was like another of bear intestines, also made
by Mary Evanoff, which is on display in the Resurrection Bay Historical Society's museum in Seward, it was gay and pretty, decorated with little tufts of bright blue and red thread.

Hannah and the Nielsens were grounded in the notorious mile-wide
Kaskanek Flats of the Kvichak River, still regarded as a boatman's
nightmare, John Branson tells me.

At the time Daluska was married, she was sixteen and Kusma was
sixty.

Chapter 16: *Waiting for the Steamer*
The roadhouse proprietor who arranged Hannah's trip over the
winter trail to Iliamna Bay was Frank Brown, a prospector who had
been born in New York and at this time was thirty-six.

The Katmai volcanic eruption created the many hot gas vents in
what is now known as the Valley of Ten Thousand Smokes. The ash
from Katmai darkened the skies of Afognak, Kodiak and Wood Island for three days; nobody could venture outside; gardens were

smothered and roofs imperiled. The one village, Katmai, close to the volcano, simply disappeared.

Chapter 19: Last Assignments
In recent times the Wrangell garnet mine has been operated by the Boy Scouts as a fund-raising project; the garnets are sold to tourists.

Walter Harper was a member of the four-man mountain-climbing team, led by Hudson Stuck, which was the first to reach the summit of Denali (Mt. McKinley).

Douglas and Juneau are now classified as one metropolitan area. In Douglas people call it Douglas-Juneau; in Juneau it's Juneau-Douglas.

In a referendum to show Washington their feelings, Alaskans voted nearly two to one in favor of prohibition of alcoholic beverages; this is what especially heartened Hannah at the time she left Alaska; in response to this plebiscite Congress enacted what was called the "Bone Dry Law" putting prohibition into effect in Alaska in 1918, before the Eighteenth Amendment to the Constitution permitted nationwide prohibition.

COMMENTARY NOTES
Unless otherwise indicated, letters quoted or alluded to are from a file designated as Commissioner of Education, Washington, DC, Dept. of Interior RG 75, Microfilm Roll 10, in the department of Archives and Manuscripts, Consortium Library, University of Alaska, Anchorage.

Educational Policy and Sheldon Jackson
Quotations on policy are taken from Sheldon Jackson, Report on *Education in Alaska, 1886;* Washington, Government Printing Office, 1886.

For biographical information on Jackson I am deeply indebted to J. Arthur Lazell, *Alaskan Apostle: The Life Story of Sheldon Jackson;* New York, Harper and Brothers, 1960.

Jackson's 1880 *Alaska* was published in New York by Dodd, Mead and Co.

Jackson on the vulnerability of educated native girls is from his 1886 report.

The 1880 rationalization of mission fields is from Lazell and as commonly outlined in other Alaskan references. But eighteen years later the Reverend Dr. Curtis Coe in *Baptist Home Mission Monthly,* January 20, 1898, differed slightly by adding that the Swedish Evangelical and Roman Catholic churches were assigned portions of the west coast and "are conducting successful missions." Other remarks by Coe in the same article illustrate the Protestant missionaries' objections to the Russian church and its clergy. He condemned it for doctrinal reasons, gross immorality, drunkenness, debauchery, swearing, gambling, preventing people from imbibing American ideas and encouraging a belief that "the Czar will eventually again rule Alaska."

An account of the Sitka school custody case and other conflicts between civil authorities on the one hand, and the Sitka school and Jackson personally on the other hand, is included in Jackson's 1886 report and Lazell. The four civil officials removed in response to pressure from Jackson were: John H. Kinkead, governor; Ward McAllister, Jr., federal judge; E. W. Haskett, U.S. attorney; and M. C. Hillyer, U.S. marshal. All had been appointed by President Chester Arthur after Congress passed the first civil code for Alaska in 1884. Jackson gloated righteously over their removal in his 1886 report. (Under the district form of civil government and later, also, under territorial government, federal judges could be removed without being impeached as mandated by the Constitution.)

Jackson's letter to Hannah was among her papers; it is in custody of the editor.

The Reindeer Project

Jackson's own description of the reindeer project, his sweepingly extravagant promises of its worth, and the minutiae of reindeer husbandry are set forth in his report on *Education in Alaska, 1892–93;* Washington, Government Printing Office, 1895. The account of the jinxed voyage is drawn from Lazell, as are statistics on herds and herders, and Grenfell's admiration.

Jackson despised Siberian herders not only as sneaky and cruel, but "passionate, obstinate, jealous and conceited," ironically enough much the same traits attributed to Jackson by his enemies.

Reasons for the impracticality and consequent failure of the project were described by John Branson, historian on the staff of the Lake Clark National Park and Preserve; personal communication.

An annual Alaskan excitement is the Iditarod Trail dogsled race from Anchorage to Nome, commemorating a historic mercy mission when diphtheria serum was rushed from Seward by dogsled to a stricken Nome gold mining camp. Sprint dogsled racing (twenty and thirty miles) is popular. The annual Yukon Quest, which takes off from Fairbanks, is considered by Alaskans to be perhaps the toughest race of any kind in the world. Some dogsleds are still even employed functionally in preference to snowmobiles. One might suppose, offhand, interest in reindeer sledge racing or reindeer breeding, but it does not exist.

Lazell quotes Jackson as saying outright that he took authority for his actions straight from God—a hauteur that dumbfounded people who found themselves in disagreement with him, and even some of those on his side. Lazell says people tended to be wholly for Jackson or wholly against him; he left them little scope for compromise, accommodation or middle ground.

The Bureaucracy
This material is almost entirely drawn from the letter file cited at the beginning of "Commentary" notes.

The brief biographical material on William Lopp is taken from Lazell, as is also information on the Churchill Report.

Dr. Henry O. Schaleben was born in 1881 in Minnesota; he was thus twenty-nine or thirty at the time he became Hannah's superintendent. He died in 1949 in Texas.

Fort Yukon Troubles
The Fairbanks trial and events leading up to it are taken from David M. Dean, *Breaking Trail: Hudson Stuck of Texas and Alaska,* Ohio University Press, 1988; and from the *New York Evening Post,* "Saving Alaskan Indians," by Hudson Stuck, February 14, 1914.

Robert Service's "The Low-Down White" is from *The Spell of the Yukon,* New York, Dodd Mead and Co., 1907; republished in Service, *Best Tales of the Yukon,* Philadelphia, Running Press Book Publishers, 1983.

Lazell points out that only a very small minority of prospectors managed to make a living; most "chased each rainbow to where it touched the earth only to find that others had gotten there first and seized the treasure . . . a bedraggled lot . . . often desperate, starving." Failed prospectors and unemployed miners in the Yukon area, turning expediently to the fur trade, poisoned animals wholesale with strychnine, which attacked the foundation of the far northern Indian economy.

Governor Brady thought the roots of white American debauchery of Indians went back to the initial military government, when soldiers supplied Indians with liquor and raped both Russian and Indian women with impunity; he said that sending soldiers into Alaska was the most foolish thing a government could have done. Jackson tended to lay blame for white-influenced debauchery on traders and miners; Stuck laid blame on Americans and other whites across the board, missionaries and teachers excepted.

Among Hannah's letters (in custody of the editor) were several to her from Stuck relating to complaints against her:

March 10, 1913, from Fairbanks: ". . . It rejoices me to know that there is no intention of removing you from Fort Yukon. I am so assured from both Washington and Seattle. It is good to know that someone is holding the fort there . . ."

February 10, 1914, from New York: ". . . I saw your high superiors at Washington and spoke very frankly and freely of your admirable courage at Fort Yukon . . ."

May 28, 1914, from New York: "Although I think it was quite unnecessary I have just written to Dr. Claxton advising him to pay no heed to the complaints of the evil disposed at Fort Yukon. I think he understands the situation pretty well and since my personal interview with him I feel very much more in touch with the Alaska school situation than I was before . . ."

A signed copy of Mr. Crossley's letter to W. T. Lopp was among Hannah's papers (in custody of the editor).

Regarding Stuck's mentions of Hannah by name in the talks he was giving, this letter from him to Hannah of February 10, 1914, from New York: ". . . Whenever I have gone lecturing and speaking about our affairs I have shown a lantern slide made from a photograph I took of you and your whole school and have made mention of your faithfull stand against the evil that surrounds you there . . . standing out against the general corruption and debauchery and the connivance of that corruption and debauchery on the part of those whose profit they serve."

Hudson Stuck is perhaps best remembered in Alaska today as a mountain climber, first to reach the top of Denali (Mt. McKinley), in 1913. In the same letter, above, about his lectures, he wrote Hannah that Tiffany and Co. (the New York jewelers) were sending her "a little lace pin enclosing a fragment of the highest rock on Denali. Now please don't tell people that this rock comes from the top of the mountain because there is no rock on top. The last 1,500 feet of the mountain is all permanent ice and snow. The rock from which this fragment was chipped stands at about 19,000 feet and so is very easily the highest rock in all North America. The design of the pin pleased me so I had yours and Mrs. Burke's made alike."

Fellow Teachers

The Reverend Dr. Coe is the missionary quoted earlier in "Commentary" notes regarding Protestant attitudes to the Russian church and clergy. In McMinnville he was a professor at the Baptist teachers' college (later secularized as the still-flourishing Linfield College) and pastor of a church a few miles out of town.

McMinnville is in the Willamette Valley, southwest of Portland. An article in *The Oregon Daily Journal,* "A Live Wire City," of May 28, 1918, praises the McMinnville city park for its flowerbeds cared for by various women's societies, its swimming pool fed by a waterfall, its children's playgrounds, its bear pit and deer park, and the two buildings flanking the park entrance, a public library and a public auditorium. It goes on to say that "No locality in Oregon is more progressive. The farmers are modern and alert in their methods." Their outputs were processed in the town's "fruit dryer, milk condenser, creamery, cannery and other factories." I am indebted to Alana Probst for a copy of this old news clipping portraying the town the year Hannah took up residence and teaching there. For all its advantages, life in McMinnville was not Hannah's first choice, however; it was from McMinnville, in 1915, that she wrote her spurned letter of application to the Indian teaching service.

Who Was Gregory?

Information on Saint Herman is drawn from Afonsky, Bishop Gregory, *A History of the Orthodox Church in Alaska 1794–1917,* Kodiak, Saint Herman's Theological Seminary, 1977; and an article celebrating the twentieth anniversary of Saint Herman's canonization, *Kodiak Daily Mirror,* August 17, 1990.

Information on Father Gerasim is drawn from Eliel, R. Monk Gerasim, *Father Gerasim of New Valaam,* Ouzinkie, St. Herman's Press, 1989; and *Alaska History,* vol. 4, no. 2, "Rasputin Is Alive and Well and Living in Kodiak"—a sardonic title—by Gary Stevens; Anchorage, Alaska Historical Society, 1989.

Although I inquired through all avenues I could find, ignorance of what became of Bishop Innocent after his Russian recall seems total; not even the tantalizing word-of-mouth report about Tibet seems to have been recorded elsewhere than in Hannah's memoir.

EPILOGUE NOTES

Much of this material is from personal observation in July 1994.

The abundant governmental presence in Fort Yukon in part reflects the fact that Alaska has been spending almost four times as much per capita on government as the average U.S. state; one in five employees is on a government payroll. Oil royalties are the major source of funds; there is no state income or sales tax. *The New York Times*, "Sunset for the Oil Boom and Alaska's Life Style," April 24, 1994—reporting worries about finances when oil wealth dries up.

Sharing oil wealth with citizens directly, through an annual personal dividend, was the idea of Jay Hammond, governor from 1974 to 1982. His reasoning was that the state's ideas of how to help people were not necessarily better than people's own ideas, so the oil bonanza should not be monopolized by the state. Hammond's autobiography, *Tales of Alaska's Bush Rat Governor*, Seattle, Epicenter Press, 1994. Although there are no strings on how individuals use this money, let alone any means tests, a visitor hears no complaints that it is frittered away. Some people use it for small productive ventures, as micro-capital.

Historical reasons for village mobility, apart from epidemics and a wish for better quality of life on a clean site, include: changes in river channels or fluctuations in beach levels; availability of game and fish; depletion of other resources such as wood; modification of economic cycles owing to cultural changes; natural disasters; defeat in warfare or deaths in raids. Ellanna and Balluta, *The People of Nondalton and Nuvendaltin Quht'ana*, Washington, Smithsonian Institution Press, 1992.

Hannah evidently did not realize that, historically, villages were mobile nor that villagers were perfectly capable of shifting location when they themselves judged it desirable or necessary. She was so shocked by Iliamna when she first arrived there that she wrote Washington (to her discredit, in my opinion), "The only way to better the condition of this people is to build new homes—burn these old pest-ridden, filthy houses. Then make it *obligatory* to keep clean both in house and person." Hannah would find little or nothing to criticize in the self-relocated successor village to Iliamna, consequence of the portage extension in 1937.

The history of the portage is related in *The Bristol Bay Times,* "Iliamna Portage Long Used by Bears, Humans," by John Branson, December 10, 1993. It was first made passable for horse-drawn wagons in the 1920s; by 1932 small trucks used it; five years after that came the extension to Pile Bay.

Homer, on the Kenai peninsula, where Annie and Walter Johnson live in winter, was a small fishing village that in the 1960s became attractive to hippies, and has now slightly surpassed better-known Seward in population and size of economy. Both Homer and Seward are linked to Anchorage by intercity buses (rarities in Alaska).

Yule Chaffin's book, in collaboration with Trisha Hampton Krieger and Michael Rostad, is *Alaska's Konyag Country,* Woody Island, Chaffin, Inc., 1993.

Expectation of a booming commercial future for Wood Island was set forth by Mrs. James McWhinnie, *History of Kadiak* (sic) *Orphanage,* Chicago, Women's American Baptist Home Mission Society, 1912.

Afognak was a pre-Russian settlement, much older than Kodiak and, at the turn of the century, larger. Why their forebears chose so unprotected and impractical a site has puzzled their descendants. Until recently, the most common explanation was that stiff sea winds were an advantage for processing fish. But fishing camps are chosen for such advantages, not village sites, and Afognak had a separate fishing camp. Now it is more plausibly speculated that in pre-Russian days when native groups were continually raiding one another's settlements, the open site with its long, wide reach of uninterrupted water was protection from surprise attacks.

The life story of Mrs. Neseth and much else about Afognak and many of its other people is told by Lola Harvey, *Derevnia's Daughters: Saga of an Alaskan Village,* Manhattan, Kansas, Sunflower University Press, 1991; an exhaustively researched, detailed history of a mixed Swedish-native family with both deep local roots and surprisingly cosmopolitan connections.

A fireweed and clover raw-honey recipe is included in a cookbook by Charles and Joan Budai, *The Taste of Hospitality,* Anchorage, Hospitality Press, 1993. Alaska Honey & Pollen, Inc., Eagle Harbor, produces raw fireweed honey commercially.

The drunk-driver vehicle confiscation program in Anchorage was instituted in April 1994. Seven seized vehicles auctioned by the municipality on July 23, 1994, had belonged to three drivers with three previous convictions each of driving while intoxicated; one driver with at least one previous conviction; and three who were caught driving in spite of suspended or revoked licenses. Driving a snowmobile while intoxicated incurs the same penalties as driving a car or truck. *Anchorage Press,* "Drunk Cars for Sale," July 21–27, 1994.

Information on Mrs. Pajoman (Matrena Salamatov) is drawn from a monograph by Lydia Black of the Department of Anthropology, University of Alaska in Fairbanks, and from an interview with Mrs. Pajoman's son, Carl, by Gary L. Stevens, *Kodiak Daily Mirror,* Aug. 7, 1991.

ACKNOWLEDGMENTS

Kinfolk of Hannah's by blood or marriage who tracked down information, took photographs, or supplied suggestions I used are Carol Bier, Patricia Broms, James and Kay Butzner, Judge John D. Butzner, Pete Butzner, Burgin Jacobs, Dr. James K. Jacobs, Ned Jacobs, Mel Manchester, the Reverend David E. Robison; and I am especially indebted to Mary Ann Code for research and for conducting me through archival labyrinths, and to Robert H. Jacobs, whose idea it was that we should go to Alaska.

So many in Alaska were both helpful and kind that it is impossible to mention them all, but I'm particularly indebted to John B. Branson, Charles and Joan Budai, Margaret Carroll, Yule Chaffin, Connie Chya, Ruth A. Dawson, Willie Hall, Lola Harvey, Sara Hornberger, Annie and Walter Johnson, Marian Johnson, the late Reverend Fr. Peter Kreta, Dustin Lang, Mark Lang, Peter Olsen, the late Nina Olsen, Mary Patterson, Bill Ray, Alice Ryser, Dan Seavey, Sergai Sheratine, Melvin Squartsoff, Fred Thomas, the staffs and resources of the Alutiiq Center, the Church of the Holy Resurrection, the Community Baptist Church of Kodiak, the Consortium Library of the University of Alaska, the Kodiak Historical Society and Baranov Museum, the Kodiak Public Library, the Lake Clark National Park and Preserve and the Resurrection Bay Historical Society and Seward Museum.

Others to whose help I'm indebted are Patricia Cairns, Peter A. Frey, Sheila Kay, David Kent, Hugh Lessig, Joy de Menil, Alana

Probst, Teresa Spurlock Vessels, Elaine Hutton Woodward; and I am so grateful for the resources of the Augustana Library of Rock Island, Illinois, the Charles A. Cannon Memorial Library of Concord, North Carolina, the Richmond Public Library, the South Carolina State Library and the Toronto Public Library.

I'm especially grateful to Jason Epstein and Douglas Pepper, whose editorial suggestions and encouragement have been indispensible.

INDEX

————◇————

Note: *Italicized* page numbers indicate illustrations.

A

Patterson, Mary, 265
Pavlof, Nicholai, and daughters Mary
    and Annie, 75–6
Pedro, Matrona, 96–7, 136
Pedro Bay, 259–60
Permafrost, 125–6
Petellin: Albert, 9, 13–5, 40; Mary,
    40 3; the Raw Fir, 17, 23 30,
    38–42, 44, 47, 83, 245; wife,
    39–40, 42
Peter the Great. *See* Czar
Pile Bay, 258–9
Pneumonia. *See* Epidemics
Point Barrow, 201, 211
Population, Alaskan: native peoples,
    269; totals, 268
Porcupine River, 174
Port Alsworth, 260
Port Lions, 263–5
Portages, 62–3, 66–7, 92–3, 122–5,
    146–50, 152, 160–3, 280–9,
    214, 258–60, 285 n.
Prejudice: anti-Aleut, 17–8, 99, 142,
    144; anti-Eskimo, 142; anti-
    native, 142, 199–201, 205–6,
    207, 233, 237; anti-Russian
    Orthodox, 202, 279 n.
Presbyterians, 24, 221–2, 227; mis-
    sion allocations, 201
Presbyterian missions: Alaskan pan-
    handle, 201; Fort Wrangell, 199;
    Point Barrow, 201; Rocky
    Mountains, 198; Sitka. *See*
    Jackson, Sheldon
Prices, xii, 36, 42, 57, 58, 68, 91,
    100, 115, 172, 215, 218,
    219–20
Prince William Sound, 6
Princeton Theological Seminary, 198
Probst, Alana, 283 n.
Prohibition. *See* Alcohol
Prospectors, 44, 77, 87, 97, 108,
    118, 121, 131, 208–9, 275–6 n.,
    281 n.
Pullen's, Mrs., boarding house,
    168–9

R

Rabbits, 124, 150, 172
Railroads, 7, 57, 60, 68, 86–8, 165,
    169, 183, 193, 274 n.
Rasputin, 246–7
Rather, Peter, 210
Ruville, Mrs., 50–9
Redmyer, Hedley E., ix, xvi, 61–2,
    65, 70, 91, 208–10, 213–4, 224,
    268
Reindeer, 208, 214–5, 220, 224,
    227–8, 267; apprentices,
    110–1, 144, 212, 214; express
    system, 210–1; failure, 214;
    herders, 211–2, 214, 215,
    227–8; project, xvi, 208–14;
    220–1, 222; statistics, 211, 214;
    vicissitudes, 212–3. *See also*
    Jackson, Sheldon; Redmyer,
    Hedley E.; Schaleben, Dr. Henry
Reindeer Man. *See* Redmyer,
    Hedley E.
Resurrection Bay, 88. *See also*
    Seward
Rickteroff, 98–9, 275 n., 277 n.;
    Agafia, 95, 96, 113; Daluska,
    142, 277 n.; Daria, 95; Epheme,
    xvii, 95, 96, 99, 105, 113,
    119–20, 136, 152; Kusma, 66,
    68, 95, 99, 100, 102, 120, 136,
    142, 277 n.; Maria, 95; Mary, 95;
    Michael, 137; Paraskovia, 95;
    Pete, 102–3; Stephen, 95;
    Thedoska and daughter
    Wassalissa, 66–8; Vera, 96;
    William (Old), 94–5, 99, 109,
    138, 154; William Mike (Young
    William), 95, 137
Robison, Martha, 227
Rocky Mountains, xi, 63, 198
Roman Catholic Missions, 279 n.
Romig, Dr., 223
Roosevelt, President Theodore,
    206 n., 221–2
Ruby, 178, 231–2

Born in Pennsylvania in 1859, HANNAH BREECE taught in Pennsylvania and the Rocky Mountains before accepting a government post to teach in Alaska from 1904 to 1918. She died in 1940.

JANE JACOBS was born in Scranton, Pennsylvania, and now lives in Toronto. Her previous critically acclaimed books include *The Death and Life of Great American Cities, Cities and the Wealth of Nations, The Economy of Cities,* and *Systems of Survival.*